Labour and Employment in the USSR

Also by David Lane

Soviet Economy and Society (New York University Press, 1984)
State and Politics in the USSR (New York University Press, 1984)

Labour and Employment in the USSR

EDITED BY

DAVID LANE
Professor of Sociology
University of Birmingham

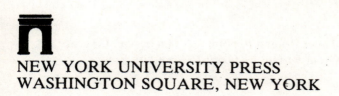

NEW YORK UNIVERSITY PRESS
WASHINGTON SQUARE, NEW YORK

© David Lane, 1986

First published in the USA in 1986 by
NEW YORK UNIVERSITY PRESS,
Washington Square, New York, N.Y. 10003

Library of Congress Cataloging-in-Publication Data
Main entry under title:

Labour and Employment in the USSR.
   Papers presented at a conference organized at the University of
Birmingham in May 1984.
   Includes index.
   1. Labor supply—Soviet Union—History—20th century—
Congresses.   2. Soviet Union—Full employment policies—
History—20th century—Congresses.   I. Lane, David Stuart.
HD5796.L33   1985   331.1′0947   85-15565
ISBN 0-8147-5019-2

Typeset in Times Roman 10 point medium by MC Typeset
Printed in Great Britain by Oxford University Press

Contents

Preface   vii

1. Marxist-Leninism: An Ideology for Full
   Employment in Socialist States?   1
   David Lane

PART I: THE HISTORICAL BACKGROUND

2. The Ending of Mass Unemployment in the USSR   19
   R.W. Davies
3. A Note on the Sources of Unemployment Statistics   36
   R.W. Davies and S.G. Wheatcroft
4. The Development of Soviet Employment and
   Labour Policy, 1930–41   50
   John Barber

PART II: THE ECONOMICS OF FULL EMPLOYMENT

5. Lessons of Soviet Planning of Full Employment   69
   Mark Harrison
6. The Serendipitous Soviet Achievement of Full
   Employment: Labour Shortage and Labour
   Hoarding in the Soviet Economy   83
   Philip Hanson
7. Systemic Aspects of Employment and Investment in
   Soviet-Type Economies   112
   D.M. Nuti
8. Heterogeneity of the Soviet Labour Market as a
   Limit to a more Efficient Utilisation of Manpower   122
   Silvana Malle

PART III: SOCIO-ECONOMIC PROBLEMS

9.   Geographical Mobility – Its Implications for
     Employment   145
     Ann Helgeson
10. Shortage of Labour and Motivation Problems of
     Soviet Workers   176
     Anna-Jutta Pietsch
11. Productivity Campaigns in Soviet Industry   191
     Peter Rutland
12. Transition from School to Work: Satisfying Pupils'
     Aspirations and the Needs of the Economy   209
     Sheila Marnie
13. Underemployment and Potential Unemployment of
     the Technical Intelligentsia: Distortions Between
     Education and Occupation   223
     Eduard Gloeckner

PART IV: LABOUR AND THE LAW

14. The USSR Law on the Work Collectives: Workers'
     Control or Workers Controlled?   239
     Elizabeth Teague
15. Job Security and the Law in the USSR   256
     Nick Lampert

Index   278

Preface

This book originated in a conference organised at the University of Birmingham in May 1984. With rising levels of unemployment in the West, one of the aims of the conference was to consider the claim that socialist societies provided work for the population concurrently with the maintenance of a dynamic economy. Such a topic requires an interdisciplinary perspective involving history, sociology, economics and politics. In the papers that follow, employment is considered from the perspective of these individual disciplines, and we await a macro analysis of labour under socialism as much as we do under capitalism. The papers included here reflect not only various disciplinary perspectives but also ideological ones. Full employment is seen by Mario Nuti as a systemic characteristic of the economy, while Martin Harrison regards it more as the working out of a social and political policy, and I consider it to be a result of a complex political interchange. Full employment is conceded by all contributors to be a fact of Soviet society, but some argue that this also entails considerable countervailing costs—in unacceptable levels of inefficiency (Philip Hanson), underemployment (Ed. Gloeckner) and overinvestment (Mario Nuti). Nick Lampert and Elizabeth Teague point to pathologies which continue in the Soviet Union—arbitrary dismissal and authoritarian political control.

My thanks have to be expressed to the following, who participated in the conference, either as discussants or as presenters of papers, and helped make it a success: Dr J. Cooper, Dr R. Garside, Mr M. Kaser, Dr C. Lane, Dr C. Littler, Professor C. Mako, Professor M. Peil, Dr J.L. Porket, Dr A. Pravda, Professor D. Stark and Dr S. Wood. Ms Sheila Marnie and Mrs June Brough provided much administrative assistance and the

vii

former also gave considerable help in editing some of the papers. Finally, I would like to thank the BUAS/NASEES Ford Foundation Committee and the Nuffield Foundation for financial assistance in support of the conference.

Birmingham, November 1984   David Lane

1 Marxist-Leninism: An Ideology for Full Employment in Socialist States?

DAVID LANE*

It is a well known fact, which is brought out in many papers in this book, that state socialist societies utilise a high proportion of the population in paid labour. This is common to all socialist societies and should not be obscured by caveats which are also made in papers presented here; for instance, whether such labour has been administratively directed, is inefficient or is subject to arbitrary dismissal. Rapid industrialisation, both in countries of the First World and the Third World, has not given rise to the institutionalisation of such high rates of labour utilisation as in contemporary socialist societies. The question may be posed as to why such a high-employment and low-wage policy has become normal.

It is not being claimed in this paper that the explanation may be derived solely from the ideology of Marxism-Leninism, which is said to guide the policy of the society. One has also to take into account the level of development of the economy—the demand for, and supply of, labour and the psychological attitudes of the population to work. It will be argued in this paper that the Marxist conception of man entails that work activity be conceived as a human need. In distinction from some Western Marxist commentators, who have stressed the negative characteristics of work activity in terms of alienation, it is contended here that Marxists also regard work as self-fulfilment. But there is a contradiction in Marxism between work being conceived as the basis of production and a creator of wealth and hence a human need, and work activity considered as alienated labour under capitalism. In the earlier periods of Soviet power, it is the former aspect—that of work as the creator of wealth—which guided the Soviet political

* Department of Sociology, University of Birmingham. This research is part of a study financed by a grant from the British ESRC.

leadership. There has also been a particular and unique historical dimension: in the early years of the Revolution, labour (like military service) was an obligation, a *povinnost'*, as it was described in the 1918 constitution, not a duty (*obyazannost'*), as defined in those of 1936 and 1977.[1]

In the development of the USSR up to around 1956, work was regarded as an essential component of building socialism. The emphasis was not on the content or form of labour but on the socio-political necessity of work. Hence Marxism-Leninism, as it developed under Stalin in the USSR, became an ideology which was used to develop work attitudes necessary for industrial development. These attitudes were transmitted to the peasantry, to the newly arrived townspeople. While John Barber (Ch.4) is correct to point out that coercion was used to prize some of the peasantry away from the countryside and to deploy many on labour intensive projects, there were also many massive campaigns to glorify the factory and its work in general which sought to create a positive attitude to labour in an urban setting.

In this paper the Marxist view of labour in contemporary socialist society is examined, and it is shown that labour as a need and as a form of alienation coexist in Soviet discussions. A 'positive attitude to work' is particularly necessary under conditions of full employment in order to encourage labour productivity. However, full employment, coupled to a low-wage economy, may in the 1980s be a brake on such development. The Soviet ideology of labour now provides greater constraints on the political leadership than is found under capitalism; not only is there an expectation that paid work will be provided for all, but such work is required to be 'satisfying'.

Compared to earlier periods of industrialisation, when movement to the town and to a paid job was a social advance for the peasantry, contemporary cohorts of school-leavers expect 'satisfying' work. This is not quite the same as having a 'positive attitude' towards labour. This new attitude may be derived from the claim that under 'developed socialism' people should have a choice of occupation. There is again a difference compared to capitalist states where levels of expectations tally more exactly with the supply of jobs and are mediated through the instrumentality of money.

The role of ideology is to act as a constraint on policy. It makes it politically impracticable to move to a market-type high-wage, low-employment policy. To improve labour productivity and levels of economic growth, changes will have to take place within the present structure of a full employment economy. The dilemma for Soviet planners is how to improve efficiency and labour discipline and to meet expectations for 'satisfying' work without undermining the political legitimacy of a planned system which would follow from redundancies and the development of a capitalist-type labour market.

THE NATURE OF WORK IN MARXIST THEORY

Labour and the work process is a fundamental component of Marxist theory:

The work process resolved . . . into its simple elementary factors, is human action with a view to the production of use-values, appropriation of natural substances to human requirements; it is the necessary condition for effecting exchanges of matter between man and nature; it is the everlasting nature-imposed condition of human existence, and therefore is independent of every social phase of that existence, or rather, is common to every such phase.[2]

For Marx, the maintenance and reproduction of material life is the prime human need. In a well-known passage in *The German Ideology* Marx writes, 'The first historical act is . . . the production of material life itself. This is indeed . . . a fundamental condition of all history, which today, as thousands of years ago, must be accomplished every day and every hour merely in order to sustain human life.'[3] Work is not only a fundamental category in Marxist approaches but is also a major component in the classical bourgeois sociologists' concept of an acquisitive society, such as that found in Weber and Durkheim.

In Marxist thought it is labour that creates value; that is, it is the labour power that is embodied in a good or service that gives it social value. Use-values are produced by conscious or purposeful human activity; such activity may be defined as work. Work has two social aspects. First, it fulfils a social need on the part of the worker—it uses mankind's creative power. Expending such effort is man's 'life-activity'.[4] What distinguishes the human race from other species is the ability to transform nature to a world of its own making. The second aspect of such activity is that goods and services are produced which are consumed. Material and spiritual human needs are met through the consumption of goods and services. Production and consumption are both aspects of the fulfilment of needs in the Marxist conception of man.

In Marxist theory the kind of activity or work that characterises a society (and the requisite structure of needs) is dependent on a given mode of production. The labour process in pre-capitalist societies was linked to the direct satisfaction of needs; the typical peasant laboured to fulfil his material and spiritual wants, and to pay taxes. Domestic labour under capitalism is a form of direct creation of use-values. The growth of the division of labour, of paid labour and the employment of workers, gives rise to a different constellation of needs: production and consumption are differentiated. In the expansion of labour activity through a market system, men and women need jobs or employment; they become wage labour. The fulfilment of human needs in a market system is dependent on employment in order (a) to express one's creativity and (b) to fulfil needs to consume goods and services. These two aspects of employment are quite separate.

While human activity and work fulfil human needs, the Marxist notion of class structure modifies the ways that work is organised and labour is performed. Work as fulfilment of human needs, it is argued by many Marxists, is vitiated, even precluded by the capitalist class structure. The division of societies into classes gives rise to a dominant and exploited class. The significance of this division is that the dominant class, as such, does not participate in labour activity. It lives off the surplus of the exploited class. While consumption requirements of members of the dominant class are met, they do not make any contribution to fulfiling human needs. Class relations also have their impact on the activity, labour and work of the exploited class. Exploitation means that the workers' exchange with nature is not an expression of his or her will but is determined by the domination of the ruling class. Under capitalism, much (not all) work is instrumental; it is organised by the capitalist class for the realisation of exchange-values and for the extraction of surplus, though in the process use-value is produced.[5] Under such conditions the fulfillment of the workers' needs, it is argued, is made impossible. The worker becomes *alienated*.

In the late 1960s and 1970s in Western countries, alienation was the primary focus of concern of Marxists. 'Alienation' is one of the most ambiguous words used in the social sciences. I would distinguish between three meanings of the term. First, 'alienation' is used in a very general sense to describe a lack of correspondence between people (as individuals or groups) and society; it depicts a state of malaise in social relationships involving feelings of isolation, powerlessness, self-estrangement and normlessness. Second, Marxist writers particularly have focused on control of the product of labour. As ownership of the means of production is vested with the capitalist class, the worker's product is alien to him and, in a societal perspective, there arises a disjunction between production (for profit) and human needs. This approach sees the primary source of alienation (both at work and in society) to lie in ownership relationships. Third, many writers (Marxist and non-Marxist) have found the essence of alienation to lie in the modern process of production; for this school the nature and context of work performed are alienative.

The thrust of most recent Western scholarship has been on the third approach and has been inspired by Marx's *Economic and Philosophical Manuscripts*. Such writers have emphasised the fact that mass-production-process manufacture leads to the fragmentation of production and the extreme division of labour. The repetitiveness of jobs in mass production, the deskilling of manual and non-manual work and the increasing domination of manager over worker have led Marxists to deny that work fulfils human needs. Such critics are agreed that rather than developing a person's potential powers, 'capitalist labor consumes these powers without replenishing them, burns them up as if they were a fuel, and leaves the individual worker that much poorer. The qualities that mark him as a human being become progressively diminished'.[6] Writers such as Braverman emphasise the deskilling process involved with the advance of capitalism.[7] An individual becomes 'a living appendage of the machine'.[8]

It would be mistaken, however, to regard work, even under capitalism, as alien to people's needs. Needs are relative to the development of society and are socially defined. Under conditions of modern capitalism, wage labour is a means to meet the necessities of life: it is an instrumentality to fulfil the prime needs of reproduction (food and shelter). It is also valued in itself. To be gainfully occupied or employed is a mark of social recognition of one's contribution to society. Even the dominant class legitimates itself by claiming to contribute to wealth creation—profit is a reward for risk-taking, and royalty performs the ceremonial aspect of government and is claimed to contribute to the 'tension-management function' of society. For Marxists a distinction here is between the parasitical class which lives off labour and the productive class which creates value.

This line of reasoning, which posits work as a major dynamic of modern society, has been questioned in recent years. Writers such as Claus Offe[9] have argued that in advanced Western societies work no longer has such an important role. Following sociologists such as Dahrendorf and Bell, he argues that labour and wage dependency no longer play a major role as the focus of collective concern.[10] In their stead, as organising principles, Offe suggests concepts such as 'way of life', 'post-industrial society', and 'the home'.[11]

In the 1980s the advent of high levels of unemployment in the West has led to a different emphasis on work and employment. The stress on the 'alienative' character of work current in the 1960s has been put to one side and replaced by a concern for the 'right to work'. There has developed a recognition of the deprivation which ensues if work is denied to a person and this has eclipsed the writings of Bell and Offe and led to a reappraisal of work. Jahoda analyses work into four dimensions (for the individual): the provision of income, the granting of social status, an activity to occupy the day and the making of an environment in which social conviviality may be enjoyed.[12] The moral and social values engendered by capitalism make work—and especially an occupation and employment—a human need. Unemployment is not only a potential cost to the economy in that labour is underutilised, but it is a cost to the unemployed individual and to society. The burden of unemployment is socially differentiated, often the poorest groups bear the brunt of the costs, and politically it may be socially divisive and destabilising. What is true about the critique of Dahrendof, Bell and Offe is that as incomes and consumption have risen to very high levels, the marginal utility of money has fallen. Under capitalism the 'motivation' effect of additional money has declined for *certain* (mainly middle-class) social groups who have sought satisfaction outside the work role. On the other hand, when income is reduced, as it is with unemployment, dissatisfaction increases.[13] In a nutshell, increases in money do not make some people more satisfied, but reductions in money invariably lead to increases in frustration and dissatisfaction.

WORK UNDER SOCIALISM

Marxists in socialist states have always adopted a more positive attitude towards the necessity for people to work. Soviet Marxism with regard to labour may be called the 'Protestant ethic of socialism'.[14] Lenin's analysis of work recognises its prime necessity for the building of socialist society. For Lenin work was not only conceived of as the fulfilment of man's 'species being' but was bound up with the development of the productive forces. Capitalism (and its form of labour) was progressive compared to feudal society. Lenin stressed the economic and social advance of wage labour over serfdom. As he put it in *The Development of Capitalism in Russia*, 'Compared with the labour of the dependent or bonded peasant, the labour of the hired worker is a progressive phenomenon in all the branches of the economy'.[15]

In distinction from capitalist countries, where wage labour was taken for granted, the Soviet state went about creating conditions for the growth of a class of wage labourers. In *The Immediate Tasks of Soviet Power*, Lenin considered that a major task of the Soviet government was 'to teach the people how to work'.[16] Large-scale factory production, then characteristic of capitalism, was regarded as being capable of fulfilling a higher level of human needs than artisan labour. The most advanced forms of labour organisation had to be copied from the West. For Lenin, Taylorism was 'the last word of capitalism' and 'its greatest scientific achievements [lie] in the field of analysing mechanical motions during work, in the elimination of superfluous and awkward motions, in the working out of correct methods of work, and in the introduction of the best system of accounting and control, etc'.[17] Subsequently, domestic work was transformed by the massive industrial employment of women and collective farm labour also became a form of wage labour.

In creating the conditions of a socialist attitude towards work, the Soviet political leadership was confronted not by workers who had become alienated by capitalist conditions of labour but by peasants who had experienced the rhythm of traditional agricultural production. The cultural background to the Soviet industrialisation process is a conditioning factor of immense importance. The 'Protestant ethic' contingent to the rise of capitalism in Western Europe did not provide an analogous value basis on which the Soviet leaders could build. Hence Stalinism as an ideology had elements of the provision of a motivating work ethic. In the early period of Soviet power the Soviet leadership encouraged full employment primarily to bring about economic advance—to create the material basis of communism. Also a new type of labour process under socialism was thought to be possible. Work as salvation is a common element in the puritan's and Stalin's world view. 'Alienation' played little part in Soviet Marxist philosophy during the period before the death of Stalin. The major disjunction between producers and society was analysed in terms of the second approach to alienation defined alone (p.5)—the separation of the product of labour from the producer. During the 1950s, even the discussion of the *Economic and Philosophical Manuscripts* did not lead to alienation being considered to lie in the work process.[18] The political conditions present in the USSR necessary for the abolition of alienation as a structural condition were the public ownership of the means of production, the demise of the capitalist class and the replacement of production for the market by planning. 'Socialist emulation' (*sorevnovanie*) was a Soviet device intended to augment Taylorism in the work process.

The emphasis on the duty to labour, which has been made explicit in the Fundamental Laws or Constitutions of the Russian Republic and of the USSR, should be interpreted in this way. In distinction from capitalist states, the Constitutions have always defined work as a right and duty of citizens, and the state has a duty to provide employment. In the twentieth century, Western capitalist governments put their policy emphasis on consumption rather than work. Unemployment is mitigated by the provision of a minimum standard of consumption through unemployment benefit. Full employment in socialist states is a vindication of the Marxist notion that labour is the source of value and that idleness is degenerate. It also shows recognition of the fact that industrial development requires a different work ethic from the traditional peasant one. The Bolsheviks in 1918 were conscious that they should define the essence of the socialist system in a similar way to that of the French revolutionaries in 1789. As Sverdlov put it, 'Just as in the days of the French bourgeois revolution . . . there was proclaimed a Declaration of Rights of Man and of the Citizen . . . so today our Russian Socialist Revolution should likewise make its declaration.'[19] The Declaration abolished private ownership of the means of production, ratified workers' control and 'in order to do away with the parasitic classes of society and [to] organise the economic life of the country, universal labour duty is introduced'. The first constitution of the RSFSR, published on 3 July 1918, reiterated the obligations of all citizens to work, and proclaimed the freedom of citizens from economic exploitation. Constitutional rights were restricted to those who laboured; clergymen and 'those who employ others for profit' (Articles 64, 65) were excluded. Similar sentiments have been expressed in the 1936 and 1977 constitutions. In 1936 it was declared that 'Work in the USSR is a duty, a matter of honour for every able-bodied citizen—He who does not work shall not eat'. Citizens had the right to work and to 'guaranteed employment'. In the 1977 constitution citizens were not only given the right to work but also the choice of a trade or profession.

CHANGING CONCEPTIONS OF WORK

The declarations of the 1936 and 1977 constitutions of the USSR have changed in emphasis concerning the role of work. The earlier constitutional claims (and policy which derived from them) emphasised the social necessity of work in order to provide the necessities of life; work was a duty to create the conditions of the first stage of the communist mode of production. Work was seen as a human necessity and was counterposed to the idleness of a parasitical ruling class. The individual need for creativity in work—to satisfy some psychological striving on the part of the individual—was ignored. However, as I have just said, the 1977 constitution recognises the right of the individual to a choice of trade or profession. This recognition signals a development in the Soviet conception of work under 'mature socialism'. Individual satisfaction in and with work is now of greater importance to policy-makers. As the late Leonid Brezhnev put it, 'Socialism as a social structure has within it great possibilities for the rational and human use of society's main productive force—human labour'.[20] Under socialism, work should become 'a need and a pleasure'.[21] Such sentiments take account of people's attitude towards work and the labour process.

Offe and other critics of the work process under contemporary capitalism have pointed to the developing crisis of 'exchange-rationality' when market conditions do not act as 'effective and reliable' spurs to individual action.[22] Soviet society, however, anticipates this condition by stressing more the collective necessity (rather than individual instrumentality) for work activity. If Habermas and Offe are even partially correct in pointing to the limitations of 'market incentives' (including the reserve army of unemployed) as a motivating force for work, then paradoxically orthodox Soviet economists and sociologists are theoretically correct to seek improved motivation for work outside the market nexus.

There is a tension in Soviet society between the necessary requirements of the economy and the aspirations of many people. The provision of work is a traditional social goal—both for the individual and the society of which he or she is part—and has to be reconciled with the aspirations for different types of work expressed by individuals. (See Ch.12, Sheila Marnie's paper, where this will be considered in detail.) Soviet policy-makers are therefore constrained by two basic ideological objectives which have not been adopted by governments under capitalism: (a) the provision of work for all the population and (b) the requirement of giving opportunities to people to find satisfaction in work.

Under the conditions of socialist states we must distinguish between different types of alienation. Prior to the 1960s, Soviet writers were mainly concerned with the structurally induced types of disjunction between the labourer and his product involving the production of exchange rather than use-values. In more recent times attention has focused on a type of alienation occurring when individual workers are dissatisfied with the conditions of their labour and with the jobs that they are required to do under conditions of modern technology. This latter sense of work alienation has been developed by Western writers such as Seeman and Blauner.[23] Such writers shift the emphasis away from structural factors associated with a mode of production to the individual's perceptions of his or her labour which are shaped by the technology of modern production. 'In modern industrial employment, control, purpose, social integration and self-involvement are all problematic.'[24]

Many Soviet studies have pointed to the rise of such attitudes in the labour process in the USSR.[25] The expansion of consumerism in the USSR has led to a greater 'instrumentality' in the attitudes of workers towards work, and the rising levels of education have led to a growth in desire for interest and self-satisfaction in work.[26] Women, for instance, in recent years have made claims for interesting work which are now similar to men's.[27] Soviet sociologists and other commentators have advocated greater participation in management in the enterprise and various schemes of team-work assembly to overcome monotonous work. Lenin's ideas of Taylorism and the importation of Western methods of the work process have been somewhat updated by the advocacy of the more humane face of contemporary Western procedures and the modernisation, as it were, of brigade and team methods and various other types of 'socialist emulation'. These are not only, as invariably interpreted in the West, ways to increase labour productivity but are intended to develop a moral tone appropriate to a socialist form of work behaviour. Indeed, some Soviet sociologists (particularly Yadov and Zdravomyslov) have been at pains to argue that greater 'satisfaction' with work will not necessarily increase labour productivity. Similarly, recent Soviet discussions on the election of managers are also indications of ways in which a more 'socialistic' labour process may be created.[28] The imbalance between people's aspirations for jobs with the array of posts available is a problem which is to be resolved through the 'lowering of ambition' and a different form of school, socialisation—particularly the provision of vocational education.[29]

In considering these disjunctions between aspirations for work and the kinds of jobs available, one must bear in mind that (unlike under capitalism) the dominant ideology requires not only that work for all has to be provided but that this work should give satisfaction to the worker. the relatively high proportion of income provided by 'social consumption' (highly subsidised housing, travel, health, education, leisure) makes the use of material incentives less potent as an incentive to labour than under capitalism. There are, therefore, structurally induced expectations which make the fit between aspiration and reality more difficult to achieve than under capitalism. Getting the 'right attitude' towards work is not just a way of increasing labour productivity but has 'a direct relationship to the moral state of the entire people, the entire society'.[30]

A major difference between socialist states and capitalist ones is that there is less differentiation between 'the individual realm of work'[31] and the collectivised provision of welfare. The Soviet factory is the hub of the distribution of welfare benefits; leisure provision, recreation and housing are closely linked to the enterprise through the trade union and ancillary organisations. This gives the work place a greater role in the life of the individual than it does in the West. As pointed out in Malle's paper (p. 125), the larger the enterprise the greater the provision of welfare and the lower the rate of labour turnover. The high effective labour-participation rate also precludes the development of counter-cultures, as in the West, where non-work may be normal and legitimate.

SOME PROBLEMS OF A LOW-PAY, FULL EMPLOYMENT ECONOMY

The Soviet policy of a fully employed but low-paid workforce is a response both to the ideological assumptions discussed above and to the requirements of modernisation under conditions of state ownership of the means of production and central planning. It fulfils the economic need to utilise the workforce, and at the same time it provides employment fulfilling the political objectives mentioned. In the early period of Soviet power, industrialisation and economic growth may have been the primary objective of the Soviet government, but once full employment had been achieved, it became a sacred element in Soviet social policy. The duty to provide full employment is derived from the legitimating ideology of Marxism-Leninism. It cannot be abrogated without seriously weakening the integrity of Soviet society. The provision of full employment and the overcoming of alienation at work are legitimating factors for the regime in the world order. There is an international dimension to internal policy: the weakening of a policy of full employment (perhaps more so than a decline in the rate of economic growth) would cast in doubt the Soviet claim to be a socialist state. The low-pay, full-employment economy creates its own problems. It is often argued that the desire for 'satisfying' work, the absence of a 'reserve army' of unemployed and ineffective wage incentives lead to a poorly motivated workforce, and this in turn undermines another tenet in the Soviet concept of building socialism—the steady rise in material welfare. While such factors undoubtedly make increases in labour productivity difficult to obtain, one should not put all the fault on the policy of full employment since countries experiencing unemployment also have difficulties in raising labour productivity. The market has been faulted by some Western commentators as a means of satisfying human wants.[32]

The maturation of the Soviet economy in the 1980s has brought in its train not only new economic problems but also a different pattern of needs on the part of the population. Rather than to increase growth extensively by adding to the labour force, the economy now requires intensive growth entailing an increase in labour productivity. The traditional 'capitalist' solution to some of the Soviet Union's economic problems would be a movement away from a full-employment, low-wage economy to a high-wage, low-employment one. Material 'stimulation' of labour to achieve greater efficiency has many implications for social policy. First, wage payments linked to 'material incentives' may distort differentials between groups of workers, thereby undermining the principles of distribution thought appropriate for the development of 'mature socialism'. Second, the utilisation of wages as a stimulus will only be effective if payment can be realised through consumption. This is not just a problem of adjusting the economic mechanism but involves the development of different products and the introduction of market prices for many highly subsidised services. A consumer society fulfils a particular pattern of needs: it encourages production to respond to the pattern of demand given by the distribution of income. The consumption needs of the richer groups might be met at the cost of those of the poorer ones. Such a policy is at variance with the political goals and ideological outlook of the Soviet political leadership (or at least with elements of it). Third, improving material incentives involves not only rewarding those who work efficiently but penalising workers who default. The organisation of work on the basis of efficiency, where for the enterprise marginal cost equals marginal revenue, is likely to involve a reduction in the workforce. Unemployment may follow in the train of a move to a Western-type economy based on maximising the efficiency of production units and giving priority to consumption needs. Unemployment is not only a consequence of substituting capital for labour but it also acts to discipline the labour force and as a reservoir to meet changing industrial requirements for labour (by sector and geographical location).

A policy involving a significant shift from a full-employment, low-pay economy is not likely to be adopted. Ideology can only be effective in terms of social policy if there are dominant and subordinate groups in support of it. The maintenance of the present employment policy may be considered to be (a) in the interests of the Party political (rather than the economic) leadership, (b) supported by economic managers at the point of production who rely on labour surpluses in the enterprise to ease their production bottlenecks (labour size is also a criterion of management earnings) and (c) required by the masses of employed people who fear unemployment and, in the absence of unemployment benefit, poverty. A move to a high-wage, low-employment policy would undermine the legitimacy of the political leadership, and the essence of a socialist society as it has been conceived of in the Soviet Union would be threatened. Another way of putting it is that certain groups' interests are met by present policy which would be undermined by a market-type economic reform. The present system of planning gives the Party and government leadership prerogatives over the allocation of resources that would pass to 'the market'. This not only diminishes the political power of the economic ministries and Party but would be likely to divert resources away from defence and welfare policies to consumption. A weakening of the right to employment would be feared by the mass of wage workers and qualms about the effects of labour unrest (in a socialist society) are probably strong enough for the Party leadership to give priority to the maintenance of loyalty on the part of the working population albeit at the expense of economic efficiency.

The Soviet political leadership is not only legitimated by the provision of work and full employment but also by an economy that fulfils the material and spiritual needs of the population. It is faced here with a number of contradictions. Improving the level of production in the Western style through wage incentives leads to a greater 'instrumentality' in the attitude to work which is contrary to the socialist goal of fulfilling the psychological needs of the worker through satisfying work. There is some evidence that some strata of management and workers may be sufficiently confident of their position to advocate a policy of efficiency involving lay-offs rather than of 'overful employment' giving loyalty.

If one is a pessimist, one might argue that the Soviet economy will progressively weaken, or even colllapse, unless it adopts a labour policy in line with this latter kind of perspective. If one is an optimist, one would believe that economic change and advance may be achieved through the adaptation of existing Soviet methods—through improvements in planning and the evolution of alternative methods to improve the productivity, discipline and mobility of the workforce. The experience of the USSR in maintaining to date full employment is one major way that it is differentiated from the capitalist West. Have we anything to learn from such experience? Is such full employment only characteristic of the early stage of socialist industrialisation, and is it now a brake on the development of the productive forces? If so, how will ideology change to incorporate a new labour policy? The answers to such questions are not only of importance to the future of the Soviet Union but also to the economies and societies of the West. One must be reminded that the advanced Western economies have not solved their own problems of maintaining growth with full employment, and the labour process is characterised by alienation.

The Soviet Union in particular and the socialist states in general will have to work out new policies. These seem likely to occur in the context of a full-employment economy. Merely copying the practice of the West would not only import the labour problems of capitalism but, because the legitimating ideology is not one of competitive individualism, would also have serious destabilising effects on the political order.

NOTES

1. I am indebted to Steve Wheatcroft for pointing out this distinction.
2. Karl Marx, *Capital*, vol.1, (Moscow, 1958) pp.183–4.
3. 'The German Ideology', reprinted in T.B. Bottomore and M. Rubel, *Karl Marx: Selected Writings in Sociology and Social History* (London: 1963), p.75.
4. *Economic and Political Manuscripts of 1844* (Moscow, 1959) p.75.
5. See *Capital, op cit*, p.177.
6. B. Ollman, *Alienation: Marx's Conception of Man in Capitalist Society* (Cambridge, 1976), p.137.
7. *Labour and Monopoly Capitalism* (New York. 1974).
8. Marx, *Capital, op. cit.*, p.484.
9. Claus Offe, 'Arbeit als sotsiologische schlusselkategorie', in *Krise der Arbeitsgesellschaft*? (Frankfurt, 1983).
10. *Ibid.*, pp.45, 50.
11. *Ibid.*, pp.59
12. M. Jahoda, *Employment and Unemployment: A Social-Psychological Analysis* (Cambridge, 1982).
13. Offe, *op. cit.*, p.53.
14. D. Lane, 'Leninism as an Ideology of Soviet Development', in E. de Kadt and G. Williams (eds.), *Sociology and Development*, (London, 1974).
15. V.I. Lenin, *Collected Works* (Moscow, 1960–70), vol.3, p.598.
16. *Ibid.* vol.27, p.259.
17. *Ibid.*
18. *See* the useful discussion of Soviet views by M. Yanowitch, 'Alienation and the Young Marx in Soviet Thought' *Slavic Review*, no. 1 (1967).
19. 'The Opening of the Constituent Assembly' (18 Jan. 1918). Report in James Bunyan and H.H. Fisher, *The Bolshevik Revolution 1917–18. Documents and Materials*, (Stanford, Calif., 1934), p.372.
20. L.I. Brezhnev, *Leninskim kursom*, (Moscow, 1982), vol.9, p.310.
21. *Ibid.*, (1970), vol.2, p.270.
22. Offe, *op. cit.*, p.55.
23. M. Seeman, 'On the Meaning of Alienation', *Amer. Soc. Rev.*, vol. 24 (1959); R. Blauner, *Alienation and Freedom* (Chicago, 1967). Blauner's work has been well received in the USSR; *see* discussion in Yanowitch, *loc. cit.*, p.48.

24. Blauner, *ibid.*, p.15.
25. Particularly, A.G. Zdravomyslov *et al.*, *Man and His Work* (New York: IASP 1967). On the increase of monotonous jobs, *see* discussion in: *Znanie-sila* no. 2, 1980; N.A. Aitov, *Sotsiologicheskie issledovaniya*, no. 3, 1979.
26. *See:* N.F. Naumova in V.I. Dobrynova (ed.), *Sovetski obraz zhizni segodniya i zavtra* (Moscow, 1976); V.A. Yadov and A.A. Kissel, *Sotsiologicheskie issledovaniya*, no. 1, 1974.
27. This is one of the findings of the replication of the Leningrad study, reported by Yadov in *Komsomol'skaya Pravda*, 9 Feb. 1978.
28. *See:* Ya. S. Kapeliush, *Obshchestvennoe mnenie o vybornosti na proizvodstvo* (1969), translated in M. Yanowitch (ed.) *Soviet Work Attitudes* (New York; 1979), pp.60–80; *Literaturnaya Gazeta*, 3 Nov. 1976. O.I. Kosenko, in *Ekonomika i organizatsiya promyshlennogo proizvodstva*, No. 1, 1977, pp.89–95; O.I. Kosenko, *Pravda*, 5 April, 1983.
29. *See* S. Marnie's paper in the present collection, Ch.12.
30. A.G. Zdravomyslov, *op. cit.*, p.146.
31. Offe, *op. cit.*, p.54.
32. Robert E. Lane, 'Markets and the Satisfaction of Human Wants', *Journal of Economic Issues*, vol.12, no.4 (Dec. 1978) pp.799–827.

PART I

The Historical Background

2 The Ending of Mass Unemployment in the USSR

R.W. DAVIES*

The end of mass unemployment in the USSR, which occurred in the course of a mere eighteen months in 1929 and 1930, has a strong claim to be considered one of the most important events in twentieth-century world history. In many Western capitalist countries, the level of unemployment in the 1920s was much higher than it had been before the First World War, and in 1929–30, when mass unemployment was largely eliminated in the Soviet Union, the onset of the world economic crisis resulted in a vast increase in the already large numbers of unemployed in Western Europe and the United States. Even towards the end of the 1930s, industrial production in several major countries was lower than at the end of the 1920s, and unemployment remained very high. The Soviet Union, with its full employment and its high rate of industrial growth, seemed to many in the West to have provided fundamental proof that socialism, or at any rate comprehensive planning, offered the only way forward.

After the Second World War, for about a quarter of a century the balance of economic advantage and disadvantage between Soviet socialism and democratic capitalism seemed to have changed substantially. Between about 1950 and the early 1970s it was abundantly clear to most Western socialists, and even liberals, that Western capitalism, applying Keynesian prescriptions, had managed to emulate Soviet success in eliminating mass unemployment and had smoothed out cyclical booms and slumps. This achievement of bourgeois-democratic states lent itself to Marxist as well as Keynesian analysis; almost all Marxists at that time explained capitalist economic crisis in terms of underconsumption

* Centre for Russian and East European Studies, University of Birmingham.

or overproduction rather than of a fundamental tendency in capitalism to produce major economic disproportions. As the years passed, empirical observation seemed to confirm that these major changes in the economic behaviour of Western capitalism were permanent. It now seemed that the main advantage of Soviet planning lay not in the presence of full employment but in its remarkable (and also evidently permanent) ability to promote very rapid growth. This growth was so striking that many were prepared to argue that it would result in the emergence of the Soviet Union as the world's most powerful economy by the 1970s, or at any rate the 1980s. Perhaps the Western economies could introduce more socialist planning into their democracy, and the communist countries could introduce more democracy and individual freedom into their socialism. To achieve this would require major political changes in East and West. But once these bridges were crossed, Utopia would be well on its way.

In the 1970s, dark clouds gathered slowly and unexpectedly above both West and East. The West, more gently than in the 1930s, but equally relentlessly, plunged into an economic crisis which brought back a high level of mass unemployment: in Britain, unemployment steadily rose from 2 to over 14 per cent of the employed population, a figure higher than in all but the worst years of the 1920s and 1930s. In the Soviet Union, on the other hand, the annual reports on the fulfilment of the plan still continue to proclaim, more or less correctly, that 'as in previous years, the full employment of the population capable of work was ensured'. But the onset of mass unemployment in the West did not result in a corresponding onset of mass conversions to Soviet socialism. This was partly, perhaps, because the slowness of the descent hindered us from comprehending the depth and degradation of the abyss into which the world capitalist economy was descending; in the industrialised countries it was certainly also partly due to the mitigation of the immediate effects of the hell of unemployment by higher welfare benefits than were available between the wars. But it was mainly due to widespread and growing disenchantment with the performance of the Soviet economy.

During the 1970s, in the unpropitious context of the unwillingness of the Soviet authorities to widen the bounds of individual freedom, Soviet industrial growth gradually slowed down, and latent inhibitions on innovation became much more obvious and damaging. Many Western observers, including some of those sympathetic to planning, concluded that the Soviet Union needed to infuse not only more democracy but also more competitive market forces (perhaps even some unemployment?) into its socialism. And as for the West, no one except the monetarists seemed to be able to state confidently what should be done with the Western economies in order to pull them out of unemployment and crisis. The easy assumptions about economic progress in the 1950s and 1960s, which took it for granted that the right to employment was inalienable, were thus shattered by the crisis of the 1970s.

This is not the whole story. In my view there is far from sufficient indignation in the West about the rebirth of the scourge of unemployment; and, because of the great stress placed in virtually all Western writings on the undoubted weaknesses of Soviet-type economies, there is insufficient recognition of the significance of the success of the communist world in eliminating unemployment. 'Modernisation without unemployment' should be inscribed on our banners when we boldly march upon the Kremlin, the White House and 10 Downing Street with recommendations for economic reform.

Following the Bolshevik revolution of October 1917, between 1919 and 1920, during the civil war, mass unemployment seemed to have been eliminated for ever in Soviet Russia. But with the introduction of the New Economic Policy (NEP) in 1921, the restoration of the market economy brought with it the re-emergence of the scourge of mass unemployment in 1922 and 1923.[1] As early as the beginning of 1922, an authoritative labour official wrote of the 'repulsive phenomena of capitalist accounting behaviour, bringing about competition between men and women and between adults and adolescents'.[2] Throughout the golden age of NEP, mass unemployment was a major and durable deficiency. The definition of 'unemployment' is, of course, much disputed. In a peasant country like the Soviet Union in the 1920s, many people in the countryside are 'unemployed' in the straightforward sense that work which they would like to take on is not available to them in their village and many more are 'underemployed' in the more ambiguous sense that the marginal productivity of their labour is very low indeed. Figures varying between 5 and 20 or more million persons were suggested in the 1920s for the level of Soviet rural underemployment. Here I shall confine myself to unemployment in the stricter sense of 'failure of a person to obtain employment when seeking it', and will deal mainly with unemployment in the towns.[3]

Even in the case of urban unemployment there are many problems of measurement. Like unemployment statistics in capitalist countries in the inter-war years, Soviet statistics for unemployment varied greatly.[4] (Some of the major problems are discussed in Ch.3 of this collection.) The most reliable figure is provided by the population census of December 1926. Here the definition of 'unemployment' is strictly confined to those entirely without work at the time of the census, and people with temporary or part-time work, or engaged in public works, are excluded from the category of 'unemployed'. The census total was 1,013,383, excluding Turkmenistan.[5] Two other series, from the labour exchanges of the People's Commissariat for Labour (Narkomtrud) and from the trade unions, provided substantially higher figures for the number of people registered as unemployed on approximately the same date; these series both included people with temporary and part-time work who registered in order to seek more permanent employment. The number registered with the 281 urban labour exchanges of Narkomtrud on 1 January 1927 was 1,310,000. This figure included some half a million non-trade-unionists.[6] In the alternative series compiled by the trade unions, the number of trade unionists alone registered as unemployed on the same date was as many as 1,667,000.[7] The commissariat for industry, Vesenkha, estimated from these two series that the total number of unemployed on that date of trade unionists and non-trade-unionists together was at least 2,300,000, and one estimate of the State Planning Commission, Gosplan, was 2,275,000, including 600,000 seasonal workers.[8]

Most authorities at the time agreed that the labour-exchange series was too low, and the trade-union series and the Vesenkha and Gosplan estimates were too high. The two time-series were not very reliable as a measure of the rate of change of unemployment, as significant changes occurred in their coverage in the course of 1924–1930 (see Ch.3).

The general level of unemployment was undoubtedly high. Unemployment even on the narrow definition of the population census amounted to some 9 per cent of the employed population, and the labour-exchange series shows unemployment amounting to 11.2 per cent of the employed population for the economic year 1926/27.[9] This level of unemployment was higher than the British level of the 1920s, roughly comparable with that of the second half of the 1930s, though lower than in either Britain or the United States in the worst depression years.[10]

According to both the labour-exchange and the trade-union series, unemployment was rising continuously throughout almost the whole of the 1920s, both in absolute numbers and as a proportion of the employed population. In the labour-exchange series it rose in the economic year 1925/26 by 16.4 per cent. In the economic year 1926/27 a slight decline by 2.8 per cent was in large part a purely statistical result of restrictions on the right to register at labour exchanges. Unemployment rose rapidly again in 1927/28, by as much as 31.1 per cent. Even on 1 April 1929, the month in which the five-year plan was approved, unemployment was 10.5 per cent higher than on the same date in the previous year. By this time unemployment, as recorded in this series, equalled some 13 to 14 per cent of the employed population. The upward trend shown by this series must be regarded with some caution, at least as far as its magnitude is concerned (again, see Ch.3 for further discussion). But, by all accounts, unemployment during NEP was far higher than unemployment before the revolution. The estimate of a Soviet economist, an average of between 400,000 and 500,000 in 1900–13,[11] is certainly less than half the level of unemployment in the Soviet Union in 1928 by the same definition.

As in the Western capitalist countries, unemployment in NEP Russia was seen as an ever-present menace by large numbers of urban workers. A survey by the information department of the party central committee for 1925 admitted that, because of unemployment, workers were constantly afraid of losing their job.[12] But unemployment during NEP was in one major respect strikingly different from unemployment in Western capitalist countries. In the USSR it was not due to economic depression. On the contrary, it persisted and expanded in spite of a rapid and continuous expansion of employment. The number of job vacancies increased rapidly;[13] between 1924/25 and 1929 the number of employed persons increased from 8.5 to 12.4 millions, an expansion sufficient to absorb far more than the whole of the natural expansion of the able-bodied urban population.[14] But simultaneously labour migrated in substantial numbers from underemployment in the countryside to seek employment in the towns. Estimates of migration vary widely. But there is no doubt that in the middle and late 1920s the pull of the towns was far greater than before the revolution. According to some Soviet estimates, annual net migration from country to town increased

from about one third of a million a year to over a million a year in
the course of the period 1923–28.[15]

Rural–urban migration, encouraged by the growth of opportunities for work in towns and on building sites, was the driving-force
which exerted a constant pressure on the authorities to provide
more work, and it strongly influenced the pattern of urban
unemployment. According to the labour-exchange statistics, as
many as 28.5 per cent of the 1,478,000 persons unemployed on 1
April 1927 had never previously been employed (Table 3.5); over
one-third of these were new arrivals from the countryside.[16] The
number temporarily declined after a decree of the Council of
People's Commissars restricted registration of those never previously employed to the children of employed persons.[17] Owing to
the seasonal character of building and of several other industries,
variation in unemployment within each year was very high: in the
four years from 1925/26 to 1928/29 the percentage increases in
unemployment between October 1 (when seasonal employment
was high) and April 1 (when seasonal employment was low) varied
between 15 and 50 per cent.

In the USSR in the 1920s, the liberating effect of the revolution
encouraged women to seek work and to strive for economic
independence from men, and the unemployment regulations gave
unemployed women the same rights as unemployed men. In
consequence, women registered as unemployed to a substantially
greater extent than in other countries in the inter-war years.
Women constituted 43.8 per cent of the unemployed registered at
the labour exchanges on 1 April 1927 (see Table 3.5), but were less
than 30 per cent of the number of employed persons.[18] In addition,
a substantial number of unemployed was registered in the category
'intellectual labour' (including clerical labour), amounting to 19.2
per cent of unemployed registered at labour exchanges on 1 April
1927 (see Table 3.5).

But in some other important respects the pattern of unemployment resembled that familiar to us in industrial countries. Over 50
per cent of those registered as unemployed on 1 April 1927 were
unskilled. The proportion of young people among the unemployed
was also very high. In 1928, on the eve of the first five-year plan,
74 per cent of registered unemployed were between the age of
eighteen and twenty-nine.[19] A Narkomtrud report of 1926
characterised unemployment among young people as 'huge in
scale and in the severity of the situation'.[20] A resolution of the
fifteenth Party conference in October/November 1926 admitted

that many children of workers:

> lack opportunity for training not only in educational establishments but also in the factory. . . They disintegrate morally and together with the adolescent homeless [*bezprizornye*] form the main cadres on our disturbed streets, turning into an anti-social element which poisons a considerable part of working youth with its psychology, and even the least stable strata in the Young Communist League [resulting in] . . . a wave of hooliganism even in the best proletarian areas.[21]

But the level of unemployment was relatively low among members of the metalworkers', chemical workers', miners' and textile-workers' trade unions (see table 3.7, p.46), and various types of skilled workers were already in extremely short supply.[22]

In preparing to industrialise the Soviet Union, Soviet political leaders and officials were at first pessimistic about the prospects for eliminating mass unemployment. In 1926 the Gosplan economist Strumilin predicted a possible labour shortage by 1932, but this unusual optimism was apparently based on the unrealistic assumption that the able-bodied urban population would increase by no more than a couple of million during the forthcoming five years.[23] A year later the spring 1927 Gosplan draft of the five-year plan estimated that unemployment, 1.2 million in 1926/27, would remain more or less stable throughout the period up to 1930/31, in spite of a substantial increase in employment; only during the second five-year plan (1931/32–1935/6) was unemployment likely to decline, primarily as a result of a decline in the number of adolescents entering the labour force.[24] The Vesenkha draft of the five-year plan, also compiled in the spring of 1927, more pessimistically estimated that unemployment was as much as 1.9 million in 1926/27 and would increase to over 2.3 million in 1931/32.[25] Kraval', head of the Labour Department of Vesenkha, declared that it would not be the expansion of industry but the introduction of labour-intensive crops in agriculture which would solve the problem of unemployment.[26] Kuibyshev, chairman of Vesenkha, also acknowledged that the rate of recruitment to industry would be insufficient to solve the problem of unemployment, and called for more attention to the expansion of artisan industries.[27]

The intractability of the unemployment problem in the short term appeared to be dictated by the fundamental conditions of NEP. All the drafts of the five-year plan assumed that industrialisation must be financed almost exclusively by the urban economy itself. The strengthening of the 'worker-peasant alliance' required that peasants should not be exploited in the interests of industrialisation; instead, labour productivity must rise and costs fall in industry, building and transport, and savings must be obtained by reducing administrative costs. The 'regime of economy' in 1926 and the rationalisation drive in 1927 were particularly directed towards restricting labour costs. The increase in the number of employed persons, which amounted to 1,641,000 in the single year 1925/26 when the economy was still recovering to its pre-war level, was only 771,000 in 1926/27 and 394,000 in 1927/28.[28] These figures, together with the relentless migration into the towns, explain the substantial rise in unemployment in these years. Both in 1926/27 and 1927/28, the economy drive resulted in a substantial increase in the already large number of unemployed in the group 'intellectual labour', as a result of the dismissal of officials both in government and in the economy.[29]

The high absolute level and substantial increase of unemployment in 1927 provided the United Opposition with one of their most telling criticisms of official policies. The United Opposition platform of September 1927, assessing the number of unemployed at about 2 million as compared with the official figure of 1.5 million, claimed that 'the number of unemployed is growing incomparably faster than the total number of employed workers'. The platform argued that the number of unemployed would reach at least 3 million by the end of the five-year plan in 1931, resulting in an increase in the number of 'homeless children, beggars and prostitutes'; this rise in unemployment was attributed to 'the slow growth of industrialisation'.[30] But, committed like the Party leadership to the stability of the currency and to the market relation with the mass of the peasantry, the Opposition was not able to indicate a realistic alternative road to rapid industrialisation.

While the persistence of unemployment, and its undesirable social consequences, were undoubtedly a source of anxiety for the Party leaders, in my judgement the deliberate aim of eliminating unemployment quickly was not a decisive factor in the switch to rapid industrialisation between 1927 and 1929. Unemployment was not a prominent issue in the speeches of Stalin and his associates justifying accelerated industrialisation; these were primarily couched in terms of such factors as the need to overtake the capitalist countries in the interests of the defence of the USSR, and to provide the base for the industrialisation of peasant agriculture.[31] It was rather that, having decided to undertake rapid industrialisation primarily for other reasons, the Party leaders gradually came to realise that the prospects for eliminating unemployment were much brighter than they previously assumed.

The first major policy measure holding out the prospects of a substantial reduction in unemployment was the decision in the autumn of 1927 to reduce the standard working day, with its corollary that in some industries a three-shift system would be introduced, so that more workers would be employed on the same equipment. From the spring of 1927 onwards, these policies were pressed upon the authorities by prominent advocates of industrialisation—such as Larin, Strumilin and Sabsovich—who were not tainted with association with Trotsky and the United Opposition.[32] But, even after the adoption of these measures, Kuibyshev still anticipated that unemployment would continue throughout the five-year plan, falling only to 848,000 in 1931/32 as compared with 1,268,000 in 1926/27.[33] Eighteen months later, in the spring of 1929, the optimum Gosplan variant approved by the sixteenth Party conference assumed that unemployment would amount to 511,000 in 1932/33 as compared with 1,100,000 in 1927/28, and claimed that 500,000 unemployed was 'approximately the size of the free reserve necessary in the system of the Soviet economy for a normal turnover of labour power'.[34] The figures are dubious as they were obtained as a residual in labour balances: the starting-point of 1.1 million unemployed in 1927/28 is certainly an underestimate. And the argument that 500,000 unemployed, 3.5 per cent of the employed labour force, was a 'necessary' level was soon to be dismissed as a heresy. But the significance of this variant of the plan was that it anticipated, for the first time in an official document, that the elimination or drastic reduction of mass unemployment was possible within a few years.

For most of the economic year 1928/29, registered unemployment was substantially higher than on the same date in the previous year: on 1 April 1929 it was 10 per cent higher than on 1 April 1928. But the rapid growth of the number of registered unemployed characteristic of the previous two years had slowed down; the Gosplan control figures for 1929/30, prepared in the autumn of 1929, proclaimed this to be a 'definite breakthrough'.[35] A large part of this improvement was evidently due to the increase in the number of employed persons by 696,000 during 1928/29, a substantially larger number than in the previous year.[36] During 1928/29, skilled workers were increasingly absorbed into the labour force; the percentage of unskilled workers, adolescents and women in the total number of unemployed substantially increased (see Table 3.5). The head of the Moscow labour exchange reported a shortage in 1928/29 of skilled workers in building and in a number of other industries.[37] The Moscow electrical engineering factory, Elektrozavod, complained that the labour exchange had supplied only 15 per cent of its requirements for skilled labour and had been unable to supply any technical personnel, including draughtsmen.[38] Similar statements appeared frequently in the economic and industrial press from the summer of 1929 onwards.

In spite of these shortages, and the booming industrial economy, much scepticism continued about the prospects for full employment. As late as the autumn of 1929, a Narkomtrud official, surveying the prospects for the next five years, declared that 'we must recognise with Bolshevik straightforwardness that we have stagnant unemployment, which is far from fully reflected in our balances and in the file cards of the labour exchanges' and insisted that during the first five-year plan 'we shall not be able to reduce the number of unemployed to the reserve of labour power normally necessary for the economy'.[39] This was promptly denounced by a prominent labour specialist as 'Right-wing opportunist panic'.[40] But Gosplan's estimates of the likely effect of industrialisation on unemployment during the economic year 1929/30, prepared in the summer and autumn of 1929, remained cautious. This was partly because so many of the unemployed were unskilled and inexperienced. But it was also due to the retention in the 1929/30 control figures of the optimistic assumption that the efficiency of labour would substantially improve throughout the economy in spite of the large planned expansion of industry and capital construction, the total number of employed persons was intended to increase by only 9.4 per cent, 1.1 million persons.[41] According to Gosplan, the average number of unemployed, in view of the continued influx into the towns, would accordingly fall by less than 10 per cent in 1929/30, from 1,224,000 to 1,106,000.[42] But Krzhizhanovsky, chairman of Gosplan, while repeating the estimate that the total number of unemployed would fall by only 10 per cent, assured the Plenum of the Central Committee in November 1929 that only those seeking work for the first time would be unemployed by the end of 1929/30, while skilled workers would be in short supply.[43] The deputy commissar of Narkomtrud anticipated a reduction of unemployment by as much as 25 per cent in 1929/30.[44]

In the event, the decline in unemployment during 1929/30 was precipitate. The story is greatly complicated by the decision of the authorities to remove 'bogus unemployed' from the register on at least two occasions in 1929 and 1930—people were removed for unjustified refusal of jobs offered or because they were 'alien' or 'declassés', or eventually, in September 1930, because they 'registered for trades for which there was no demand' over a long period.[45] According to one report, 230,000 names were removed from the register at the labour exchanges in the course of 1929/30.[46] But these Thatcherite devices to improve the records should not obscure the main feature of the labour market in 1929/30—the enormous expansion in jobs available. The average annual number of employed persons (excluding agriculture) increased from 9.9 million in 1928 to 10.6 million in 1929 and 13 million in 1930.[47] Over two-thirds of the total increase in employment of 3.1 million in 1928–30 took place in industry and capital construction. In industry, primarily owing to the introduction of the continuous working week, the seven-hour day and an increased number of shifts, substantially more labour was able to be employed, even though the capital stock of industry did not greatly increase. In the long term the continuous working week proved inefficient and was abandoned, but in the short term it enabled substantial increases in employment and production. In construction, with the launching of the feverish investment programme of the expanded five-year plan, the number of persons employed increased by 77 per cent in the single year 1930.

The number of persons seeking work in the town also increased rapidly in 1928–30; according to Soviet estimates, the net number of persons settling in the towns increased from 1.06 million in 1928 to 1.39 million in 1929 and 2.63 million in 1930.[48] But in the winter of 1929/30, for the first time since the civil war, the increase in employment was greater than the increase in the number of persons seeking jobs. According to the labour-exchange statistics, unemployment fell by over 150,000 between 1 October 1929 and 1 April 1930; while part of this decline was purely statistical, it included a substantial genuine reduction of unemployment in a period when unemployment normally rose sharply.[49] The number of jobs on offer per registered unemployed person greatly increased.[50] By the spring of 1930, skilled workers were generally registered at the labour exchange merely for very short periods when changing jobs;[51] the industrial newspaper claimed that skilled workers were able to obtain a job within a couple of days and that unemployment (in Russian, 'lack of work': *bezrabotitsa*) had been replaced by 'lack of workers' (*bezrabochitsa*).[52] The pool of unemployed increasingly consisted of unskilled workers, many of them female, many of them adolescents, whom factory managements regarded as unprofitable because of their lack of skill and the special conditions attached to employing them.

During the spring and summer of 1930, unemployment undoubtedly decreased more rapidly than the normal seasonal decline. By the summer the labour shortage spread to the construction industry. The number of building workers, while much higher than in previous years, declined between August and October; normally it tended to increase.[53] The paradox was intensified: a substantial pool of unemployed existed simultaneously with increasing scarcity of labour. At the sixteenth Party congress in June/July 1930, Stalin castigated the 'big muddle' in Narkomtrud and the trade unions, who simultaneously claimed both that there were about one million unemployed and that there was 'a frightful shortage of skilled workers'; he drew the conclusion that there was no longer either 'a *reserve* army or still less a *permanent* army of unemployed for our industry'.[54] During the summer, the number of registered unemployed declined from 778,000 on July 1 to 335,000 on 1 October.[55] This was partly a real decline due to the increasing availability of jobs; in addition, large numbers of adolescents were recruited for a rapidly expanding programme training skilled workers through factory schools (FZU). An unsatisfied demand for 1,067,000 workers was reported for 1 September 1930.[56] But the figures were also reduced, as already described, by the large-scale removal of names from the register, particularly in September 1930.

In its original plans for the economic year 1930/31, Narkomtrud envisaged that unemployment would continue at a level of between 400,000 and 500,000, and that many of these would continue to receive unemployment benefit.[57] Unemployment was particularly expected to continue among two major groups: untrained youth, and housewives unable to take certain jobs or to transfer to certain areas because of their domestic conditions. Narkomtrud also expected that some of the migrants from the countryside would not succeed in finding work once the summer season was over.[58]

In the weeks after the Party congress, the Party decided to cut through these doubts and difficulties by adopting what one Soviet historian has called 'a forced-draft course to eliminate unemployment'.[59] On August 3, Uglanov, the People's Commissar for Labour, a former associate of Bukharin and the Right-wing, was dismissed.[60] On 3 September 1930 a Central Committee declaration rebuked Narkomtrud for 'publishing bureaucratic data about hundreds of thousands of unemployed and paying out tens of millions of rubles of so-called "unemployment" benefit', instead of struggling against 'selfish elements, flitters and those who refuse to work'. By this time, many of the key officials in Narkomtrud had already been replaced; some, including the respected labour economist L. Mints, were later accused of deliberate sabotage.[61] A far-reaching order from Narkomtrud dated October 9 attempted to end unemployment in a single blow. It cancelled all payments of unemployment benefit in view of the labour shortage and ruled that unemployed persons were to be allocated to vacant jobs forthwith, including unskilled work not related to their own past training. Anyone who refused to take the job offered would be removed from the register, unless producing a medical certificate.[62] This was reinforced by a Central Committee resolution and by further Narkomtrud orders; and on December 15 a decree of the Central Executive Committee and Sovnarkom announced 'the complete elimination of unemployment'.[63]

Precisely when unemployment came to an end in the USSR has been hotly disputed by Soviet historians.[64] But all agree that the process was completed by the end of 1931. If the term 'unemployment' includes structural and frictional unemployment, then these claims are unjustified; some unemployment in this sense has of course continued till the present day. But certainly mass unemployment came to an end in 1930; and henceforth severe shortages of labour were a prominent and perpetual feature of the Soviet scene.

The Soviet leaders, while claiming the maximum amount of credit—and not without justification—for the elimination of mass unemployment, at the same time recognised that the removal of the curb of unemployment, and the ready availability of alternative jobs, made it easier for the workforce to resist managerial efforts to improve labour discipline. In the autumn of 1930 the attitude temporarily came to prevail that, with the introduction of socialist planning and the elimination of unemployment, labour as well as the means of production must be directly planned by the state. The new deputy People's Commissar for Labour, Kraval', an associate of Stalin's, insisted that 'the words "labour exchange" and "labour market" should be finally driven out of our vocabulary, as it is entirely inappropriate for the proletarian state that the labour force should be quoted on some "market"'.[65] A corollary of the view that workers in a socialist economy were not commodities subject to market forces was that they must be subject to much greater planned control. Legislation, discussion and economic practice at this time all reflected a rapid movement towards the training and allocation of Soviet citizens in accordance with the needs of the central plan; principles and practices familiar in the years of War Communism were revived.

These far-reaching measures failed to establish a coherent system for direct planning and allocation of labour in any way comparable to the system of planning and allocating industrial production. The compulsory powers frequently worked badly; in practice, outside the growing forced-labour sector, workers normally remained free to change their jobs and were not subject to compulsory direction. Economic incentives were restored and strengthened in the course of 1931–35; a labour market, though an imperfect one, continued to exist. The problem of improving labour discipline in a full-employment society, and of planning an economy in which labour is partially directly planned, partially a commodity on a state-managed market, have continued to haunt the Soviet authorities ever since 1930.

NOTES

1. *See* E.H. Carr, *The Interregnum, 1923-24* (1955), pp.46–59.
2. A. Anikst, 'Sovremennaya bezrabotitsa v Rossii i bor'ba s neyu', *Vestnik truda*, No.2(17), 1922, p.12.
3. James Tobin plausibly argues that 'If people are at unproductive work, whether as hired wage earners, family farm hands, or self-employed, the best statistical symptom of this social malady is low, per capita income, not unemployment'; in *The Measurement and Behaviour of Unemployment* (Princeton, 1957), p.599.
4. Unemployment estimates for the USA, for example, varied between 464,000 and 2,080,000 for 1926, and between 2,896,000 and 4,825,000 for 1930; a 'best' figure has been suggested of 880,000 for 1926 and 4,340,000 for 1930 (*ibid.*, p.218).
5. *Vsesoyuznaya perepis' naseleniya 1926 goda*, vol. LII (1931), pp.86–7.
6. L.S. Rogachevskaya, *Likvidatsiya bezrabotitsy v SSSR, 1917–30gg* (Moscow, 1973), p.249.
7. *Materialy k pyatiletnemu planu razvitiya promyshlennosti (1927/28–1931/32gg)* (Moscow, 1927), p.93.
8. *Ibid.*, p.93.
9. Average unemployment in 1926/27 was reported by the labour-

exchange series as 1,240,000; the average number of employed persons was 11,007,000 (excluding all self-employed persons but including employment in the private sector); see *Kontrol'nye tsifry narodnogo khozyaistva SSSR na 1928/29 god* (Moscow, 1929), pp.156–7, 452–5.

10. For Britain, *see* Sir William Beveridge, 'An Analysis of Unemployment', *Economica*, Nov. 1936, pp.360–87. In *The Measurement and Behavior of Unemployment* (Princeton, 1957), p.280, E. Ginzberg characterises the US unemployment level of 25–33 per cent in the 1930s as a 'gross pathological condition'.

11. *See* L. Mints, in *Bol'shaya sovetskaya entsiklopediya*, v (1930), col. 214; this figure excludes unemployed persons not previously employed, which amounted to about one-third of the 1928 labour-exchange figure.

12. Cited from the archives in K.I. Suvorov, *Istoricheskii opyt KPSS po likvidatsii bezrabotitsy* (Moscow, 1968), p.80.

13. *See also* comments on the tendency of 'intensity' of unemployment to decline in Ch.3.

14. *Narodnoe khozyaistvo SSSR* (Moscow, 1932), pp.410–1; these figures include employment in agriculture; the equivalent figures excluding agriculture were 6.7 and 10.4 millions; of course, none of these figures include the independent producers in the 25 million peasant households and the independent artisans in the towns.

15. *See* E.H. Carr and R.W. Davies, *Foundations of a Planned Economy, 1926–29*, vol.1 (London, 1969), p.454.

16. *Kontrol'nye tsifry . . . 1928/29* (Moscow, 1929), p.156, reported that on average in 1925/26 13.7 per cent, in 1926/27 11.9 per cent and in 1927/28 10.0 per cent of registered unemployed were new arrivals.

17. *Sobranie zakonov, 1927*, art. 132; this was an attempt to reinforce earlier legislation (*see* Ch.3 in this collection).

18. In the USA and in Britain in the 1930s the rate of registered unemployment was lower among women than among men.

19. *See* Carr and Davies *op. cit.* (London, 1969), pp. 457–8.

20. Cited from the archives in Rogachevskaya *op. cit.*, p.134.

21. *KPSS v rezolyutsiyakh*, vol. 2 (Moscow, 1954), p.325; the resolution added that this hooliganism was 'often exaggerated in a panicky fashion by our sensation-seeking press'.

22. *Kontrol'nye tsifry . . . 1928/29* (1929), p.158.

23. *Torgovo-promyshlennaya gazeta*, 16 May 1926 (report to Communist Academy).

24. *Perspektivy razvertivaniya narodnogo khozyaistva SSSR na 1926/27–1930/31gg.* (Moscow, 1927), pp.9–10, and Appendix, pp.15–6. The expected decline in the number of adolescents was a result of the low birth-rate during the world war and civil war.

25. *Materialy k pyatiletnemu planu razvitiya promyshlennosti SSSR (1927/28–1931/32gg.)* (Moscow, 1927), pp.91–3. Both the Gosplan and Vesenkha estimates were obtained as residuals by deducting estimates of 'utilised' from 'non-utilised' labour, and so should not be taken as equivalent to the number of registered unemployed (though Gosplan and Vesenkha themselves sometimes discussed their estimates as if these concepts were fully interchangeable).

26. *Torgovo-promyshlennaya gazeta*, 10 October 1926.
27. *Ibid.*, 25 September 1927 (speech to the 'active' party members of Krasnaya Presnya, Moscow).
28. *Trud v SSSR* (1936), pp.10–1; *Kontrol'nye tsifry . . . na 1928/29*, (1929), pp.454–5; there are slight differences between these two series, but these amount to less than 1 per cent of our estimates.
29. The number unemployed in this group rose from 210,500 on 1 October 1926 to 317,800 on 1 October 1928, increasing from 19.7 to 23.3 per cent of the total; in *Trud v SSSR, 1926–1930: spravochnik* (Moscow, 1930), p.36.
30. *The Platform of the Joint Opposition (1927)* (London: 1973), p.17.
31. *See*, for example, Stalin's speech at the Plenum of the Party Central Committee, 19 November 1928 (*Sochineniya*, Moscow, vol.xi, pp.245–57).
32. Strumilin was in charge of perspective planning in Gosplan, and Sabsovich was head of the planning department of Vesenkha. *SSSR: 4 s"ezd sovetov* (Moscow, 1927), pp.369–72 (Larin, April 1927); S.G. Strumilin, *Na planovom fronte* (Moscow, 1958), p.377 (speech of 2 April 1927 at a Gosplan congress); L. Sabsovich in *Torgovo-promyshlennaya gazeta*, 19 October 1927.
33. *See* Carr and Davies, *op. cit.* (1969), p.463.
34. *Pyatiletnii plan narodno-kho zyaistvennogo stroitel'stva SSSR* (3rd edn., 1930), vol.ii, part ii, p.178.
35. *Kontrol'nye tsifry narodnogo khozyaistva SSSR na 1929/30 god* (Moscow, 1930), p.239.
36. *Ibid.*, p.487; for increases in employment in previous years *see* p.23 above.
37. *Torgovo-promyshlennaya gazeta*, 26 December 1929.
38. *Ibid.*
39. B. Spektor, in *Ekonomicheskoe obozrenie*, no. 9, September 1929, p.94.
40. S. Kheinman, in *ibid.*, no.11, November 1929, p.49.
41. *Kontrol'nye tsifry . . . na 1929/30* (1930), p.487.
42. *Ibid.*, pp.249, 486.
43. Cited from the archives in Suvorov, *op. cit.*, pp.203–4.
44. *Torgovo-promyshlennaya gazeta*, 5 September 1929.
45. M. Romanov, in *Voprosy truda*, nos. 7–8, 1930, pp.49, 53; *Industriali-zatsiya SSSR, 1929–1932 gg.* (Moscow, 1970), p.386 (report of Narkomtrud).
46. *Industrializatsiya, ibid.*, p.385.
47. A. David Redding, 'Nonagricultural Employment in the USSR, 1928–55', Ph.D. thesis, Columbia University (1958), p.35.
48. *Trud v SSSR* (Moscow, 1936), p.7.
49. It was claimed that only 1.2 per cent of those registered were removed from the labour-exchange lists in the 'cleansing' of early 1930 (*Voprosy truda*, nos. 7–8, 1930, p.49).
50. The number of jobs available at labour exchanges per 100 unem-ployed persons was 68.3 in 1925/26, 98.1 in 1926/27, 125.2 in 1927/28, 142.1 in 1928/29 and 181.4 in the first five months of 1929/30; in *Trud v SSSR 1926–30* (1930), p.36.

51. M. Romanov, in *Voprosy truda*, nos. 7–8, 1930, p.50.
52. *Za industrializatsiyu*, 19 June, 1930.
53. *Trud v SSSR* (Moscow, 1936), p.244. This was partly because some seasonal workers returned to their villages, attracted by the good harvest and repelled by the poor conditions on building sites (the net overall seasonal outflow from the villages was, however, much higher than in previous years). How far in addition to this the collective farms succeeded in holding back labour from moving to or remaining in the towns is much disputed; *see* R.W. Davies, *The Soviet Collective Farm, 1929–1930* (1980), p.166, and N. Shiokawa, in *Annals of the Institute of Social Science* (Tokyo: University of Tokyo), no. 24 (1982–83), pp.138–9.
54. I.V. Stalin, *Sochineniya*, vol. xii (Moscow, 1949), pp.292–3 (Stalin's emphasis).
55. Rogachevskaya, *op. cit.*, p.279.
56. *Ibid.*, p.281.
57. *Ibid.*, pp.274, 276.
58. *See* the discussion in A.S. Sycheva, in *Uchenye zapiski Moskovskogo oblastnogo pedinstituta*, vol.cxxxv (Moscow, 1964), pp.208–9.
59. *Ibid.*, p.208.
60. *Sobranie zakonov 1930*, vol.ii, arts. 266–7; he was replaced by A.S. Tsikhon.
61. *See* G. Gimmel'farb in *Problemy ekonomiki*, nos. 4–5, 1931, p.33.
62. *Pravda*, 11 October, 1930.
63. *Sobranie zakonov, 1930*, art. 641. The resolution of the Central Committee Plenum of 17–21 December 1930, however, more cautiously stated that 'we have the elimination of unemployment in the main *[v osnovnom]*', in *KPSS v rezolyutsiakh*, vol.iii (1954), p.76; this modification was apparently introduced at the behest of a Narkomtrud report prepared in the same month (*see* Sycheva, *loc. cit.*, citing the archives).
64. A.S. Sycheva, *op. cit.* (1964), p.209, argued that some unskilled persons, mainly women and adolescents, were unable to find employment at the end of 1930, and claimed that 'if one considers the moment of full and final location of an unemployed person in training or in work to be the moment when he or she ceases to be unemployed, then the process of eliminating unemployment lasted until the end of 1931'. The number of registered unemployed was 236,700 on 1 November 1930, 259,300 on 1 December 1930, 236,000 on 1 January 1931, 205,700 (including 57,200 adolescents) on 1 April, and 18,000 on 1 August (*ibid.*, p.209; Suvorov (1968), pp.224–7, V.Z. Drobizhev, *Sovetskii rabochii klass* (Moscow, 1961), p.36; *Trud v SSSR* (1932), p.9). But Rogachevskaya, *op. cit.*, pp.282–3, and Suvorov, *op. cit.*, pp. 226–7, argue that these were not unemployed persons, merely persons seeking to find work via the reorganised labour exchanges, adducing in proof the large number of job vacancies throughout this period; 'those wishing to find jobs obtained work in 3 to 5 days'.
65. *Za industrializatsiyu*, 17 November 1930; italicised in original.

3 A Note on the Sources of Unemployment Statistics

R.W. DAVIES and S.G. WHEATCROFT*

Unemployment data are available from four major sources: the population censuses (the urban population census of March 1923 and the general population census of 17 December 1926); the data of the labour exchanges of Narkomtrud on registered unemployed; the current data of the trade unions on the unemployed trade unionists registered with them; and the censuses of unemployed trade unionists of October 1925 and October–November 1927.

The fullest data are provided in the population census (Table 3.3), in which a volume is devoted to unemployment: *Vsesoyuznaya perepis' naseleniya 1926 goda*, vol. LII (1931). This provides data on numbers of unemployed by age, length of unemployment, region (including place of origin) and in great detail by type of former work; it includes data both on those previously in work and on those who are seeking work but have never been employed. Only those actually unemployed on the day of the census are included: the instruction to the census-taker reads, *'Persons are considered as unemployed only if they have no work at all at the time* and are seeking it. Those with any earnings (even though temporary and not in their own trade) are considered as employed'; this included unemployed who are engaged in public works. The population census data are discussed in L.I. Vas'kina, *Rabochii klass SSSR nakanune sotsialisticheskoi industrializatsii* (1981), pp.162–82; they deserve comprehensive examination.

The labour-exchange statistics (Tables 3.4–3.6) provide a series from 1922 to 1931. The data suffer from several defects. First, the coverage is not comprehensive by area. Labour exchanges existed only in medium- and large-size towns; even at the end of the 1920s

* Centre for Russian and East European Studies, University of Birmingham.

36

there were only 281 labour exchanges. As a result, many inhabitants of small towns, and of villages, were unable to register as unemployed. Second, some unemployed did not register with the labour exchanges but sought jobs through other channels, though this proportion greatly declined in the mid-1920s. Third, the regulations about who was entitled to register as unemployed changed in the course of the 1920s and generally aimed to exclude new arrivals from the countryside from registration. In 1924 registration was confined to trade-union members, skilled workers who had worked for at least three years and employees and manual workers who had worked for five years. This legislation temporarily drastically cut the number registered.[1] But it was evidently ineffective. A decree of March 1927 again restricted registration to 'real unemployed', including persons with previous employment for a stated period and children of workers and employees, and resulted in a substantial cut in the total.[2] Even so, according to Gosplan, 10 per cent of those registered in 1927/28 were migrants from the countryside.[3] Further legislation introduced in 1929 and 1930 is described in Ch. 2 above.

All these measures would tend to reduce the number registered below the true level. But other factors operated in the opposite direction. First, people registered, or remained registered, as unemployed, although not actively seeking work, so as to obtain various privileges available to the unemployed or to retain their official length of labour service *(trudovoi stazh)*.[4] Second, the trade unions insisted (apparently with incomplete success), especially on two occasions at the end of 1926 and 1928, that all unemployed trade unionists should register with the labour exchanges as well as with them.[5] Third, the proportion of vacancies filled via labour exchanges increased, and this led to an increase in the number of skilled workers and others who registered at the exchanges when seeking new jobs.[6] Fourth, the proportion of temporary jobs greatly increased.[7] This was a major source of uncertainty and frustration for those not in permanent work, but it presumably resulted in a rise in job turnover and increased the total number of persons registered as unemployed.

The third series was the register of unemployed kept by the trade unions (Table 3.7), generally believed to be exaggerated. Registration was quarterly, so people who found work remained on the register during the quarter; members, including housewives, registered, although not really seeking work, in order to retain their right to trade-union membership, an important lever in seeking work in the future.[8]

These three sources may be compared for the period of the population census, the winter of 1926–27. The census gave the lowest figure. The biggest discrepancy as compared with the labour-exchange statistics was the low figure for persons seeking work for the first time; this is something of a puzzle, as the provision that persons with temporary work should not count as unemployed would not be expected to affect this group. The number of 'previously employed persons' seeking work is roughly comparable in the two series (an exact comparison is impossible, as a breakdown of labour-exchange data has been available only for 1 October 1926 and 1 April 1927). But the number of women unemployed is substantially lower in the census, as is the number of unemployed builders.

The trade-union current series of registered unemployed is very much higher. On 1 January 1927 as many as 1,667,000 trade unionists were registered with the trade unions as unemployed;[9] but the number of trade unionists registered as unemployed by the labour exchanges was 515,000 on 1 October 1926 and 795,300 on 1 April 1927. This discrepancy led investigators in Gosplan and Vesenkha to conclude that the true number of unemployed in the spring of 1927 must be at least 2,300,000. According to Vesenkha, 'If we bear in mind that there were only 55 per cent of trade unionists registered at the labour exchanges, then the labour exchanges appear not to have included at least 850,000 unemployed members of trade unions. This means that the total number of unemployed in the USSR has reached at least 2,300,000'[10] (presumably this is made up of 1,478,000 registered at the labour exchanges on 1 April 1927 plus 850,000). But these figures are entirely incompatible with the population census. Here is an important batch of statistical inconsistencies meriting further examination.

The trade union censuses of October 1925 and October–November 1927 (Tables 3.1–2 and 3.8) provide a check both on the labour-exchange data as far as trade unionists were concerned and on the extent to which trade-union current unemployment statistics were exaggerated by the system by which unemployed registered even if they had secured employment. They do not, however, provide direct information on the extent to which trade unionists were registering in order to retain various rights even though not genuinely seeking work, both in the trade union and in the labour-exchange data.

In October 1925 the number of unemployed registered in the census (excluding agriculture and forestry) was 581,300; a comparison of this figure with the current statistics was said to show that 'the ballast which is included in the records as a result of the [quarterly] system of registration by unemployed is about 10 to 15 per cent'. The census figure, however, was in turn believed to be underestimated by 10 per cent because some members who lived far from the registration points had been unable to register.[11]

In November 1927 the total number of unemployed registered in the trade union census was 842,000 (excluding agriculture and forestry and trade) as compared with 969,000 in the current statistics:[12] according to the Soviet analysis the census figure was underestimated by 5 per cent due to the failure of unemployed to register in the census, while the current statistics were overestimated by 10 per cent due to the quarterly system of registration.[13]

After various adjustments, the number of unemployed registered in the November 1927 census (including trade but excluding agriculture and forestry) was approximately 1,080,000[14] as compared with 581,300 in October 1925. Table 3.8 presents a rough comparison of the two censuses as reclassified by major occupations.

The data for the November 1927 trade-union census fit fairly well with the data for the number of unemployed trade unionists registered at labour exchanges on 1 October 1927. According to the trade-union census, 69.5 per cent of unemployed trade unionists registering with the trade unions (excluding trade) were registered at labour exchanges, or 611,000; to this must be added an unknown proportion of the 236,000 members of the union of trade employees. According to the labour-exchange statistics, the number of registered unemployed trade unionists on 1 October 1927 was 652,000.[15]

Table 3.1: *Trade union censuses data on the period of unemployment (in % of total unemployed)*

	Up to 3 months	3–6 months	6–12 months	Over 12 months	TOTAL
October 1925	37.8	15.0	18.9	28.3	100.0
November 1927	43.4	14.7	16.2	25.8	100.0

These are returns for 872,000 unemployed (excluding trade and agriculture and forestry) in November 1927, almost a complete coverage, and 406,940 (excluding agriculture and forestry) out of 581,300 in October 1925.
Source: S. Iozefovich, in *Statistika truda*, no.3 (1926), p.6; *ibid.*, nos.3–4 (1928), p.8.

Both the trade-union censuses supply data on the period of unemployment (Table 3.1).

The November 1927 census provides some data on the extent to which unemployment was involuntary, on the basis of statements from the last place of work. The 838,700 unemployed on whom information was available left work for the following reasons:

Table 3.2: *Reasons for leaving employment—November 1927 trade-union census (in %)*

Reduction in number of personnel	38.8
Employing organisation closed down	11.0
Season or period of hire complete	23.1
Long illness	3.2
Own wish	12.0
Others	11.1
	100.0

Source: S. Iozefovich, in *Statistika truda*, nos.3–4 (1928), pp.15–16.

The first three categories, amounting to 72.9 per cent of the total, are clear cases of involuntary unemployment. The Soviet study of the trade-union census suggests that one of the major reasons for the high level of involuntary quittings is the high proportion of temporary jobs; this proportion greatly increased in the mid-1920s and evidently played an important role in increasing the general level of unemployment in these years.[16]

The labour exchanges also collected data on job vacancies, showing both the number of jobs offered and those actually filled through the exchanges. From these figures labour economists estimated indicators of the 'intensity' of unemployment, usually in terms of the ratio of jobs offered per month to the total stock of unemployed (the lower the ratio, the greater the intensity of unemployment). The crude data show a fairly low intensity of unemployment in 1922, increasing dramatically in 1923, and remaining at a high level in 1923–25. In the late 1920s the number of jobs on offer greatly increased, and the 'intensity of unemployment' declined.[17] However, the data are somewhat contradictory, and in order to interpret their significance it would be necessary to disentangle the effect of the increase in temporary employment both on the number of jobs on offer and on the total number of unemployed.

Text continued on p.45

Table 3.3: *Numbers unemployed according to population census of 17 December 1926, excluding Turkmenian SSR (in thousands)*

	Male	Female	Total	Length of Unemployment:					Years of age:								
				Less than 3 months	3–5 months	6–11 months	1 year and over	Not known	Less than 16–17	18–19	20–24	25–29	30–39	40–49	50 and over	Not known
1. Previously employed as:																
Workers in:																
Agriculture	22	12	35	14	10	3	4	4	2 / 3	5	8	5	6	4	3	–
Factory industry	115	58	173	54	40	30	38	12	1 / 5	16	42	33	40	24	14	–
Artisan industry	30	12	42	12	10	8	10	3	– / 3	5	10	7	9	5	3	–
Building	21	1	22	14	4	1	2	7	– / 1	2	5	4	5	3	2	–
Railway transport	26	4	30	12	7	4	5	2	– / 1	4	8	5	6	4	3	–
Other transport	24	3	26	14	5		4	2	– / –	2	6	5	7	4	2	–
Other	73	25	99	34	22	13	19	11	1 / 4	10	21	16	22	14	10	–
Total Workers	311	115	427	154	99	63	80	31	3 / 17	44	99	74	94	59	36	–
Employees	204	219	423	111	90	64	123	33	1 / 6	21	91	89	107	61	46	–
Total formerly employed	516	334	849	265	188	125	204	67	4 / 23	66	190	163	201	120	82	1

Table continued on p.42

Table 3.3: *Numbers unemployed according to population census of 17 December 1926 (continued)*

	Male	Female	Total	Length of Unemployment:					Years of age:								
				Less than 3 months	3–5 months	6–11 months	1 year and over	Not known	Less than 16	16–17	18–19	20–24	25–29	30–39	40–49	50 and over	Not known
2. Total formerly self-employed, etc.	17	5	22	7	5	3	5	2	–	–	1	4	4	6	4	3	–
3. Formerly in armed services.	5	–	5	2	1	–	1	1	–	–	–	2	1	1	–	–	–
4. Former employment not stated	10	5	15	2	2	1	2	8	–	1	1	3	2	3	2	2	–
Total of 1–4	547	344	891	277	194	130	212	79	4	24	68	199	171	211	126	87	1
5. Seeking work for first time	50	69	119	–	–	–	–	–	7	31	35	29	8	6	3	1	–
Total Unemployed	597	414	1010	–	–	–	–	–	11	55	104	228	178	217	128	88	1

Source: Adapted from *Vsesoyuznaya perepis' naseleniya 1926 goda*, vol.LII (1931), pp.86–7.

Table 3.4: *Number of unemployed registered at labour exchanges, 1922–31 (in thousands)*

1 January 1922	160(i)[a]	1 January 1929	1616(ii)
1 July 1922	408(i)[a]	1 April 1929	1741(iv)
1 January 1923	641(i)[a]	1 July 1929	1473(v)
1 January 1924	1240(i)[a]	1 October 1929	1242(iv)[f]
1 July 1924	1344(ii)[a]	1 January 1930	1316(ii)[f]
1 January 1925	952(ii)[a,b]	1 February 1930	1236(vi)[f]
1 October 1925	920(iii)	1 April 1930	1079(vii)[f]
1 January 1926	951(ii)	1 June 1930	937(vi)[f]
1 April 1926	1057(iii)	1 July 1930	778(vii)[f]
1 October 1926	1071(iv)	1 September 1930	525(vii)[f]
1 January 1927	1310(ii)[c]	1 October 1930	335(vii)[f]
1 April 1927	1478(iv)	1 November 1930	237(viii)
1 October 1927	1041(iv)[d]	1 December 1930	259(viii)
1 January 1928	1352(ii)	1 January 1931	236(ix)
1 April 1928	1574(iv)[e]	1 April 1931	206(viii)
1 October 1928	1367(iv)	1 August 1931	18(ix)

Notes:
(a) These are apparently estimates of total unemployment based on returns from a limited number of labour exchanges (70 in 1923–4, less in 1922, as compared with 281 from 1926 onwards). The number of unemployed registered at these exchanges was 363,000 on 1 January 1923, and 754,000 on 1 January 1924 (*Ekonomicheskii byulleten' Kon"yunkturnogo instituta*, no.11–12, 1926, p.51; *Sotsialisticheskoe khozyaistvo*, iv (July 1925), pp.413–4).
(b) Towards the end of 1924 'dead souls' were removed from the register and the categories of unemployed entitled to register sharply reduced (*see* p.37 above; Rogachevskaya, *op. cit.*, p.81; Vas'kina (Moscow 1981), p.163).
(c) In the autumn of 1926 the trade unions (without great success) required all unemployed members to register at the labour exchanges (*see* Suvorov, *op. cit.*, p.151).
(d) In March 1927 the restrictions of the right to register at labour exchanges were reinforced by a Sovnarkom decree (*see* p.37 above).
(e) In 1928 the trade unions again required all their unemployed members to register (*see* p.37 above).
(f) In 1929/30 several drastic reductions were made in the unemployed permitted to register (*see* p.29 above).

Sources:
(i) L.S. Rogachevskaya, *Likvidatsiya bezrabotitsy v SSSR, 1917–30 gg* (Moscow, 1973), pp.75–6.
(ii) *Narodnoe khozyaistvo SSSR* (Moscow, 1932), pp.xxi–xxiii.
(iii) Rogachevskaya, *op. cit.*, p.142.
(iv) *Trud v SSSR, 1926–1930* (Moscow, 1930), p.36.
(v) Rogachevskaya, *op. cit.*, p.251.
(vi) *Ibid.*, pp.268–9.
(vii) *Ibid.*, pp.279.
(viii) K.I. Suvorov, *Istoricheskii opyt KPSS po likvidatsii bezrabotitsy* (Moscow, 1968), pp.224–7.
(ix) *Trud v SSSR* (Moscow, 1932), p.9.

Table 3.5: Numbers of unemployed registered at labour exchanges, 1926–30 (in thousands)

	1 October 1926	1 April 1927	1 October 1927	1 April 1928	1 October 1928	1 April 1929	1 July 1929	1 October 1929	1 April 1930	1 July 1930	1 September 1930	1 October 1930
Previously employed:												
Industrial group (excluding unskilled)	182	239	165	226	207	264	231[a]	206	144[a]	120[a]	75[a]	47[a]
Builders (including unskilled)	41	126	63	208	89	208	117[a]	47	115[a]	54[a]	10[a]	5[a]
Intellectual labour group	211	284	262	352	318	317	243[a]	212	150[a]	116[a]	75[a]	60[a]
Unskilled/other	273	407	321	488	401	546	438[b]	360[b]	328[b]	209[b]	130[b]	79[b]
Total previously employed:	707	1056	811	1274	1015	1335	1029	825	737	499	290	191
Of which, trade unionists	515	795	652	1079	832	1113	823	670	549	361	203	140
Not previously employed:	364	422	230	302	340	406	419	416	342	269	230	143
Of which, adolescents							259		211	185	140	102
Total unemployed:	1071	1478	1041	1576	1365	1741	1448	1242	1079	778	525	335
Of total, adolescents	144	163	169	197	240	258	281	291	229	199	149	109
Of total, women	520	647	487	622	642	758		730				
Of total, unskilled	586	758	508	743	696	894		831				

Sources: 1 October 1926 to 1 April 1929, and 1 October 1929: *Trud v SSSR, 1926–30* (1930), p.36. 1 July 1929, and 1 April 1930 to 1 October 1930: Rogachevskaya, *op. cit.*, p.278, citing the archives.

Notes: (a) Excludes a small number of adolescents previously employed in this group: the total number of adolescents previously employed (in thousands) was: 1 July 1929, 21; 1 April 1930, 18; 1 July 1930, 14; 1 September 1930, 3; 1 October 1930, 7.

(b) Includes a small number of adolescents previously employed in other categories; see note (a) above.

On the basis of the various sets of employment and unemployment statistics, Soviet economic agencies responsible for preparing long-term plans sought to prepare estimates of future unemployment. Both Vesenkha and Gosplan constructed 'balances' of labour availability and labour utilisation; unemployment, or rather the unutilised available labour force, was obtained more or less as a residual. Examples of such balances may be found in the Gosplan and Vesenkha drafts of the five-year plan of the spring of 1927, and in the basic and optimum variants of the Gosplan five-year plan, the optimum variant of which was approved in the spring of 1929.[18] Not surprisingly, these estimates are unreliable. The five-year plan approved in the spring of 1929, in order to obtain a reduction of unemployment by 50 per cent over the five years, adopted quite casual assumptions about the success of the policies of agricultural intensification in retaining labour in the villages and about the proportion of housewives in the towns who would not seek work; fairly minor changes in the assumptions could have sharply increased the level of unemployment estimated for the last year of the plan, or completely eliminated unemployment.[19] In the event, the accelerated pace of industrialisation and collectivisation overturned all the assumptions about the supply and utilisation of labour; but, even within the framework of NEP, the estimates were quite arbitrary.

Table 3.6: *Number of industrial unemployed adults registered at labour exchanges by sub-categories, 1929–30 (in thousands)*

	1 April 1929	1 July 1929	1 October 1929	1 April 1930	1 July 1930	1 September 1930	1 October 1930
Metal workers	79.8	71.6	55.4	38.4	26.3	17.0	12.7
Textile workers	36.7	41.5	43.0	28.6	34.9	24.6	15.0
Food workers	40.8	33.0	30.2	24.4	20.7	9.8	5.3
Other workers	103.8	85.0	74.5	52.1	38.0	23.6	14.1
Total in industrial group	261.1	231.1	203.1	143.5	119.9	75.0	47.1

Source: Rogachevskaya, *op. cit.*, p.278, citing the archives.

Table 3.7: Number of unemployed registered with trade unions, 1927–29 (in thousands)

	1 October 1927			1 October 1928			1 October 1929		
	No. unemployed	Total membership	% unemployed	No. unemployed	Total membership	% unemployed	No. unemployed	Total membership	% unemployed
1. Agriculture and timber	251.9	1243.5	20.2	255.3	1359.1	18.8	273.8	1627.8	16.8
2. Industry:									
Paper	3.8	44.0	8.6	4.5	43.5	10.3	4.4	44.3	9.9
Mining	28.7	474.7	6.0	44.6	522.9	8.5	26.8	521.7	7.1
Woodworking	34.4	176.6	18.5	38.2	186.6	20.4	24.3	189.7	12.8
Leather	24.7	120.5	20.5	19.8	130.0	15.2	15.9	151.0	10.5
Metals	87.1	892.5	9.8	86.1	975.8	8.8	90.2	1085.6	8.3
Printing	26.3	135.3	19.4	23.5	129.6	18.1	16.5	126.8	13.0
Food	118.0	451.6	26.1	132.5	464.4	28.5	148.8	457.4	32.5
Sugar	27.3	104.9	26.0	43.7	111.1	39.3	42.8	104.1	41.1
Textiles	53.3	838.4	6.4	64.0	883.1	7.2	92.0	873.4	10.6
Chemicals	26.8	250.0	10.7	27.8	264.4	10.5	23.6	279.9	8.4
Sewn goods	17.4	80.3	21.7	15.3	100.8	15.2	16.6	109.8	15.1
Total, industry	447.8	3568.3	12.5	500.0	3812.2	13.1	501.9	3943.7	12.7
3. Builders	98.1	923.7	10.6	122.0	953.8	12.8	92.2	1053.8	8.7
4. Transport and communications:									
Water transport	17.7	175.4	10.1	23.1	176.7	13.0	19.3	184.8	10.4
Rail transport	90.6	1122.4	8.1	140.5	1131.8	12.4	122.3	1092.5	11.2
Local transport	32.0	181.3	17.6	30.5	175.8	17.3	23.6	180.1	13.1
Communications	13.9	115.9	12.0	16.4	116.3	14.1	14.8	116.1	12.7
Total, transport and communications	154.2	1595.0	9.7	210.5	1600.6	13.2	180.0	1573.5	11.4

	1 October 1927			1 October 1928			1 October 1929		
	No. unemployed	Total membership	% unemployed	No. unemployed	Total membership	% unemployed	No. unemployed	Total membership	% unemployed
5. Institutions:									
Art	21.7	88.0	24.7	24.4	90.4	27.0	24.4	93.2	26.2
Medical and Health	68.9	517.5	13.3	75.7	548.6	13.8	71.6	568.6	12.6
Education	89.2	751.4	11.9	93.0	792.9	11.7	87.6	835.5	10.5
Trade	235.9	1223.8	19.3	257.2	2365.8	20.3	200.1	1282.4	15.6
Total, institutions	415.7	2580.9	16.1	450.3	2697.7	16.7	383.7	2779.7	13.8
6. Municipal economy	33.7	248.0	13.6	39.4	256.4	15.4	37.7	260.5	14.5
7. Public catering	102.6	281.5	36.4	131.2	314.8	41.6	136.2	346.3	39.3
TOTAL	1504.0	10441.4	14.4	1708.6	10994.6	15.5	1605.5	11585.3	13.9

Source: Trud v SSSR, 1926–30 (1930), p.65.

Table 3.8: *Number of unemployed registered in trade-union censuses of October 1925 and November 1927, by occupational groups (in thousands)[a]*

	October 1925(i)[d] Number	%	November 1927(ii) Number	%
Industrial workers (excluding unskilled)	156.8	27.0	278.2	25.8
Building workers	23.8	4.1	53.4	4.9
Unskilled (chernorabochie)	90.7	15.6	126.1	11.7
Transport and posts	26.0	4.5	81.8	7.6
Employees in services[b]	214.3	36.9	357.5	33.1
Workers in service industries[c]	69.7	12.0	183.1	17.0
TOTAL	581.3	100.0	1080.1	100.0

Sources:
(i) *Statistika truda*, no.3, 1926, p.4.
(ii) *Ibid.* no.3–4, 1928, p.3.

Notes:
(a) The two censuses are not strictly comparable—for details see the Soviet sources.
(b) Trade, health, education, art.
(c) Catering, municipal economy, junior personnel (cleaners etc.).
(d) This column was estimated in the Soviet source on the basis of data from 540,500 unemployed.

NOTES

1. L.I. Vas'kina, *Rabochii klass SSSR nakanune sotsialisticheskoi industrializatsii* (Mościow, 1981), p.163 and E.H. Carr, *Socialism in One Country, 1924–1926*, vol. 1 (1958), p.411.
2. *Sobranie zakonov, 1927*, art. 132; *see* E.H. Carr and R.W. Davies, *Foundations of a Planned Economy, 1926–29*, vol. 1 (London, 1969), p.456.
3. *Kontrol'nye tsifry . . . na 1928/29* (Moscow, 1929), p.156.
4. *See* L.S. Rogachevskaya, *Likvidatsiya bezrabotitsy v SSSR, 1917–30 gg* (1973), p.145.
5. *See* K.I. Suvorov, *Istoricheskii opyt KPSS po likvidatsii bezrabotitsy* (1968), p.151 (September 1926); Rogachevskaya, *ibid.*, p.144 and *Kontrol'nye tsifry . . . na 1928/29* (1929), pp.156–7 (1928).
6. In factory industry in the RSFSR, the proportion hired via labour exchanges increased from 25.2 per cent in October–December 1925 to 56.6 per cent in July–September 1927 (estimated from data in *Statistika truda*, nos. 1–2, 1928, pp.22–3); in the USSR as a whole, the percentage of all jobs supplied via labour exchanges rose from 61.7 in 1926/27 to 77.3 in 1927/28 (*Statisticheskoe obozrenie*, no.6, 1929, p.53).
7. In provincial and okrug towns of the RSFSR, temporary jobs as a percentage of all new jobs increased from 45.1 per cent in

October–December 1925 to 65.0 per cent in July–September 1927; in factory industry in the whole RSFSR the percentage increased from 41.7 to 64.3 between the same dates (estimated from data in *Statistika truda*, nos.1–2, 1928, p.25).

8. *Kontrol'nye tsifry . . . na 1928/29* (1929), p.159.

9. *See Materialy k pyatiletnemu planu razvitiya promyshlennosti (1927/ 28–1931/33 gg)* (Moscow, 1927), pp.91–3.

10. *Ibid.*, p.93.

11. S. Iozefovich, in *Statistika truda*, no.3, 1926, pp.1–2; pp.1–17 summarise the results of this census.

12. Some areas did not make returns. The comparable figures for the whole USSR were estimated at 900,000 (see *ibid.* nos.3–4, 1928) and 1,016,200 (*see* our Table 3.7, pp.46–7—total excluding agriculture and forestry and trade).

13. *Ibid.*, nos.3–4, 1928, pp.1–2; pp.1–32 summarise the results of this census.

14. 1,092,000 from Table in *ibid.*, nos.3–4, 1928, p.3, less 'demobilised' and 'studying' categories not included in October 1925 (this table includes the number of unemployed members of the union of trade employees from the special trade-union census of April 1927, who were excluded from the November 1927 census—the seasonal numbers of unemployed in this trade union did not fluctuate substantially).

15. *Ibid.*, nos.3–4, 1928, p.14, and Table 3.5 (p.44).

16. *See* footnote 7 above.

17. The ratio of number sent to work to the total number of unemployed declined from 37.2 per cent in November 1922 to 17.0 per cent in November 1923 (*Ekonomicheskii byulleten' Kon"yunkturnogo instituta*, no. 11–12, 1924, pp.51–2); in October–December 1928 the ratio (monthly equivalent) was 29.6 per cent (Yu. Kalistratov, in *Statisticheskoe obozrenie*, no.12, 1929, p.19). The ratio was naturally much higher in the summer and autumn months of high seasonal employment than in the winter months. For data for the RSFSR in 1927/28, see *Statistika i narodnoe khozyaistvo*, no.1, 1929, pp.116–7; no.3, 1929, pp.236–7; no.5, 1929, pp.206–7; breakdown by occupational category is available.

18. Brief accounts of the balances will be found in *Perspektivy . . .* (1927), pp.9–10, and Appendix pp.15–6 (Gosplan); *Materialy . . .* (1927), pp.91–3 (Vesenkha); *Pyatiletnii plan* (3rd edn, 1930), vol.ii, part ii, pp.176–81.

19. For the assumptions of the optimum variant of the plan, *see* S.A. Kheinman, in *Ekonomicheskoe obozrenie*, no.11, 1929, pp.50–9; this article was a reply to B. Spektor's article in *ibid.*, no.9, 1929, pp.88–94, in which he made a rather ill-informed attempt to criticise the Gosplan labour balance.

4 The Development of Soviet Employment and Labour Policy, 1930–41

JOHN BARBER*

Like many of the basic policies and institutions of modern Soviet society, present-day employment and labour policy in the USSR had its origins in the period of the pre-war industrialisation drive. This paper will examine some aspects of employment and labour policy in large-scale industry during the first three five-year plans. First, however, the main features of the context within policy evolved should be outlined. The period may be divided into the following phases.

1929–33:
The time of most rapid economic expansion, especially of heavy industry; a huge increase in the size of the industrial workforce, which more than doubled; major dislocations and disproportions between different sectors; a serious shortage of labour; a drastic fall in workers' living standards, with real wages declining by half; rationing; the beginning of socialist competition and shock work; the intensification of labour; the collectivisation of agriculture, with disruption of peasant migration.

1934–36:
More balanced economic growth; the end of rationing and a rise in living standards; Stakhanovism; an increase in wage differentials; the raising of norms; a rise in productivity.

1937–41:
Slower economic growth, except in the defence industry; the level of employment nearly static; serious labour shortage; a decline in

* Social and Political Sciences Committee and King's College, University of Cambridge.

living standards; disruption in management caused by the purges.

These conditions created numerous problems for the authorities. The two with the greatest implications for employment policy concerned recruitment and discipline. How was the necessary manpower for industry to be obtained? And how, with a sellers' market now existing for labour, was discipline to be maintained and improved? In the event, the attempts to find solutions to these problems reflected the limitations rather than the extent of the government's power.

ORGANISED RECRUITMENT

During the years of NEP, a free labour-market existed in the Soviet Union, subject to relatively little state regulation. The hiring of labour was essentially a private matter between employer and worker. Workers were either signed on 'at the gates' of the enterprise, or were recruited by the enterprise's agent, or were engaged through the labour exchange. Though there were attempts, particularly on the trade unions' part, to make the last the sole means of hiring labour, in practice employers retained the freedom to hire workers as they wished.

Greater regulation of employment may have been implied by the launching of the first five-year plan. But what actually produced it was the end of unemployment in 1930 and an acute labour shortage. The first steps towards a new system were taken at the end of 1930. The labour exchanges of the Commissariat of Labour (Narkomtrud) were replaced by 'labour administrations'. These were ordered to provide 'systematic estimates and the planned distribution of available manpower'. They were further directed to 'wage a decisive struggle against the unorganised attitudes of economic agencies concerning the hiring of manpower' and to provide for the latter's 'organised recruitment', in particular through agreements with collective farms. To curb managers' tendency to hoard labour, they were also instructed to check on enterprises' use of manpower. To strengthen their influence, the hiring of labour through labour administrations was made compulsory.[1]

None of this, however, solved the problem of manpower supply. Though strenuous efforts were made to tap the urban labour reserves, and particularly to attract women and youth into industry, the labour shortage worsened during the first half of

1931. The labour administrations were unable to cope with the demand for workers. In May 1931 Narkomtrud itself proposed to Sovnarkom that their formal monopoly over hiring be abolished;[2] and eventually, in September, enterprises regained the right to hire workers directly. By this time new workers for industry were increasingly being provided by the countryside ('almost the sole and the basic source of supplying enterprises with manpower', Narkomtrud acknowledged in November).[3] Attention thus turned to the question of regulating the flow of rural labour to industry. With the majority of the rural population now collectivised and more accessible to the authorities, the idea emerged of a state-regulated contract system for the supply of labour to the towns.

In April 1931 a Gosplan report on the building industry recommended the establishment of 'a permanent link of specific kolkhozes with specific new sites by means of the conclusion of a special agreement between the new construction site and the kolkhoz'.[4] Over the next few months a number of local agreements were made. The decision soon followed to establish a general system of organised labour recruitment in the countryside. At the Conference of Industrial Managers on 23 June 1931, Stalin singled out the provision of manpower as the most crucial current economic problem. The spontaneous flow (*samotëk*) of labour from the countryside into industry and building, he asserted, had ceased because of the end of unemployment and the improvement of conditions in the countryside. It was therefore necessary 'to move from the policy of *samotëk* to the policy of the organised recruitment of workers for industry. But for this there exists only one path—the path of agreements between the economic organisations and kolkhozes and kolkhozniks'.[5]

The kind of 'orgnabor' agreement envisaged was spelt out a few days later in a government decree. It combined incentives with pressure on the kolkhozes to release manpower. The earnings of kolkhozniks who left to work elsewhere were to be liable neither to deductions by the kolkhoz nor to tax. Work in the kolkhoz was to be guaranteed on their return, and members of their families remaining in the kolkhoz would still receive work, food and access to services. Kolkhozes were to be given assistance to improve their output from organisations recruiting their labour, as well as preferential provision of agricultural machinery, schools, child-care facilities and cultural amenities. Pressure took the form of an obligation on kolkhozes to compile lists of their members with industrial skills and to allow them to depart to work elsewhere, 'leaving only those most needed for work in the kolkhoz'. All necessary documents were to be provided immediately, and the recall of kolkhoz members before the end of the contracted period of work was expressly forbidden.[6]

Further aspects of the new system were elaborated in August 1931. To end competition for manpower, Narkomtrud was instructed to allocate areas for recruitment to enterprises and economic agencies, after these had informed it of their requirements. The kolkhoz unions were ordered to work out labour balances, with production plans for 1932 including estimates of the numbers of qualified workers in kolkhozes. Control figures for recruitment totals were to be sent to the areas concerned, though expressly not to individual kolkhozes (thus avoiding the appearance of a compulsory labour draft).[7]

A full-scale campaign to implement the new system soon got underway. Socialist competition was declared between kolkhozes to deliver the maximum number of workers. Migrant workers appealed to their fellow countrymen to join them. Groups of experienced workers were sent into villages to organise meetings, lectures and film shows about work in industry and construction. 'Consultation points' and 'enquiry tables' for orgnabor were set up. Impressive results were claimed for the new system almost immediately, and there does appear to have been a large growth in a number of rural recruits for industry in autumn 1931. Some kolkhozes were reported to have achieved up to 200 per cent of their quota. Orgnabor, however, had numerous shortcomings, which soon became obvious. Despite the incentives offered to the kolkhozes, their relationship with the enterprises was hardly an equal one. They were supposed to part with labour in return for promises of assistance whose fulfilment they had no means of compelling and which often amounted to little of practical value. In place of technical assistance, enterprises generally provided kolkhozes with goods or simply money (four or five roubles per hired worker). The terms of agreements concluded were frequently still more disadvantageous to the kolkhozes. Although enterprises were supposed to be responsible for recruiting—the kolkhozes were obliged only to assist recruitment—kolkhozes were in fact often made responsible for selecting workers and delivering them to the enterprises. In some cases they were financially liable for their members' failure to fulfil contractual obligations or for any damage done to machinery or were obliged to replace 'deserters' with new workers.[8] One model agreement produced by Soyuzstroi even made kolkhozes liable to pay compensation if the workers recruited did not correspond to the professions required. A Narkomtrud report of November 1931, describing it as 'a typical model contract of sale, not an agreement of socialist mutual assistance between kolkhoz and enterprise', commented that in practice it would have resulted in the 'compulsory migration of kolkhozniks'.[9]

The quality of the recruiting personnel also left much to be desired. As a Soviet historian writes, recruiters were 'in many cases illiterate, politically ignorant people, drunkards, rowdies, embezzlers'.[10] An official responsible for appointing as a recruiter for railway workers in the Leningrad oblast in 1931 a man only just released from prison, explained that 'a person with a criminal past could not be entrusted with any work other than recruitment'. The high-handed conduct of recruiters was much reported. One was typically quoted as announcing to a kolkhoz that he had brought the 'warrants' (*naryady*) for the delivery of workers.[11]

For workers recruited under the system, orgnabor in practice meant a reduction of their limited ability to determine their conditions. Though official statements emphasised its voluntary nature, in fact it could contain a real element of compulsion. Formally agreements had to be concluded between enterprises and individual kolkhozniks, as well as between enterprises and kolkhozes. In fact, the former were rare.[12] It is clear that decisions about people leaving the countryside to work elsewhere were frequently taken by the kolkhoz administration, not by the individuals affected. The latter might even be unaware of the agreements under which they were engaged. As one Soviet historian remarks, 'in the majority of cases, kolkhozniks did not know about the existence and content of agreements, as they were not discussed at general meetings. Thus they did not take a direct part in deciding whether they would go to work in a state enterprise or not'.[13]

Sometimes all pretence of individual recruitment was dropped. A model agreement used in the Central Black-Earth region obliged the kolkhoz to send with new recruits a list of those being dispatched and details of their professions, since the receiving enterprise would have no knowledge of who was coming.[14]

The rights and 'privileges' guaranteed the recruit under orgnabor in practice added nothing to his or her existing rights. Since the government could not control the movement of population sufficiently to make orgnabor the only means of rural recruitment of industrial labour, the unregulated flow of peasants, including kolkhozniks, to the towns had to be permitted. Indeed, kolkhozes were still obliged to release individuals wishing to leave to seek work independently. But since such kolkhozniks still remained members of their kolkhozes, they retained their rights as members. Unlike those of many orgnabor recruits, furthermore, theirs were not dependent on the fulfilment of contracted duties or of the term of their agreement (usually for one or two years). For the individual peasant, collectivised or not, the traditional system, in contrast to orgnabor, allowed some degree of job-choice and more possibility of mobility between jobs.

Not surprisingly, therefore, despite its initial impact, orgnabor failed to replace traditional migration, the free flow of peasants to the towns. Not only did it meet resistance from kolkhoz administrations keen to retain manpower, even factory managers showed reluctance to embrace the new system. They disliked both its inflexibility, the costs of recruitment and their obligations towards kolkhozes and workers. As Stalin in his June 1931 speech observed, some managers 'do not want to work in the new way and sigh for the "good old times", when the workforce came to the enterprise by itself'.[15] One such manager was quoted in 1932 as declaring that 'those who come *samotëkom* do not make any demands and they are no trouble; but those who come in an organised way make numerous demands'.[16] Enterprises were said to be bypassing kolkhoz managements in order to deal directly with kolkhozniks, and to be ignoring the boundaries of recruitment zones established by Narkomtrud.[17]

After its initial impact, the limitations of organised recruitment were soon reflected in official reports and statistics. 'In the first half of 1932, *samotëk* in many areas of economic construction has shown a marked tendency to grow', commented one source. In the first three months of 1932, orgnabor was said to have provided only a quarter of all recruits to industry and building in the RSFSR.[18] At Magnitogorsk, 30 per cent of recruits came via orgnabor in 1932 and 70 per cent independently.[19] In March 1933, the government tightened up the regulations governing migration. Privileges for kolkhozniks leaving to work elsewhere and the rights of members of families remaining were made dependent on agreements having been signed.[20] But this failed to prevent widespread evasion of the system. The abolition of Narkomtrud in 1933, moreover, worsened the situation. In its place a Sovnarkom

Commission on the Organised Recruitment of Manpower was created, but lacking Narkomtrud's experience and its network of agencies, it made little impact. Reports in the mid-1930s continued to show that many, perhaps most, new workers were being recruited in the traditional way.

The problem of recruitment became more acute in the years preceeding the war. Mobilisation for the armed forces aggravated the labour shortage in industry and increased migrants' ability to choose their jobs. Improvements in rural living standards may also have reduced the flow of labour to the towns. In 1937 the plan for organised recruitment was only 47.9 per cent fulfilled.[21] Orgnabor was officially said in July 1938 to be in a state of 'disorganisation'. In many cases, tens or hundreds of enterprise representatives were recruiting in the same region. This 'unhealthy competition' was resulting in recruited workers sometimes being lured away by other enterprises. A new apparatus was therefore created to administer the system. Permanent commissions of Sovnarkom were to allocate commissariats to each region.[22] However, recruitment still fell far short of its targets: in 1938 by 1.5 million, in 1939 by 1.7 million.[23] A Gosplan report in May 1940 stated that 'despite a certain improvement in manpower recruitment, there are still serious failings'. Kolkhoz managements still impeded migration, refusing documents to those wishing to leave or providing inaccurate labour balances. Independent migration continued on a mass scale: 'In the kolkhozes investigated by us, the number of kolkhozniks leaving the kolkhoz without agreements exceeds the number leaving by means of orgnabor'.[24]

It is clear that the attempt to regulate the labour market through organised recruitment fell a long way short of achieving its objective. The claim that 'from 1931 organised recruitment became the chief means of providing the most important branches of industry with manpower' is quite unjustified.[25] On the contrary, it is likely that the majority of new workers entered industrial employment in the traditional, individual way. One Soviet historian states unequivocally that 'orgnabor supplied the Urals metal factories with no more than 20 to 25 per cent of the total number of new workers, and only on the largest new construction sites did this figure reach 45 to 50 per cent. The basic form [of recruitment] was the direct engagement at the enterprises of people who had spontaneously come to the towns and the construction sites.[26]

This was probably true of Soviet industry as a whole. The old and the new systems of recruitment coexisted, with the former continuing to play the dominant role.

THE STATE LABOUR RESERVES

The only other major innovation in recruitment policy came on the eve of the Soviet Union's entry into the Second World War. On 2 October 1940, the Presidium of the Supreme Soviet ordered the mobilisation of between 800,000 and 1 million male youths aged between fourteen and eighteen not still attending secondary school to undergo vocational training.[27] This consisted of six-month courses to train semi-skilled workers for jobs in 'mass trades' and two-year courses training skilled workers. A network of trade schools was to be set up to provide workers for priority industries. On completing the courses, young workers would be required to work in state enterprises for four years, as directed by the Chief Administration for State Labour Reserves. The compulsory nature of the new scheme was qualified only by the fact that it was selective (the quotas being set considerably below the total number in the age group concerned), and that obligatory recruitment was to be employed only if there were insufficient volunteers for the courses. In the initial phase, at any rate, the element of compulsion seems to have been relatively small scale. It was said that 1,100,000 people volunteered for enrolment in November 1940, of whom 450,000 were accepted. Only 152,000 out of the total entry of 602,000 appear to have been drafted. (The urban and rural contingents were roughly equal, with 303,600 and 288,900 respectively.)[28]

The immediate reason for the introduction of the State Labour Reserves is not difficult to perceive: the growing labour shortage and the increasing threat of war. Nazi Germany had triumphed in Western Europe and Soviet-German relations were worsening. But it must also be seen as a response to the inadequacies of the labour recruitment system. The combination of a cumbersome system of organised recruitment for part of the rural labour reserve and a simple reliance on market mechanisms for recruitment of the remainder of the rural and the whole of the urban reserve was obviously unsatisfactory, particularly given the growing labour shortage and the absence of unemployment as a stimulus to recruitment. The State Labour Reserves did not replace existing methods of recruitment, but they were a rational and potentially effective addition to them. Guaranteeing the provision of at least part of industry's labour requirements, they also offered more chance that new workers so recruited would be committed to industrial employment, unlike the much less stable orgnabor recruits.

But the impact of the new system on employment in the pre-war Soviet Union was to be zero. The new courses got under way in December 1940. The first students at the six month courses, 335,000 in all, were due to graduate and begin work in summer 1941. In June 1941, however, Germany invaded the USSR. With the whole economy now on a war footing, *all* workers were henceforth subject to compulsory regulation.

FORCED LABOUR

Analysis of Soviet employment policy in the 1930s must involve some account of the role of forced labour. While its precise scale and its economic significance are matters of serious controversy, there can be no doubt that it was an integral feature of manpower distribution. Forced labour took several forms. Two illustrate the indistinct boundary between free and forced labour, since elements of compulsion and choice were both present. Compulsory work at the worker's own place of employment for a period of up to a year and for a substantially reduced wage was a punishment often imposed for breaches of labour discipline. Exile to specified areas was the more serious fate of many, including large numbers of kulaks in the early 1930s. Sometimes kept under armed guard, obliged to do work provided by the authorities, exiles were technically still free workers earning wages. The main forms of forced labour, however, were the corrective labour colonies (ITKs) and camps. The inmates of the former were prisoners serving sentences of up to five years in colonies generally attached to enterprises or construction sites. As such, they comprised part of the general labour force. By contrast, labour camps, occupied by longer-term prisoners, typically situated in remote and climatically harsh regions, were run by the NKVD and provided the whole labour force for the work involved.

Estimating the size of the forced labour population in the USSR in the 1930s is a complex task beyond the scope of this paper.[29] But two points emerge clearly from the available evidence. First, the number of people performing involuntary labour was substantial.

Though estimates of 20 million and more prisoners made by some commentators for the late 1930s seem greatly exaggerated, even 2 or 3 million would constitute a significant proportion (perhaps a fifth or a sixth) of the non-agricultural manual labour force. Second, forced labour was a significant feature of manpower distribution throughout the period. It already existed on a large scale before the end of the first *pyatiletka* and expanded greatly from 1937.

The main uses to which forced labour was put appear to have been construction, mining and the timber industry. But its use in manufacturing indusry was far from insignificant.[30] Labour colonies were a common feature of new enterprises and construction sites, especially in the remoter regions, even where the labour force primarily consisted of free labour.

Whatever the motives for the mass arrests of real or suspected opponents of the government in the 1930s, the resulting captive workforce performed an important economic function in providing labour for industries and for regions to which free labour was difficult and costly to attract. In this sense it remedied some of the deficiencies of the labour recruitment system. That it did so cannot have been fortuitious. It seems an unlikely coincidence that the two largest expansions of the labour-camp population, in 1930–31 and 1937–39, took place at times of acute labour shortage.

LABOUR DISCIPLINE

A major objective of Soviet labour policy in the 1930s was to combat the upsurge of labour indiscipline, and particularly of turnover and absenteeism, that had followed the launching of the industrialisation drive. By 1930 an industrial worker was on average staying in a job for less than eight months, a coalminer for only four months.[31] Unauthorised absenteeism reached an average for each worker of nearly six days a year in 1931; coalminers again led the field with over ten days absence.[32]

Contemporary Soviet explanations of indiscipline put heavy emphasis on the impact of new, particularly ex-peasant workers: 'workers not long arrived from the countryside, uprooted artisans, declassé urban petit-bourgeois, who have recently been swelling our factories in considerable numbers'.[33] Given the scale and rapidity of the new workers' entry into the labour force, this is quite plausible. The problems experienced by new workers in adapting to the unfamiliar routine of factory work or the environment of urban life are common to all industrialising societies. The reasons for high labour turnover noted by one American engineer working in the Soviet Union during the first *pyatiletka* would have held equally true for many other societies at a comparable stage:

Restlessness of people in unfamiliar new kinds of work and new environment; actual fear of the new machines, furnaces, etc.; opposition to the effort to transform their entire lives and habits; hope of better living conditions; the thought that they may like the new work better; wanderlust, laziness, and the old habit of taking a few days off and then searching for a new job rather than explain absence or perhaps accept penalties.[34]

On the other hand, contemporary reports indicate that turnover was often as high among skilled workers as among unskilled. Both new and established workers were subject to increased pressures at work and outside, which could result in them changing jobs. Adaptation to a new routine was not only a problem for new workers. Technological changes in this period were often accompanied by 'deskilling', by the disappearance of industrial crafts and their replacement by mechanised processes. The sense of loss of control over their work might be as great for cadre workers as for new workers, and its effects on labour discipline as pronounced. The strongest pressure, however, resulted from the steep decline in living conditions. Given this and given the demand for labour, changing jobs in the hope of finding better conditions elsewhere was a rational response on the part of workers, whatever their length of employment (*stazh*). Foreigners working in Soviet industry during the first *pyatiletka* repeatedly stressed the influence of bad living conditions:

The labour turnover was unbelievable . . . people were always on the move in a continual search for a place where they could get something to eat. Any rumour that another place had better food immediately started a migration to that place. . . A report of more food, more clothing, or a better place to live immediately caused an exodus of labour to that location. . . Primarily, food conditions caused the labour turnover. . . Men and their families roamed the country from job to job, not looking for bigger wages in paper rubles but hunting for more food and better housing conditions.[35]

The means employed to improve labour discipline were essentially threefold: material incentives, education and legal compulsion. The first two figured prominently in the early socialist competition campaigns. But the prevailing conditions of scarcity precluded the provision of real incentives for most workers to improve discipline. The authorities therefore put the main emphasis on imposing correct behaviour by the sanction of law. The first systematic attack on labour turnover came with the Party Central Committee's decree of 20 October 1930.[36] As well as introducing rewards for workers who remained in their jobs, the decree laid down that 'deserters and flitters' were to lose for six months the right to be sent by labour exchanges for employment in industrial enterprises. It did not, however, prohibit enterprises from employing them. Given the growing labour shortage, this effectively nullified the decree's effect. Late in 1932 this loophole was plugged. The Central Committee's decree of 15 November 1932 banned 'malicious disorganisers of production' (i.e. those who left their jobs without permission) from any work in industry or transport for six months.[37] The decree also attempted to curb the mounting wave of absenteeism. Automatic dismissal for as little as one day's unauthorised absence from work was to be accompanied by the confiscation of ration cards issued by virtue of employment and eviction from enterprise housing.

The 1932 measures appear to have had some effect—not surprisingly, for they were real sanctions given the harsh living conditions of the time. Labour turnover fell, and so, very sharply, did absenteeism.[38] Absenteeism statistics, however, were much easier to falsify then those for turnover. There is no shortage of evidence that factory managers, because of labour shortage, often turned a blind eye to breaches of discipline for which the automatic punishment was dismissal.

Some improvement in labour discipline does appear to have occurred. In any case, other shortcomings of the workforce attracted more attention in the mid-1930s, in particular the inefficient use of work time. It was only at the beginning of the third five-year plan that the issue of labour discipline again came to the fore. With the growing labour shortage reducing the effect of sanctions against indiscipline and increasing the opportunities for mobility, turnover and absenteeism rose. In response, the drive for discipline resumed. In December 1938 new legislation was introduced which both supplemented and superseded that of 1930 and 1932. Work books were introduced in which changes of employment were recorded together with the reasons for the changes (a measure seriously considered eight years earlier but never implemented). New punishments were laid down for violations of labour discipline such as lateness or idling, including dismissal where three such violations occurred in a month or four in two months. To counter turnover, the notice required to terminate a work contract was extended to one month, and entitlement to social insurance benefits and annual leave was made conditional on *stazh*.[39] In January 1939 absenteeism was redefined as being more than twenty minutes late—an offence punishable under the November 1932 decree by dismissal.[40] Eighteen months later, in June 1940, the weapon of the criminal law was brought into operation. Workers who left their jobs without permission were liable to imprisonment for two to four months, while the penalty for absenteeism was changed from dismissal to corrective labour at the place of employment for up to six months.[41]

Though some Western historians have found the labour legislation of December 1938, January 1939 and June 1940 'draconian', the conditions of the time, particularly the international situation, made it comprehensible. British workers after September 1939 were unable to leave their place of work without their employer's permission and were liable to be tried for absenteeism in a court of law—although not for a criminal offense. Though the USSR was not at war until June 1941, it was increasingly on a war footing economically and socially during the preceeding two years, a situation which this legislation reflected. What is surprising is that even the latter had a very limited impact. After a temporary improvement, levels of turnover and absenteeism were both rising again by spring 1941.[42]

Perhaps the most conspicuous feature of the 1938—41 phase of the drive for labour discipline was the clash of interests between the political leadership and the enterprise managers. Only three days after the decree of 28 December 1938, state procurators were ordered to prosecute managers who failed to apply it.[43] A series of well publicised cases in which offending managers received prison sentences followed. Nonetheless, reports of excessive leniency on the part of managers (and even of local courts) continued.[44] One aim of the June 1940 legislation may indeed have been to reduce the possibility of managerial obstruction. Making breaches of labour discipline criminal acts in effect took enforcement of the law out of the hands of managers, leaving them merely with the duties of informing the courts of such breaches and of implementing sentences of corrective labour.

The persistence of high levels of turnover and absenteeism during the 1930s, despite all the leadership's attempts to eradicate them, provides another illustration of the regime's limited ability to determine the workforce's behaviour. The force of objective circumstances—the labour shortage, low standard of living, difficult working conditions—proved stronger than the legal sanctions or the incentives which could be applied. It did so because managers and workers combined to circumvent official regulations and nullify the regime's policies.

CONCLUSION

A widespread theme in Western accounts of Soviet labour in the 1930s is that workers were increasingly subject to the compulsory direction of labour. One important study declares that 1930 saw 'the beginning of a shift from a controlled labour market to a directed labour supply, to the manipulation of manpower, i.e. to the planned allocation of the manpower to individual industries and individual plants'.[45] The evidence examined above, however, must cast doubt on this interpretation.

It is true that elements of compulsion were present in the system of labour allocation. Millions of forced labourers obviously had no control over the place and nature of their work. A small minority of free workers were subject to direction, namely the graduates of factory apprenticeship schools (FZUs), who were obliged to work for three years wherever they were sent by the commissariat responsible for their industry. Those who completed courses at the trade schools set up under the State Labour Reserves scheme were to be treated similarly. Organised recruitment, as shown, contained coercive features, though these were breaches of the law, not intrinsic, and were more than off-set by workers' ability to evade the system.

The general picture, however, is one of an employment policy still in practice based on a free labour-market. For the majority of Soviet workers in the 1930s, the existence of a highly authoritarian government, willing to use harsh sanctions against its population to achieve its ends, nonetheless did not mean the end of freedom to choose their place of work. The factor which eventually inaugurated the era of compulsory labour direction was not Stalinist industrialisation but war.

NOTES

1. *Industrializatsiya SSSR, 1923–1932 gg.* (Moscow, 1970), pp.417–9.
2. *Ibid.*, p.421.
3. *Ibid.*, p.430.
4. *Ibid.*, p.428.
5. *Pravda*, 5 July 1931.
6. *Izvestiya*, 1 July 1931.
7. *Izvestiya*, 10 September 1931.
8. A.M. Panfilova, *Formirovanie rabochego klassa SSSR v gody pervoi pyatiletki* (Moscow, 1964), pp.12, 55, 88, 116.
9. *Industrializatsiya SSSR, 1929–1932 gg.*, *op. cit.*, p.428.
10. Panfilova, *op. cit.*, p.90.
11. *Voprosy truda,* no.7 (1932), p.18.
12. Panfilova, *op. cit.*, p.88.
13. *Ibid.*
14. *Ibid.*, p.89.
15. *Pravda*, 5 July 1931.
16. *Voprosy truda, op. cit.*, p.7.
17. *Ibid.*, p.21; *ibid.*, 1932, nos.8–9, p.53.
18. *Ibid.*, nos. 8–9, pp.53, 103.
19. John Scott, *Behind the Urals* (London, 1943), p.217.
20. *Izvestiya*, 18 March 1933.
21. M.Ya. Sonin, *Vosproizvodstvo rabochei sily v SSSR i balans truda* (Moscow, 1959), p.185.
22. *Sobranie postanovlenii i rasporyazhenii pravitel'stva SSSR*, 1938, no.34, art.208.
23. *Profsoyuzy SSSR*, 1941, no.4, p.53.
24. *Industrializatsiya SSSR 1938–1941 gg.* (Moscow, 1973), pp.237–8.
25. Sonin, *op. cit.*, p.173.
26. N.P. Shcherbakova, 'Rabochii klass Urala v 1926–1940 gg.', avtoreferat kandidatskoi dissertatsii (Sverdlovsk, 1965), p.14.
27. *Izvestiya*, 3 September 1940.
28. Solomon M. Schwarz, *Labor in the Soviet Union* (New York, 1952), p.78.
29. For a critical analysis of the available evidence, *see* S.G. Wheatcroft, 'On Assessing the Size of Forced Concentration Camp Labour in the Soviet Union 1931–56', *Soviet Studies*, 1981., no.4.
30. S. Swianiewicz, *Forced Labour and Economic Development* (London, 1965).
31. *Byulleten' po uchetu truda* (Moscow, 1932).
32. *Trud v SSSR* (Moscow, 1936).
33. A. Khan and V. Khandros, *Kto oni—novye lyudy na proizvodstve* (Moscow, 1930), p.3.
34. W.B. Clemmitt, Hoover Institution Archive, American Engineers in Russia Collection..
35. H.H. Angst, L.M. Banks, A.J. Bone, *ibid.*
36. *Spravochnik partiinogo rabotnika*, vyp. 8 (Moscow, 1934), pp.396–8.
37. Schwarz, *op. cit.*, p.97.
38. J. Barber, 'Labour discipline in Soviet Industry 1928–41', (Cam-

bridge, 1980. Unpublished paper).
39. 'O meropriyatiyakh po uporyadocheniyu trudovoi distsipliny', *Pravda*, 29 December 1938.
40. 'Proyasnenie', *Pravda*, 9 January 1939.
41. *Sobranie zakonov i rasporyazhenii*, 1940, no.22, art.745.
42. Barber, *op. cit.*, p.14.
43. Schwarz, *op. cit.*, p.104.
44. *Sovetskoe gosudarstvo i pravo*, 1941, no.1, p.15.
45. Schwarz, *op. cit.*, p.47.

PART II

The Economics of Full Employment

5 Lessons of Soviet Planning for Full Employment

MARK HARRISON*

Two kinds of lessons are available to us from Soviet experience—the ideological lessons and the practical ones. The ideological lessons concern the validity and legitimacy of the Soviet 'model' of economic and social transformation, taken as a whole. These do not concern us here. The practical lessons involve more selective, discriminating analysis of Soviet experience in the search for guides to the solution of immediate problems on the international agenda—for example, the mass unemployment currently prevailing in Britain and the other OECD nations. Practical lessons may be obtained directly from Soviet experience of creating and maintaining a full employment economy. At the same time, to call such lessons 'practical' does not mean that they are free of moral or political judgement.[1]

FULL EMPLOYMENT IN SOVIET TERMS

What is the Soviet concept of full employment? While it has easily recognisable features, it is quite different from the full-employment concepts favoured by strict neoclassical economic theory. Full employment in Soviet terms does not start from notions of market equilibrium or market clearance at given price–wage ratios and does not yield concepts like the 'natural' rate of unemployment. The Soviet concept of full employment starts from the citizen's right and duty to work.

* University of Warwick. This is a revised version of a paper which first appeared in Keith Cowling *et al., Out of Work: Perspectives of Mass Unemployment*, Department of Economics, University of Warwick 1984. I am grateful to a number of my colleagues for helpful discussion and comments.

The idea of socialist labour as both a right and an obligation is fully reflected, for example, in the 1977 USSR ('Brezhnev') constitution. Article 40 sets out the rights of citizens to work, including the right of pay in accordance with the quantity and quality of work done, and rights of choice of trade, profession and type of job, 'with due account of the needs of society'. Article 60 imposes a corresponding obligation to work conscientiously in a chosen, socially useful occupation and to observe labour discipline. Some necessary qualifications and exceptions are also to be found. Thus article 41 guarantees the right to rest and leisure. Article 42 prohibits child labour, while article 43 guarantees the right not to work to pensioners and to sick and disabled people. The position of women is governed not only by the foregoing but also by special considerations of women's equality. The Soviet constitution reflects Engels' view of the emancipation of women as a process of drawing them into social labour, granting them economic independence and freeing them from domestic drudgery.[2] Thus article 35, in guaranteeing the equal rights of men and women, sets out separately the right of mothers to choose to work or not to work, the right of expectant mothers not to work, and the right of mothers with small children to a shortened working week.[3] In the 1920s Soviet society was characterised by widespread agrarian underemployment and the associated phenomenon of open unemployment in the towns. At the end of the decade there was a dramatic mobilisation of labour in order to meet the goals of Stalinist industrialisation. In October 1930 the Soviet authorities announced that employment had been eliminated; associated with this announcement came the abolition of labour exchanges and unemployment benefit and the direction to work of the few remaining unemployed. Ever since then a feature of the Soviet economy has been the virtual absence of involuntary joblessness, with the exception of individual cases of political discrimination. Moreover, except for the period of Soviet involvement in the Second World War, state employment in the USSR has grown in every year since 1922, without cyclical or periodic downturns.

In contrast to the rapid elimination of full-time or 'open' unemployment, 'disguised' unemployment or underemployment took longer to disappear. There were two main categories of underemployed labour: women and farm workers. In 1926 women accounted for only 23 per cent of state employment, but in the years of rapid industrialisation their participation in social labour grew steadily, reaching 39 per cent by 1940. As in other countries it was sharply increased by the employment needs of the Second World War, and in the postwar period the trend was not reversed. By 1982 women accounted for 51 per cent of state employment in the USSR as a whole, although behind this average there existed a range from 55 per cent in Latvia in the west to 39 per cent in the middle-eastern Tadzhik SSR.[4]

Over the same period, reserves of rural underemployment have been largely exhausted. In the mid-1920s the Soviet peasant worked, on average, 220 days per year.[5] By the mid-1960s this average had risen to 230 days for full-time collective farmers and, by 1981, to 259 days—about the norm for an industrial society on a five-day week and fifty-week year.[6] At the same time, by comparison with the past, agricultural labour became far more productive, enabling a reduction in agriculture's employment share from over 70 per cent in the 1920s to 31 per cent in 1965 and 20 per cent in 1982.[7] This employment share remains high for an industrially developed, food-importing country by OECD standards, but the reason is that the labour productivity gap has not been completely closed, not that there remains a reserve of underemployed rural labour.

Thus the Soviet economy has shown a high capacity to provide jobs for all and to soak up the pools of underemployment which characterise backward agrarian countries. At the same time, another negative feature of the historical background—the massive overemployment of the minority which had access to jobs in industry—has also been mitigated. Before the First World War a fifty- to sixty-hour working week was normal in the Russian factory. In the inter-war period a much shorter working week became the norm. It was put back up to 48 hours by emergency legislation in 1940, not repealed until 1956. Since then the normal working week has been brought down to the 40-odd hours of the 1970s and 1980s.[8].

THE DEMAND FOR LABOUR

How has the Soviet economic system been able to guarantee high and rising employment over more than half a century? In the capitalist economies of the OECD bloc, the demand for labour is determined by some combination of the demand for output and the real wage, and today falls short of the supply by 32 million workers. In the USSR on the other hand, labour shortage is a systemic characteristic which results from inbuilt excess demand for goods of all kinds—both consumption and industrial goods. The demand for labour is constrained only by the availability of fixed capacity and non-labour variable inputs. The system as a whole is resource-constrained, not demand-constrained.[9]

How is labour shortage sustained? The prime objective of the economic system at all levels, from the central planning authority through intermediate agencies to the enterprise itself, is the expansion of the capital stock. Moreover, this 'expansion drive' is not constrained before the event by budget limits or by the fear of making unjustified investments.[10] Corresponding to the resulting rapid growth of the capital stock is a high rate of reinvestment of national income—30 per cent and rising in the 1970s.[11] It is the heavy capital construction programme and resulting high level of demand for industrial goods and services which have provided the main means of soaking up the pools of unemployment and underemployment inherited from the past. Thus lack of product-market constraints has eliminated the threat of unemployment arising from deficient demand.

Even in an economy where aggregate demand is always sufficient for full employment, taking the workforce as a whole, without distinction of types of labour and their location, unemployment may still arise if the structure of demand fails to match the structure of supply. How effectively has Soviet policy acted to reconcile the regional and skill composition of the workforce with the economy's employment needs?

Regional labour reserves have traditionally been mopped up through appropriate regional location of investment programmes.[12] At the same time a variety of policies aimed at labour supply have proved necessary to complement regional investment policy. Administrative controls on rural-urban migration were introduced in 1932 to prevent rural depopulation (a famine was in progress at the time) and urban overcrowding. These controls were finally ended in 1977. Different policies have been pursued at various times for securing a labour force for resource extraction and capital construction in the inhospitable regions of the far north and east. In Stalin's day the most important was the direction of forced labour through the NKVD gulag. Elements of this system still exist today under another name, but more important since 1956 have been the promise of higher wages and the impact of voluntarist appeals to the nation's politically conscious youth. A major underlying problem for today's policy-makers is the trend of migration southward to the Soviet sunbelt of the Caucasus and Central Asia, where the natural increase of the population is also most rapid[13]—away from the resource-rich northern regions, where the demand for skilled industrial labour is growing most rapidly.

A number of policy measures have also been brought to bear upon the matching of supply and demand for the various categories of skill. On the demand side a policy of technological dualism and deskilling was pursued in industry in the 1930s, and this permitted combination of large numbers of abundant, unskilled workers with small numbers of scarce, trained and experienced craftsmen and experts. The displacement of skilled labour as a result of labour-saving innovation has not proved a problem in Soviet experience. The problem has been the exact opposite—as reserves of unskilled labour have been used up, the reliance upon dual technologies has proved difficult to supersede, and the fostering of efficient labour-saving innovation and capital-labour substitution has become another major policy preoccupation. On the supply side, vigorous policies for education and industrial training have been pursued, based on 'manpower' plans and budgets; in the period from 1940 to 1956 these policies extended to direction of labour of all kinds, but since 1956 economic methods of allocating labour between jobs have been largely preferred.

In these ways the Soviet economy has demonstrated a working system for combining economic growth with full employment and a high degree of job security. At the same time a number of serious problems are associated with the functioning of the economy at permanent full employment. These problems concern the efficiency and intensity with which labour inputs are utilised within the full-employment framework. What is worse, these problems seem to stem from basic features of the economic system, and from the way in which full employment is achieved.

FULL EMPLOYMENT AND LABOUR UTILISATION

The economic system as it emerged under Stalin did not aim at any particular rate of growth of output, or of the capital stock, or at some optimal combination of investment and consumption; it aimed crudely at the destruction of the preceding economic order and the most rapid possible industrialisation.[14] This in turn required transformation of the whole country into a gigantic building site for projects of capital construction. The investment plan tended to be used not to balance capital construction with other competing needs and with the overall ability of the economy to supply them, but to mobilise all possible resources and pour them into capital construction regardless of the opportunity cost.

A result of this was the tendency to loss of investment discipline and to periodic overinvestment. An investment cycle appeared in which massive investment plans and extremely rapid growth of the capital stock resulted in surges of demand for labour and industrial goods far exceeding the supplies available at full employment. The result would be a slowdown in the rate of realised investment, inability to complete the large number of projects begun and rapid growth of the volume of capital locked up in unfinished factories and idle building sites. The increase in output associated with increases in the capital stock would dip sharply. At this point it would become necessary for makers of economic policy to reassert the needs of equilibrium and of planning investment within the framework of competing needs and overall availability of resources. Investment plans would be cut back, new projects cancelled and new resources concentrated on existing projects due for early completion; these measures would allow renewed growth of finished capacity. At the same time, renewed attention would be paid to investment criteria, including marginal efficiency concepts, and to optimality of growth rates of capacity, output and consumption.

Since Stalin's time much has changed; in particular, the completion of Russia's industrial revolution and the removal of the atmosphere of personal dictatorship and police terror have mitigated the feverish urgency with which capital construction was pursued at all costs. Overinvestment no longer emerges with the uncontrolled violence of the Stalin years. Nonetheless, investment retains a high priority, and the periodic rise in the number of unfinished projects awaiting supplies of unobtainable labour and investment goods which are necessary for completion still arouses serious concern. Such was the case as unfinished capacity piled up in the late 1960s and 1970s, with lengthening delivery dates and completion periods. Improvement in the balance between unfinished capacity and new investment has been achieved since 1979 only through strenuous rationalisation.[15]

Investment indiscipline has important secondary effects upon production management and labour utilisation. In the first place, excessive investment plans set the context of enterprise finance. Construction enterprises are provided with generous budgets to finance their work. Enterprises producing industrial and consumer goods and services are allocated ambitious plans for incremental output. As a result, the industrial economy as a whole tends to be overfinanced, and excess monetary demand for materials and labour emerges.[16] Since inflation is repressed, industrial materials become the object of administrative rationing coupled with a growing informal wholesale market. An atmosphere of 'corruption' is encouraged in which private deals are struck between enterprises and among managerial personnel, both to make good the gaps in centrally planned material supply for the good of the enterprise and for private gain. Speculative hoarding of materials and of excess capacity by enterprises is also encouraged, and this of course worsens the overall position of shortage. With regard to the results of excess demand for labour, the picture is only a little different. Money wages are held down, but, since 1956 at least, most categories of labour have not been rationed administratively. The response of enterprises to labour shortage is therefore one of unrestrained speculative behaviour—the hoarding of labour and concealment of labour reserves.

In addition, while enterprises hoard labour, labour does not work. Through receipt of wage incomes provided for by the excessive financing of industry, households too are overfinanced in relation to the consumer goods and services available. Their real entitlement exceeds supply. The result is the unintended accumulation of household cash balances, loss of motivation to work for higher pay and the encouragement of illegal exchanges on the retail market.

Thus Soviet analysts describe the cash balances of households as consisting of a transactions balance for everyday use, a target-savings balance for intended future purchases and an unwanted balance of 'floating' savings. The latter arises when attempts to make purchases in retail outlets are frustrated by the overall state of shortage. There is concern over the fact that in the decade of the seventies, household savings deposits grew by 90 per cent—more than twice as fast as money wages.[17] To the extent that such cash balances are unwanted, they reflect the incapacity of society to meet the consumption entitlement of its citizens acquired through labour, and result in damaged motivation to work.

In principle, the capital construction programme could be sustained and labour incentives restored by increasing retail prices more rapidly than wages. In the Soviet economy, it is true, price inflation is only imperfectly repressed. In state shops inflation is manifested in disproportionate mark-ups on new products and products of improved quality. The pricing of industrial goods reflects similar processes. After a long lag, energy-intensive goods and services have also been substantially priced up. Inflationary trends are most marked, of course, in unregulated exchanges between households. Comparative stability in the price level as a whole, however, reflects tremendous inertia in the pricing of basic goods. This inertia is powerfully reinforced by unwillingness of working people to see their theoretical entitlement to a share of society's output reduced, even though a rise in the price–wage ratio would mean shorter queues and fewer frustrated consumer purchases.

The price of an overfinanced economy and repressed inflation is paid also in terms of labour discipline and morale. In capitalist economies labour discipline is fostered through economic competition—the threat of dismissal and the lure of bonuses. In the Soviet economy these competitive market disciplines are rendered ineffective by overfinancing of enterprises and households. But they are not completely replaced by other means of economic discipline, whether of a competitive or a cooperative nature. Of course, many Soviet workers continue to work diligently from professional pride or from awareness of the social importance of their jobs. But for others this is insufficient.[18] Even under the conditions of 'real socialism' they are still alienated from their labour, which they continue to experience as joyless drudgery; they do not work effectively in the absence of a stimulus which is external to the work itself. Official recognition of this problem has given rise to such motivational substitutes as 'socialist emulation', the organisation of competitions directly among the workers, with medals and certificates and privileged access to scarce goods and services for reward; such competitions also play a role in educating the workers about the social valuation of their work. However, several features set limits on the motivational value of these schemes—their transitory character, the need to divert scarce resources to finance them and the likelihood of inadvertently rewarding inappropriate behaviours on the part of the competing workers.

Soviet failure to give rise to a new system of discipline intrinsic to economic life means that work remains poorly organised. As a result, workers' creative abilities tend to be underutilised, even if many of them would personally wish to contribute more to society. Disguised unemployment, once a feature of backward agrarian Russia, now reemerges in the modern world of the Soviet office and giant factory. Workers might as well be redundant, but their dole is simply paid out as a wage by the factory, not by the labour exchange. Moreover, this situation is simply accepted, and is not without benefit to those involved, since it means that for most workers for most of the time the pace of work is slow and irregular with plenty of opportunity for tea breaks and unauthorised absences. Everything is permitted as an excuse for not working. For example, in a recent survey of nearly 800 enterprises in the Moscow area, 73 per cent of the workers were found to take time off for personal business or to go shopping and stand in line for scarce consumer goods and services rather than to work hard and earn bonuses—although of course such interruptions in the flow of output simply aggravate the shortages encountered in the shops. At some plants only 10 per cent of the workers were present during the final hour of their normal shift.[19]

Of course, this does not mean that every Soviet factory is alive with the sound of restful conversation and card games, or that the shops are literally empty of goods—any more than one should assume that everything goes according to plan. Nonetheless, the problem of securing labour discipline runs deep in Soviet life. An enduring response is the tendency to periodic campaigns of tightening up. Such was the outcome of a recent large, top-level conference of political and economic leaders called to discuss labour discipline at the CPSU Central Committee in Moscow early in January 1983 (see Elizabeth Teague's discussion in this collection, Ch.14, pp.246–8).[20]

Whether disguised unemployment results in long-term dynamic inefficiency is a difficult question. Some Western analysts see long-term Soviet industrial deceleration as a direct result of inability to raise labour productivity at the required rate, whether by means of labour-saving innovation or by means of efficient capital–labour substitution. Without doubt, labour productivity growth is seen as a major problem area by Soviet economists. Others see the underlying Soviet labour productivity growth rate as standing within the international mainstream and industrial deceleration as reflecting the exhaustion of transitory factors which boosted it above trend in the early post-war period.[21]

According to the latter view, no dynamic inefficiency is associated with Soviet patterns of labour utilisation. Econometric tests do not discriminate conclusively between the alternative hypotheses. An historical perspective suggests that neither of these approaches tells the full story; there is dynamic inefficiency associated with the poor organisation of work in the Soviet office, shop and factory, but Soviet economic leaders also have a high capacity for periodic reorganisation and mobilisation to restore dynamic losses from time to time. Today's shambles may always be straightened out tomorrow—or at least that has been the historical record so far.

To summarise the argument, investment indiscipline, financial indiscipline and labour indiscipline mark the adverse effects of Soviet methods of achieving full employment on the utilisation of labour in a full employment context. Underutilisation is the usual result, but the results can usually be contained.

FULL EMPLOYMENT AND WOMEN'S WORK

In one direction a different result holds. This is the overemployment of women in Soviet society. Women account for half the state-employed workforce and share equally the burden of social labour. But at the same time they do far more housework than men. From this point of view women work a 'double shift'—they do two jobs, but the one they do in the home is unpaid. For example, if we add up the time spent each week on shopping, cooking, cleaning and washing, then the typical Soviet woman contributes perhaps between twenty-six and twenty-eight hours, the typical man only just over 6 hours (and half of that is made up by shopping, indicating his greater freedom to spend time outside the home).[22] Men's expectation of women's role is highly specific and deeply entrenched; thus child care in particular may be associated with women's reduced leisure compared to men because, when women obtain a shorter working week corresponding to the needs of their young children, they incur a disproportionate increase in their domestic burden.[23] Moreover, a shortened working week tends to result in women's loss of career prospects and damage to their participation in particularly skilled or responsible work.

In practice, Soviet women can obtain personal economic independence of men, but not with men's cooperation. According to one survey, frequent quarrels over housework are commonplace for 80 per cent of married couples.[24] One result is that women's struggle for economic independence is correlated with falling birth rates and rising divorce rates, visible both over time and in regional cross section. Thus there is a failure to realise Engels' expectation that women's emancipation would follow from their involvement in social labour under socialism. Soviet women share equally in social labour, but Soviet men do not share in domestic labour. Full employment in Soviet terms has meant full employment for men but overemployment for women and a highly inequitable distribution of social and domestic labour added together.

LESSONS OF SOVIET FULL EMPLOYMENT

In my view, Soviet experience of planning for full employment contains several lessons which can be taken to heart by those working for alternatives to mass unemployment in the West. These are that permanent full employment brings important benefits and, far from being an impracticable dream, is demonstrably feasible; at the same time, a price is paid for it, nor is it a panacea for curing all social and economic evils.

First, Soviet experience suggests that full employment can make a big contribution to the quality of working people's lives. For example, Soviet people take job security for granted. Soviet émigrés arriving in the West frequently find great difficulty in adjusting to the competitive struggle for jobs and the prospect of forced idleness on the dole. In the Soviet Union an income is easy to come by, even if it is sometimes difficult to spend it in ways which raise consumer welfare. In the West there are many attractive ways of spending money but, in the absence of the 'right to work', these are blocked off from the limited realm of choice open to the unemployed. Nor are the unemployed the only sufferers. Each year of mass unemployment in the OECD countries results in losses to society as a whole—measurable losses in output, a permanent physical and psychological deterioration of the workforce, the breakup of families, the alienation of young people from the world of work, and the spread of divisive attitudes hostile to working women and ethnic minorities—all on a scale beyond the grasp of most Soviet people.

Second, Soviet experience shows that full employment and a high level of job security can be sustained over a long period of time and are compatible with rapid economic growth. A growing economy can be run at full employment for decade after decade. This is different from the Western experience, which has been one of failure in this respect. Keynesian techniques of demand management have proved effective in bringing about full employment within capitalism, but not in running an economy at full employment for many years without intolerable consequences for inflation and dynamic efficiency. In contrast to Western failure, the key to Soviet success seems to have been an overriding political commitment to full employment for economic development and capital construction, combined with a willingness to contain and meet the costs of this commitment on a pragmatic basis.

Third, Soviet experience points to possible costs of permanent full employment, which appear to result from the weakening of traditional disciplines characteristic of a demand-constrained economy. In the West, economic discipline is provided by means of competition—by opportunities for private gain and by the periodic impact of recession which bankrupts the inefficient employer and throws unprofitably employed workers back onto the labour market. The latter source of discipline is unavailable to the Soviet economy in the context of its commitment to full employment, and legitimate opportunities for private gain within the Soviet system are often limited by shortages of goods. Failure of the system to throw up alternative, non-competitive mechanisms for individual or collective economic discipline results in periodic crises of overinvestment, repressed inflation and disrupted work—although not of mass unemployment. Because the self-discipline of economic units is poor or lacking altogether, coercive external disciplines are periodically imposed from above, placing further strain on centralised administration and its already overburdened relationship with society. Thus, if we think of competition and coercion as two of the alternative methods of securing Soviet economic efficiency, we might wish to consider the results of relying more on competition and less on coercion. Many groups in society would experience a widening of economic and social choice; greater choice for many and even for most people would be paid for by those who would now find employment with difficulty or, for a time, not at all.

Fourth, Soviet experience implies that, while full employment may be both practicable and beneficial in itself, it is not a sufficient condition for eliminating workers' alienation or powerlessness.

The 'right to work' is not the same thing as control over the means and conditions of labour—including women's domestic labour. In the absence of the 'right to work', many social evils are intensified, but they may also be reproduced under conditions of full employment, and the tendencies towards economic waste and social disintegration observed in Soviet society from time to time bear witness to this. If working people are powerless and express this condition in negative ways, then the results can only be eliminated by a redistribution of political rights and their exercise from below, not by means of a full employment policy benevolently administered from above. From this point of view, if we think of the alternative ways of improving the responsiveness of the Soviet economy to social need, then competitive and coercive disciplines alone may present an insufficient range of alternatives. A further indispensible element may be the development of cooperative self-disciplines, in the sense of more equal involvement of working people of both sexes, independently of the state, in the decisions facing government, enterprise and the community and family household. However, Soviet experience does not reveal very much about the conditions under which this might come about, or the possible results for employment in the economy and in the home.

NOTES

1. This issue is further discussed by Michael Ellman, 'Full Employment—Lessons from State Socialism', *De Economist*, 127 (1977), no.4, pp.489–91.
2. *Marx-Engels Selected Works* (Moscow and London, 1968), p.501.
3. *Constitution (Fundamental Law) of the Union of Soviet Socialist Republics* (Moscow, 1977).
4. *Narodnoe khozyaistvo SSSR 1922–1972* (Moscow, 1972), p.348; *Nar. khoz. SSSR v 1982 g.* (Moscow, 1983), p.369.
5. V.P. Danilov, *Sovetskaya dokolkhoznaya derevnya: naselenie, zemlepol'zovanie, khozyaistvo* (Moscow, 1977), p.273.
6. *Nar. khoz. SSSR 1922–1982* (Moscow, 1982), p.285 (grossed up from monthly averages).
7. *Nar. khoz. SSSR 1982 g.* (Moscow, 1982), p.362.
8. *Nar. khoz. SSSR 1922–1972, op. cit.* p.352; *Nar. khoz. SSSR 1922–1982, op. cit.* p.407.
9. These are the terms of János Kornai, *The Economics of Shortage*, vol. A, (Amsterdam, New York and London, 1980), p.27.
10. *Ibid.* pp.191–95.
11. Investment as a share of the Soviet net material product stood at 28 per cent for 1966–70, 30 per cent for 1971–75 and 31 per cent for

1976–80; *see* underlying data in *Nar. khoz. SSSR v 1980 g.* (Moscow, 1981), p.45.

12. Ellman, *op. cit.*, p.495.

13. V. Perevedentsev, 'Early Results of the 1979 Soviet Census', *Population and Development Review*, March 1980, pp.171–72.

14. Eugène Zaleski, *Planning for Economic Growth in the Soviet Union 1918–1932*, (Chapel Hill, 1970), p.300.

15. For recent trends in this balance, see *Nar. khoz. SSSR v 1982 g., op. cit.*, p.347. For a major expression of recent concern *see* the keynote speech of the late General Secretary Yu.V. Andropov to the November 1982 plenum of the CPSU Central Committee, in *Current Digest of the Soviet Press* (*CDSP*), 22 December, 1982, pp.5–6.

16. Again, *see* Andropov's speech to the workers of the Ordzhonikidze machine-tool plant in Moscow in January 1983 in *CDSP*, 2 March 1983, p.3.

17. *CDSP*, 15 December 1982, pp.14–15.

18. On labour discipline in a resource-constrained economic system, *see* Kornai, *op. cit.*, pp.255–56.

19. *CDSP*, 26 January 1983, p.6.

20. *CDSP*, 2 February 1983, p.19.

21. Stanislaw Gomulka, 'Slowdown in Soviet Growth: 1947–75 Reconsidered', *European Economic Review*, 1977.

22. *CDSP*, 15 December 1982, p.12.

23. *See* results of a local survey reported in Peter H. Juviler, 'The Soviet Family in Post-Stalin Perspective', in Stephen F. Cohen, Alexander Rabinowitch and Robert Sharlet (eds.), *The Soviet Union since Stalin* (London and Basingstoke 1980), p.239.

24. *CDSP*, 15 December 1982, p.12.

6 The Serendipitous Soviet Achievement of Full Employment: Labour Shortage and Labour Hoarding in the Soviet Economy

PHILIP HANSON*

Labour in the USSR is fully employed but poorly utilised. The economic system is, in Kornai's terminology, a 'supply-constrained system'. It is composed almost entirely of production units with soft budget constraints[1] and a corresponding tendency to hoard inputs, including labour. As a result there is inefficient resource allocation, together with low work effort and sluggish technological change;[2] consequently, once an industrial base has been created, slow productivity growth.

What this means is that Soviet citizens are never short of workplaces to clock in at and need not fear unemployment, but they also face perpetual shortages of everyday goods and services, poor product quality and only slow improvement of their modest average level of material prosperity. Soviet full employment, though desirable in itself, is not costless.

In recent years the slowing growth of the non-agricultural labour force (Table 6.1) has led Soviet commentators to pay particular attention to the costs of the Soviet employment system. There has been extensive discussion of labour hoarding and labour indiscipline.

One view, put forward in both the USSR and the West, is that the Soviet 'labour shortage' is a product of the Soviet economic

* Centre for Russian and East European Studies, University of Birmingham. I am grateful to Daniel Bond, Staszek Gomulka, Jacek Rostowski and Peter Wiles for comments on a draft of part of this paper and to conference participants for comments on a complete draft. The reference in the title to serendipity I owe to Mario Nuti. I am particularly indebted to Wojciech Charemza for assistance in applying to the monthly data on standard work time and industrial output more satisfactory (and more sophisticated) statistical procedures than the OLS regressions on unweighted data that I originally employed.

Table 6.1: *Dimensions of the soviet manpower problem*

	Increases in the population in the able-bodied ages*		Increases in the total civilian labour force		Increases in the non-agricultural labour force	
	Increment (000)	% increase	Increment (000)	% increase	Increment (000)	% increase
1951–55	10785	10.5	7296	7.5	6957	16.3
1956–60	6026	5.3	5195	5.0	10970	22.0
1961–65	3899	3.3	6362	5.7	12354	20.3
1966–70	7220	5.9	9118	7.8	11500	15.7
1971–75	12736	9.7	10586	8.4	12736	15.1
1976–80	11026	7.6	10336	7.6	12990	10.1
1981–85	2956	1.9	5986	4.1	8331	7.6
1986–90	2331	1.5	3590	2.4	5765	4.9
1991–95	2587	1.6	4888	3.1	6905	5.6
1996–2000	6523	4.0	5988	3.7	7858	6.0

*Able-bodied ages, as defined in the USSR, are sixteen to fifty-nine years for men and sixteen to fifty-four years for women. Increments calculated from populations as of 1 July.

Source: Gertrude Schroeder, 'Managing Labour Shortages in the Soviet Union' in Jan Adam (ed.), *Employment Policies in the Soviet Union and Eastern Europe*, (London: Macmillan, 1982).

system in the sense that a reform which reduced labour hoarding would cause the 'shortage' to vanish by raising labour productivity in each line of production and by reallocating labour more efficiently between jobs. Another view is that tougher labour discipline, by obtaining more effort from a given number of people, would reduce or even eliminate the problem. A case can be made for dealing with labour shortages and improving productivity by so changing the rules of the game that workers and managers face the possibility of redundancy.[3] This paper is an assessment of the present problems of labour shortage and labour hoarding, and of proposals to remedy them.

The discussion is organised as follows. First, the distinction is made between job security and full employment, and the regulations and institutions which provide both full employment and job security in the Soviet Union are identified. Second, there is a discussion of the sources of efficiency and inefficiency in the use of labour in an economy with a general regime of job security. Third, there is a review of the evidence that labour supply is in fact a binding constraint on Soviet output and has become more important in this respect in recent years. Fourth, an assessment of the practical importance of labour indiscipline is attempted. Finally, conclusions are drawn on the possible gains both from systemic reform and from policy changes within the existing system.

JOB SECURITY AND FULL EMPLOYMENT

Job security and full employment are quite different things. One could imagine a country in which all those currently employed were secure in their tenure of their jobs but there was simultaneously a significant amount of unemployment: new entrants to the labour force were not being offered jobs, and people who voluntarily quit one job could not find another. Yugoslavia in the present recession provides an example. Yugoslav enterprises very seldom close, and workers' councils have been accepting cuts in average real incomes in preference to sacking some of their fellow workers.[4] Conversely, one can imagine an economy which has full employment without job security: there are plenty of jobs for new entrants to the labour force, and for job-changers, but individual firms may be forced to declare redundancies or close down completely; those made redundant can generally find other jobs quickly. Many of us, indeed, do not need to imagine such an economy; it is one of the consolations of middle age that we can remember it.[5] It is, of course, quite possible to have full employment and job security at once; the USSR and the East European economies display both characteristics; so does Japan.[6]

According to official Soviet sources, the Soviet system provides full employment and job security through two main kinds of arrangements. First, 'planning from resources' means that output is planned to utilise all available resources; no demand influences independent of the planning system can influence the level of employment. There is therefore no reason why there should not be jobs for new entrants to the labour force. (If job-seekers outnumber vacancies in a particular region in a particular year, this is a planning error of a less-than-fundamental kind and can be rectified.) Soviet-type central planning should solve the Keynesian problem of a deficiency of aggregate demand; aggregate demand and supply, and thus *ex ante* savings and investment, are planned simultaneously and by the same small group of central planners. Second, the law requires people to have jobs and inhibits managers from making workers redundant.

It is my contention that the systemically determined behaviour of Soviet enterprises and other employing organisations is more important than either the law or the central planners in providing full employment and job security in the USSR. With respect to job security, the provisions of Soviet law may be sufficient to ensure a general regime of secure tenure of existing jobs (though they do not in practice preclude all victimisation of individuals by dismissals);[7] but there is not much pressure to break them with any great frequency. Their efficiency has therefore been little tested. With respect to full employment, the laws protecting tenure are insufficient by themselves to guarantee jobs for all since they have nothing to do with making jobs available for new entrants to the labour force or voluntary job-leavers. As for the central, planners, it is clear from the chapter in this collection by Silvana Malle (Ch.8) that the methods and information for planning an aggregate labour balance do not in fact exist; and it is clear from Table 10.5 in Anna-Jutta Pietsch's chapter (Ch.10), that the aggregate state employment figures projected in the five-year plans have been consistently and substantially wrong; but consistently wrong in the same direction: labour demand is underestimated.

Soviet law provides for dismissals for 'systematic non-fulfilment of work duties' and for other infringements of labour discipline. It also allows a kind of redundancy arrangement in the case of 'staff reductions'. The latter kind of dismissal, however, in which the worker is not at fault, is supposed to be accompanied by an offer of suitable alternative work in the same organisation or by evidence that the worker has refused such alternative work or—and this comes close to Western-style redundancy—evidence that no other such work is available.[8] Thus the law apparently would not forbid redundancies, and they could be more frequent than they are if Soviet managers were under pressure to economise on labour inputs.

The other side of Soviet labour law—concerning the obligation to work for the state—may in some ways be more important. The Soviet constitution says that the citizen has a duty to work, and the law penalises non-workers ('parasites'). This means that able-bodied citizens of working age, unless they are full-time students or mothers (not fathers, of course) of small children, are legally obliged to have state jobs. Full-time private employment or self-employment is ruled out, except for state-approved writers, artists and the like—who have to be members of the official unions of writers, artists, and so on, to get away with it.[9] There is no unemployment benefit.

In practice, some able-bodied Soviet adults do elude capture by the state labour force. The press has lately featured many complaints about them, which are likely to be genuine and not fabricated by journalists.[10] Such letters and articles tell us, for example, that the number of illegal non-workers arrested by the police in three towns in the Novosibirsk oblast' exceeded the (estimated) labour shortage for the whole oblast'.[11] Work books (which those not in employment should possess) can be conveniently lost so that the voluntary unemployed can claim, when stopped by the militia, to be employed; such is the labour shortage that a new employer can always be counted upon to provide a new work-book.[12] There is no systematic checking-up on people's homes to see if the residents are gainfully employed, though some letter-writers believe there should be; and it is firmly asserted by both letter-writers and journalists that the numbers of non-workers are simply not known, which makes one wonder about the accuracy of the employment data we have.[13] The parasite's crime in Soviet society is usually that he is working, but in the illegal private economy and not for the state.

At the same time, not all unemployment is voluntary. The ordinary job-changer is described as spending on average some two-to-three weeks between jobs.[14] Hence, if 10 per cent of the labour force changes jobs each year, the rate of frictional unemployment would be 0.4 per cent ($1/10 \times 2/50 \times 100$). But there is some longer-term involuntary unemployment as well. Some people are hard to place in work because of their previous poor work record and dismissals for breaches of labour discipline: there were said to be just under a thousand such persons in Kaluga in 1971–72. (The population of Kaluga in 1971 was 217,000. Extrapolating this number of hard-core job-seeking unemployables to the present Soviet population would give about 125,000 or 0.1 per cent of the labour force; but these should probably be considered as already incorporated in the average numbers and duration of frictional unemployment.) A Barnaul letter-writer to *Pravda* in 1984 complained that he had been unable to get a job for four months because of a past record of dismissal.[15] (The *Pravda* journalist, Novoplyanskii, commented about the latter case that refusals to offer work were illegal, but he must be wrong. Even when an enterprise has unfilled vacancies, it surely is not obliged to take whoever turns up.)

These 'hard-core unemployables' are unlikely to be numerous. In regions where the labour shortage is particularly acute, even people with bad work records are readily hired. The Uralmash-zavod works was said in 1981 to be in the following situation: for every two people it sacked for breaches of labour discipline, one of the people it hired to replace them had been sacked for similar reasons from another Sverdlovsk enterprise.[16] And Uralmash must be a prestigious workplace, with as much ability as most enterprises to pick and choose among job applicants.

In other words, the typical Soviet enterprise's insatiable demand for additional labour is sufficient to ensure both a general régime of job security and aggregate full employment. The central planners' erroneous labour balances and the law's less than cast-iron provisions are not crucial functioning parts of the mechanism that produces these results; they are more like spare wheels—and untested spare wheels, at that. People can be, and are, sacked, but not for being an embarrassment to the profit-and-loss account. They are sacked, broadly speaking, for persistent drunkenness, absenteeism, political dissent, exit-visa applications and annoying the boss. People sacked for these reasons sometimes remain unemployed for long periods. But the behaviour that got them sacked in the first place was voluntary, and there are not many volunteers.[17]

The reasons why the demand of Soviet enterprises and organisations for labour is insatiable are well known. The more inputs the enterprise can have allocated to it, the better, so far as the management is concerned. If these inputs are incorporated in the production plan, they will be covered in the enterprise's financial plan, even if planned losses are involved. In general, the enterprise cannot be penalised for high costs incorporated in its plan: there are no competitors to undercut it, and no fear of business failure. On the contrary, enterprise management can only benefit from high inputs.

There are several reasons for this so far as labour inputs are concerned. First, the larger the enterprise labour force, the higher the basic pay scales of management.[18] Second, labour is worth hoarding anyway because of the irregularity of material supplies and the associated need for 'storming'; the possibility that your plan target will be increased during the year; the possibility that the local Party secretary will call up unexpectedly and requisition some of your employees for road-building, road-sweeping, harvest work and the like;[19] and the fundamental fact that bonuses are in practice linked above all to total output. Third, the continued predominance of the output target (and the new normative net output target introduced by the 1979 decree could make no difference as far as labour is concerned)[20] has a further effect on labour demand. Even after the enterprise annual or five-year plan is set, with a maximum planned wage bill or a 'normative' coefficient linking the permitted wage bill to output, the enterprise can generally expect that exceeding the wage-bill ceiling will on balance be remunerative if it is necessary in order to meet the output target.

This is illustrated by the behaviour of Soviet enterprises with respect to so-called 'counter-plans'. The idea of counter-planning is that the enterprise is set a five-year plan (FYP) broken into individual years, but is encouraged (by the prospect of enlarged bonuses) to set itself higher annual plans in which output exceeds the original FYP targets. These are meant to be achieved from given inputs, but that is not what happens in practice. The domination of output targets is such that even officially applauded

Table 6.2: *Plans and counter-plans for 1980 (1975 = 100)*

Key: Q = output; Q/L = labour productivity; L = Labour inputs

		10 FYP		Counter-plan
1. Sverdlovsk oxygen	Q	138.3		141.3
equipment plant	Q/L	142.4		142.6
implicit % △ L from 1975		−2.9		−0.9
2. Kharkov machine-tool	Q	138.7		141.0
works	Q/L	129.8		132.7
implicit % △ L		+6.9		+6.3
3. Gomel' 'Gidroiprirod'	Q	149.5		160.5
plant	Q/L	. .	(described as 4% <)	. .
implicit % △ L			(counter-plan 3.3% > FYP)	
4. Moscow ATE-1 Factory	Q	123.9		138.3
(Electrical equipment)	QL	121.4		132.9
implicit % △ L		+2.1		+4.1
5. Moscow 'Zarya'	Q	115.5		122.9
footwear association	Q/L	116.5		126.3
implicit % △ L		−0.9		−2.7

Source: derived from *Ekonomicheskaya gazeta* (1979), no.42, p.5; no.43, p.3; no.44, p.8.

counter-plans contain increased labour inputs.

In several issues of *Ekonomicheskaya gazeta* the examples (shown in Figure 6.2) of counter-planning were praised.

In three out of these five 'exemplary' instances of counter-planning (nos. 1, 3 and 4) it can be observed that counter-plan labour inputs exceed FYP inputs.

Altogether, an aggregate 'excess demand' for labour is built into the Soviet economic system because of the incentives operating at the micro-economic level. 'Planning from resources' at a branch, regional and national level may assist in this but is probably secondary: the aggregate of approved labour plans of Soviet industrial enterprises tends, as Pietsch shows, to exceed the national-level plan for labour use in the industrial sector, since nobody can cope with the information needed to reconcile micro and macro plans. For the same reason, jobs are in general secure since the managers of Soviet enterprises and organisations have to be extremely provoked before they will wish to sack anybody.

EFFICIENCY AND INEFFICIENCY IN A RÉGIME OF JOB SECURITY

One of the most dynamic economies in the world—that of Japan—has a widespread (though not comprehensive) régime of job security.[21] Extensive 'tenure' arrangements, therefore, cannot be assumed necessarily to generate inefficient use of labour. To put Soviet labour hoarding in perspective, it is useful to consider the Japanese employment system.

So far as big Japanese firms are concerned, their 'lifetime employees' are virtually unsackable, but they are also virtually certain not to quit and go elsewhere: the commitment works both ways. The firm's investment in training is therefore reliably recouped. The heavy emphasis on seniority in determining promotion is, in its turn, a sort of return on the employee's long-term investment of himself in the firm. Loyalty on the part of workers towards the firm is high.[22] In these respects the labour market is further away from the Western model than the Soviet labour market is.

Flexibility in the use of labour is retained in various ways: the fringe of temporary employees in large firms; the small and medium firms whose workforce does not have permanent employment status; arrangements for early retirement of lifetime employees with rehiring on a temporary basis (as in British universities recently); and occupational and geographical mobility within the big corporation (I have been told of physicists in their thirties being retrained as chemists). Thus job-changing can be quite substantial, even among permanent employees who remain throughout their working lives with the same employer.

Moreover, the Japanese labour force, like any other labour force, is constantly being reallocated among different activities by the recruitment of new entrants to it and the departure from it of those who retire. Finally, rapid growth of output has ensured that sustained falls in employment in particular lines of production are infrequent, and rapid growth of capital stock has ensured that the structure of capital assets is capable of flexible adaptation to changes in technology and demand and can therefore accommodate changes in labour allocation.

The fact remains that the Japanese labour market does not resemble the neoclassical textbook model in which labour inputs are variable in the short run and labour utilisation is adapted so as to maximise short-run profits. What it has going for it is that (a) allocative efficiency with respect to labour inputs is to some extent maintained through the various means of labour reallocation just described, and (b) X-efficiency, in the form of work effort, initiative and the like, is probably enhanced by the lifetime employment system. All this takes effect, of course, in an environment in which the firm is subject to competition and strongly motivated to hold down costs and use resources economically.

Finally, the relatively low pay of young entrants to the labour force, which is part of the Japanese employment system, along with the relatively low pay in the small-firm sector, has probably helped to sustain levels of recruitment of young labour-force entrants even during the recent recession (though it has not prevented some increase in youth unemployment).

Some of these favourable factors are also present in the Soviet case: the rapid growth of capital stock, inflow to and exit from the labour force, and the scope for redeployment within the enterprise (since Soviet enterprises are typically very large and house many ancillary production units). There is also a potential advantage in the Soviet case: the fact that labour turnover (between employment units) is similar to Western levels, and above Japanese levels.[23] The Soviet worker, like the West European worker, but unlike the Japanese permanent employee, has no commitment to a particular enterprise or organisation. He seeks his livelihood in a labour market which is closer than the Japanese labour market to the Western textbook model. He is therefore free to follow market indicators in reallocating his services from lower-paid to better-paid—and presumably more productive—uses.

The disadvantages from which the USSR suffers, in comparison with Japan, in reconciling job security with efficient use of labour, are as follows.

To begin with, there is nothing remotely resembling the influences favourable to x-efficiency in Japanese labour use. Hidden reserves, including labour hoarding, depress effort, competitive pressures on management to use labour efficiently are lacking, and a two-way commitment between worker and management is also lacking.[24] Second, the returns to the Soviet enterprise to any investment in training (and retraining) are less secure than in Japan because trained workers are more likely to go elsewhere. In the USSR as in Britain, labour skills have to be treated more as a public good than in Japan. The adaptation of Soviet education and training to Soviet production needs—a subject beyond the scope of this paper—is much criticised.[25] Third, total output growth is no longer as fast as in Japan.[26] Fourth, the growth rate of the labour force has slowed (see Table 6.1). It is true that the scope for restructuring the labour force through departures remains quite high, as departures from the working-age population have been rising; but numbers of entrants have been falling, so that the expansion of labour-scarce activities is impeded, even while the run-down of labour-surplus activities may be facilitated (in crude, aggregate terms). More will be said about this in the next section. Fifth, the problems of slower labour force growth are exacerbated by the notorious regional, ethnic and linguistic characteristics of current and prospective labour-force changes.[27] There is no counterpart to this problem in the territorially much smaller and ethnically more homogeneous Japanese economy.

This qualitative description of the Soviet Union's strengths and weaknesses, relative to Japan, in reconciling job security with efficient labour use, cannot by itself demonstrate that on balance the Soviets are at a disadvantage. But there is no real doubt that they are: economic performance provides powerful, if indirect, evidence. It would therefore seem that slowing labour-force growth presents Soviet policy-makers with especially severe problems. The régime of *de facto* job security is not accompanied to the same extent as in Japan by compensating factors favouring efficient labour use. Instead, endemic labour hoarding and generally low work effort, together with acute regional labour imbalances, foster inefficient use of labour and, given the economic system, a labour shortage in the sense that job vacancies tend to outnumber job-seekers. Voluntary job-changing must to some extent alleviate this difficulty, but the movements of Soviet workers are notoriously at variance with the wishes of planners so far as regional distribution is concerned;[28] they probably do not correspond too well with plans for branch and occupational distribution, either.[29]

To summarise the argument so far: Soviet full employment and job security arise mainly from economic arrangements which entail substantial costs in the sense of poor utilisation of labour. These costs become more salient as labour-force growth slows down, though they do not necessarily rise in proportion as the rate of labour-force increase dwindles.

The sense in which there is a labour shortage, however, is complicated. The number of job vacancies has probably exceeded that of unemployed job-seekers for decades (see Ch.2, by R.W. Davies). Yet, even while vacancies exceed job-seekers by a (probably) increasing margin, labour is horded in the sense that in many workplaces in many periods of time there are more workers on hand than are needed to produce the output actually achieved. In a survey of British chemical plant contractors' experience with 32 chemical plant contracts in the USSR in the 1960s and 1970s, I found that on average Soviet manning levels on the completed plant were 1.5 to 1.7 times the level that would be considered normal for the same plant in Western Europe.[30] (Differences of a similar order have been found between British and West German car plants.[31] But the British and Soviet routes to poverty are different.)

The possibility that the current Soviet labour shortage is not really a constraint on output should therefore be considered. In other words, output rates in most production units most of the time may be constrained by material supplies, energy supplies, capacity limits or, generally, factors other than labour inputs. A more efficient allocation of labour, together with better work effort might not, in that case, by itself improve economic performance. In general, we should ask if anything has happened recently in the Soviet economy to make labour 'shortages' more important than they were in, say, the 1950s; and if so, what is it that has changed?

SOME EVIDENCE ON LABOUR SHORTAGES

Gertrude Schroeder has pointed out that 'If planners' labour force projections are accurate and their expectations about productivity are realised, a general labour shortage would be impossible.'[32]

In fact the usual state of affairs over the past half-century has been roughly as follows. Soviet planners regularly underestimate labour demand by large amounts. In other words the sum of enterprise labour-force plans (certainly after 'corrections' within the plan period, and probably even before that) tends to exceed any aggregate labour-force plan for the state sector as a whole. The actual demand for labour therefore probably exceeds the available supply. Vacancies outnumber unemployed job-seekers; or, to put it differently, the average vacancy remains unfilled longer than the average job-seeker remains out of work. This, as Mario Nuti shows in his chapter, is tied up with the 'accumulation bias' of the system.

At the same time, the demand for labour includes, for reasons analysed by Kornai, a demand for 'spare' labour; there is a tendency to hoard 'hidden reserves' of labour. This is not an irrational demand so far as the enterprise is concerned. Fluctuations in material supplies, for one thing, and the associated need for 'storming' have something to do with it. The logic of the system, however, is that Soviet enterprise management will aim at a larger reserve of labour than would an entrepreneurial capitalist management facing the same prospective fluctuations. To the Soviet manager the additional labour has no effective cost since his budget constraints are soft, not hard.

How, if at all, has the importance of this state of affairs changed in the past fifteen to twenty years? What is it that makes Soviet writings latterly so obsessed with 'labour shortage' if labour shortage has been a built-in feature of the system for fifty years? The chapters by Pietsch and Nuti both offer answers to this question. My own tentative answer differs somewhat from both of theirs.

Aggregate labour productivity depends in part on the allocation of labour between activities (occupations, branches, regions). If we make the generous, but not unreasonable, assumption that the Soviet authorities have their priority ranking of labour demands at least roughly right, in that the priority ranking of different activities is positively correlated with their marginal productivity, then failures to match branch and regional planned labour demand evenly (e.g. with an evenly distributed shortfall) with supply are harmful to labour productivity in aggregate. Labour reallocation through job-changing has been substantially more at variance with labour plans than labour reallocation through the allocation of new entrants to the labour force. (See Ann Helgeson's paper in this collection, Ch.9). Other things being equal, therefore, a decline in the rate of inflow of new entrants to the labour force will tend to slow the growth rate of productivity and to that extent exacerbate perceived labour shortages.

The growth rate of the working-age population has not in fact slowed in recent years, but the rate of net additions to the non-agricultural labour force has slowed (see Table 6.1). Notoriously, it will slow much more markedly in the present decade.

An argument by Barney Schwalberg suggests some modification of this view.[33] Schwalberg notes that the growth rate of employment in high-priority branches has been more stable than the growth rate of employment in low-priority branches. In particular, the high-priority branches appear to have been insulated from slow-downs in labour-force growth. He attributes this to fluctuations in the length of notional 'queues' of would-be entrants to more attractive occupations. In periods of particularly acute overall labour shortage, the queues shorten as the priority activities absorb a larger proportion of these upwardly mobile job-seekers. This is achieved, presumably, by labour planning. If Soviet enterprises in general hoard 'surplus' labour, the Schwalberg story should mean that the margin of labour reserves tends to be trimmed in low-priority activities.[34]

More data about, and more analysis of, the whole process of labour allocation in the USSR are needed before one could test these two possibly conflicting hypotheses. In the meantime we can at any rate look for what evidence there is to hand that bears on the degree of overall labour shortage.

Production function estimates for Soviet industry, whether for the industrial sector as a whole or for individual branches, could in principle tell us how responsive industrial output is to changes in labour supply. If we had reliable measures of this elasticity of output with respect to labour inputs, we would expect it to rise over time insofar as the scarcity of labour relative to other inputs increased, and insofar as worsening 'labour shortages' meant that labour inputs became, in an increasing proportion of production units, the binding constraint on output.

The usual Cobb-Douglas estimates of total factor productivity

growth in Soviet industry cannot shed light on this. They assume
(and do not demonstrate) that the Cobb-Douglas form of the
production function, with constant returns to scale, is appropriate.
The elasticities of output with respect to labour and capital inputs,
moreover, are not directly estimated but imputed on the basis of
strong assumptions.[35] Thus the CIA estimate of industrial factor
productivity change imputes to labour a weight ($\propto$, labour's share
in national income or the elasticity of output with respect to labour
inputs) of 0.524 on the basis of ruble labour and capital costs in
1970.[36] If the responsiveness of output to changes in labour inputs
were growing over time, this calculation would not reveal the
increase.

Closer to the sort of evidence we are looking for is Martin
Weitzman's calculation of output elasticities for Soviet industry
from regressions using a constant-elasticity-of-substitution production function. Weitzman's hypothesis is well known: it is that the
slowdown in Soviet industrial growth since 1950 can be adequately
explained by (a) the much more rapid growth of capital than of
labour inputs, (b) an usually low elasticity of substitution of capital
for labour, of about 0.5 and (c) a modest but fairly steady rate of
increase of total factor productivity of about 0.9 percent per
annum. (These particular numbers come from his estimates using
the CIA index of Soviet industrial value added.)[37] Weitzman's
measure of the elasticity of industrial output with respect to labour
inputs increases from 0.52 in 1965 to 0.73 in 1978. It is therefore
consistent with the hypothesis that output has become, over time,
more sensitive to variations in labour inputs. This in turn suggests
that the notion of a worsening labour shortage has real economic
meaning. To put it another way: the hoarding of labour may not be
so extensive, relative to the hoarding of other inputs, that labour
supplies are not an important influence, at the margin, on output.
A rise over time in the elasticity of output with respect to labour
inputs would seem to conflict with the view that the especially
marked slowdown after 1976 is due mainly to an investment
slowdown and thus an exacerbation of capacity constraints.[38]

Further evidence on this can be derived from some Soviet data
that have been little used by Western economists. To begin with,
there are the 'work-time calendars' which set out the number of
standard working days and hours throughout the year. A
'work-time calendar' is published each year in the Soviet Union.[39]
It lists for each month the number of hours for which workers on
standard forty-one-hour or thirty-six-hour work-weeks can be

expected to be at work. The number of hours varies each month according to the number of days in the month and the incidence of Saturdays, Sundays and public holidays.

On two occasions in recent years, the Soviet Central Statistical Administration (TsSU) has drawn attention to the importance of these variations in work-time.[40] Faced with particularly low growth in gross industrial output in early 1979 and 1982, the TsSU withheld the usual January and February figures, comparing the level of total industrial output with the level in the corresponding period of the previous year. When the first quarter figures were published, the TsSU commentary drew attention to the fact that output had been adversely affected by variations in work-time. It was noted that first-quarter 1979 output, though only '3 per cent' up on first-quarter 1978, was 3.8 per cent up if calculated on an output per day basis; in 1982 the same observation was made, the figures being 2.1 and 2.9, respectively. Thus the TsSU implied that variations in overtime worked did not significantly offset monthly variations in standard work-time.[41]

Clearly, this was a convenient point for TsSU to adduce as a mitigating circumstance when presenting particularly poor figures. It suggests, all the same, that the work-time figures may be of interest. In particular, they may provide the means for a direct measure of the impact on Soviet industrial output of small changes in labour inputs: an approximation, it might be hoped, to a direct measure of the elasticity of output with respect to labour inputs and, hence, of the marginal product of labour in Soviet industry. The TsSU provides, after all, industrial output figures on a monthly basis. Thus the variations in work-time might be capable of being treated as variations in labour inputs and related to monthly variations in output. The period after 1978 is of particular interest for such a test. Soviet productivity growth slowed sharply in 1979–82 inclusive, while industrial labour force growth was also slowing. The period for which data are used here is 1979–83 inclusive. For comparison with a period before the recent slowdown in labour-force growth, the same calculations are made for 1968–73 inclusive. The data are available from the author on request.

A direct estimate of the elasticity of output with respect to labour inputs requires that other circumstances affecting output be held constant. The *ceteris paribus* condition might be approximated by relating monthly variations in work-time, not to monthly variations in output, but to those monthly variations in output which deviate from the annual rate of output change for the year in question. That, at any rate, was the method adopted.

The data on standard hours were the work-time calendar figures for 1967–73 and for 1978–83 inclusive. The monthly totals of standard hours worked are for the 41–hour week, which is standard in most Soviet industry. The thirty-six-hour week is in effect in only a few industries, such as coalmining, and average standard hours for all industrial workers are reported as very close to forty-one (e.g. 40.6 hours in 1982).[42]

Initial calculations were carried out using ordinary least squares regression. An index of official cumulative monthly-reported industrial output growth over the previous years (successively for January–February, January–March, and so on), denoted CQQ, was adjusted by subtracting from it the percentage increase in industrial output per standard hour worked over the year, denoted R. This gave the dependent variable, DCQQ.

For example, in 1983 the reported annual growth in industrial output over 1982 was 4.0 per cent. Standard hours worked in the year, according to the work-time calendar, were 2088, down by 0.7 per cent from the total of 2102 in 1982. Annual growth in output per standard hour was therefore 4.7 per cent. Thus R = 104.7 and the CQQ for January–April 1983, for instance, of 104.4, yields a DCQQ of −0.3.

The independent variable was the cumulative percentage change in standard hours worked, in each period, over the same period of the previous year, DCQL.

The regression equation, then, was:

$$DCQQ = a + b\ DQCL.$$

The results for both 1968–73 and 1979–83 showed a statistically significant relationship (t for the b coefficient = 3.01 and 6.22, respectively) but one that was extremely weak in the earlier period ($R^2 = 0.12$) and still fairly weak in the later period ($R^2 = 0.44$). Autocorrelation, however, was high and the results were not satisfactory.

The problems with this estimate were three in number. First, the absence of monthly data for other likely independent variables (capital, technology, etc.)[43] had been crudely offset by the use of R, but the appearance of autocorrelation indicated that this procedure was an inadequate approximation to *ceteris paribus*. Second, the use of cumulative observations of output (the only data available) produces a complicated stochastic structure for the sample, with errors cumulated. Third, the structure is further complicated by the absence of a few monthly-output data (two months in 1969 and two months in 1982).

I owe to Dr Wojciech Charemza the following resolution of the statistical difficulties: the use of the Cochrane-Orcutt iterative technique in place of ordinary least squares and the use of R as a weight for the observations of DCQQ. (Several alternatives were tried; details available on request.)

The re-estimation of the question with these amendments gave the results shown in Table 6.3.

Table 6.3: *Relationship between monthly variations in Soviet gross industrial output and in standard hours worked, 1968–73 and 1979–83*

Sample period	n	b coefficient	t(b)	R^2	DW
January 1968–December 1973	67	0.394	8.64	0.533	2.10
March 1978–December 1983	54	0.369	4.69	0.284	1.84
1968–73 + 1978–83	121	0.387	10.32	0.471	2.02

where n = number of observations (some months excluded for lack of data, others because of transformations of lagged variables in the Cochrane-Orcutt technique)

    b = the coefficients of DQCL (variations in hours worked)

t(b) = the t statistic for the b – coefficient

R^2 = coefficient of determination

DW = the Durbin-Watson statistic calculated for unweighted but ê – transformed residuals.

Source: Derived from data published in *Ekonomicheskaya gazeta* (work-time data given in issue no.1 each year, industrial output changes reported monthly). Tables in which the basic data are assembled are available on request from the author.

The interpretation of these results, which are acceptable in that the problem of autocorrelation has been avoided and significance levels are high, seems to be broadly as follows. Variations in standard hours worked do affect industrial output, but their effect is a rather weak one. It was not clearly altered between the period around 1970 and the period around 1980; the Chow statistic is 0.307, indicating that the null hypothesis of no change between the two sub-periods in the relationship cannot be rejected.

The fact that the relationship, though weak, is strongly statistically significant suggests, surprisingly, that variations in standard hours are not offset by variations (whether planned from

above or not) in overtime, which is in line with the TsSU's claim
that these work-calendar variations are of some consequence for
the interpretation of output. If this is so, the variations in standard
hours are a reasonable proxy for variations in labour inputs
supplied in Soviet industry. Therefore the regression results imply
an elasticity of output with respect to labour that is lower than is
normally assumed in fixed-weights Cobb-Douglas 'growth
accounting' for Soviet industry, and lower than that estimated by
Weitzman for the late 1970s, using a CES production function. To
put it another way, the typical Soviet enterprise does not seem,
from these figures, to have such a margin of underutilised
man-hours on hand that its output rate is insensitive to man-hours
supplied. On the other hand, it appears that output was only very
moderately sensitive to labour inputs around 1970, and again
around 1980. Thus there is no clear evidence here that the margins
of surplus, hoarded labour in Soviet enterprises have tended to be
reduced.

It is questionable whether this is consistent with the Weitzman
interpretation of Soviet industrial development: that growth in
capital per worker together with a low elasticity of substitution of
capital for labour has led to output becoming, over time,
increasingly sensitive to variations in labour supply. Nonetheless,
the Weitzman story has a certain commonsense appeal to it. Soviet
discussion of investment policy often stresses, in a cruder form, a
similar point: that capital investment has created additional
'work-places' which cannot be filled. It is claimed, for example,
that investment in the 1971–75 plan created two million additional
work places which there were no workers to fill, and investment in
1976–80 (when investment growth was cut back) created another
one million unfilled work places.[44]

This notion of 'excessive' investment implies a low elasticity of
substitution of capital for labour. Indeed, it is often described in
terms suggesting that there are absolutely fixed technical coefficients linking capital stock and workers, in a manner illustrated in
Figure 1 for a hypothetical single-product economy.

In the figure inputs of capital (K) and labour (L) are measured
along the two axes. The isoquants I, I' and I" represent
combinations of labour and capital which give successively higher
levels of output, with given technology. Their L shape indicates
that substitution of capital for labour or vice versa is impossible:
there is a completely rigid ratio (e.g. one man per machine). The
economy can therefore expand only along a single ray from the

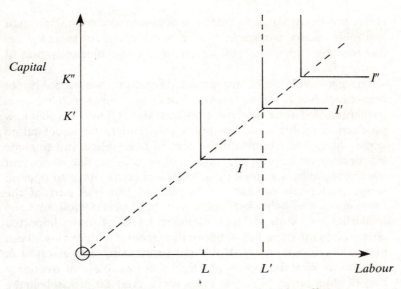

Figure 1: *Over-investment with fixed technical coefficients*

origin (the dotted line going North-east from O). The maximum labour force available in the time period pictured here is OL'. Investment which puts the economy on isoquant I leaves a margin of unemployed labour (or labour hoarded within enterprises and unused) equal to OL' minus OL. Investment which takes the economy to I' fully utilises the available labour. Investment such as that to raise the capital stock to OK" leaves OK" minus OK' capital unused.

Soviet economists and planners are of course well aware that technical coefficients can never be (for the industrial sector as a whole) quite as fixed as that. But they know that there are powerful influences hindering capital–labour substitution. One is precisely the enterprise managers' desire to maintain labour reserves. Another is enterprises' and branch ministries' insatiable appetite for investment funds, which leads to constant pressure to start more projects, build more buildings, and so on, with the aim *inter alia* of raising the number of work places rather than of mechanising or automating the work of existing personnel. This shows up in several problems which are long-established causes of complaint by Soviet economists: the inadequate mechanisation of ancillary activities such as materials handling within the factory; the unusually low rate of retirement of old capital stock; the correspondingly high concentration of labour and capital in repair and maintenance work and of investment resources in new plant construction rather than the re-equipping and modernisation of existing factories.

The gross volume of investment, therefore, has probably not been excessive. It is investment net of retirements which has been too large.[45] What we may guess is happening, typically, is that new production facilities are created which tend to be understaffed while older production facilities remain overstaffed and to some extent also overequipped; that is, they contain old equipment which should be scrapped to release workers to move to operate newer and more productive equipment. This was part of the rationale of the Shchekino experiment. (The observation, referred to earlier, of relatively high manning levels on new, imported chemical plant does not support this general proposition about new and old equipment. But this overmanning was assessed in relation to West European practice; it is possible that overmanning of older Soviet plant was even worse. And it is precisely in the chemical industry that the Shchekino method achieved much of whatever success it has had.)[46]

There are some Soviet data which might shed light on the extent of unfilled workplaces. They are data of the sort whose collection Kornai recommends: direct measures of imbalances. They come from the irregularly published 24-hour surveys of machinery utilisation in the Soviet machine-building sector. A sample (probably unrepresentative)[47] of machine-building enterprises are studied throughout a twenty-four-hour period, and the amount of machinery down-time is noted, together with the causes of it. Some of these causes are to do with labour shortages in the workplaces studied. The evidence of these surveys is used here with the greatest caution. Management records on such matters as absenteeism are very poor,[48] and it is not clear that these surveys cope adequately with this problem.

One would expect a growing man–machine imbalance to show up in one or more of the following measures: the shift coefficient;[49] the proportion of planned machine-hours actually worked; and the machinery down-time attributable to what is classified as 'staff shortages' (*neukomplektovannost' rabochimi*: freely translated, the sense is that the production process has to be operated by fewer than the approved complement of staff, like the buffet cars on British trains at a time when there are four million unemployed).

The figures from the three post-1970 surveys I have been able to locate in fact show no trace of worsening labour shortages. Except where otherwise specified the data in Table 6.4 relate to so-called 'basic production' activity on metal-cutting machine tools in machine-building enterprises under machine-building ministries.

Table 6.4: *Labour shortage evidence from TsSU machinery down-time surveys, 1973–82*

Date of survey	16 May 1973	14 May 1975	19 May 1982
Shift coefficient	1.40	1.41	1.41
% of planned machine time actually worked (all equipment)	84	85	85
The % share of staff shortages as a cause of:			
(a) complete 24-hour machinery downtime	29.4	28.9	26.3
(b) complete shift machinery downtime	45.4	44.5	39.5

Source: Vestnik statistiki (1974) no.3, pp.88–91; (1976), no.4, pp.93–96; (1983), no.4, pp.68–71.

Interpretation of these figures is not entirely straightforward. They certainly seem to provide no evidence of worsening labour shortage for the particular enterprises and activities studied.[50] It is just possible that the shift coefficient has been kept stable by a proportionate reduction in man- and machine-hours (on average for the enterprises surveyed) through all three shifts. But that is unlikely. Similarly it is possible that the proportion of hypothetically available machine time which is planned to be used has been reduced so that the ratio of actual to planned use has been maintained while actual hours worked have fallen. Again, however, this seems unlikely, if only because the planners are not generally that accurate. If the total machinery down-time per machine has in fact remained about the same, then the last two rows of Table 6.4 show 'staff shortages' as a significant source of machinery down-time, but a source which is tending, if anything, to diminish slightly.

This evidence tends to reinforce the work-time regression evidence that the margin of labour hoarding may not have been reduced over the past decade. On the other hand, it does not necessarily show that the problem of capital–labour substitution is not a growing problem for Soviet industry generally. The 'main production' of specialist machine-building enterprises is a high-priority activity. (It is possible that the survey even included defence plants.) If Schwalberg is right, staffing levels for high-priority activities are maintained through labour abundance and labour dearth, with low-priority activities taking the strain. A tentative interpretation, therefore, of these data is that they indicate the continuing protection of favoured activities from labour shortage.

To summarise: there is evidence of continued poor utilisation of labour, but there is no clear evidence that in the industrial sector in total the margin of underemployed labour has been reduced and total output has become more sensitive to variations in labour supply. Capital–labour substitution may well be low but high-priority activities may have been quite effectively shielded at least from the direct effects of labour stringency.

POSSIBLE IMPROVEMENTS

The present Soviet labour shortage problem looks to be real in the sense that industrial output is sensitive to small variations in labour supples and capital–labour substitution seems to be weak. At the same time, labour continues to be inefficiently used. Within the existing economic system an improvement in investment policy could ease labour constraints. A sharp cut in investment growth rates has already been made, in the mid-1970s. But a higher rate of retirement of old capital assets, releasing labour to man newer and more productive assets, would contribute to more flexible capital–labour substitution. This would not entail a premature writing-off of assets which were not fully amortised; the use of capital assets far beyond their planned life is a serious problem.

To call for more intelligently managed investment is to repeat innumerable calls over the decades by Soviet economists and policy-makers: denunciations of *raspylenie sredstv*; demands for the share in total investment of modernisation and re-equipping to be increased, and so on. The incentives of branch ministry officials, enterprise directors and construction managers go against these appeals, and nowhere is the de facto decentralised control of the centrally administered Soviet economy more apparent than in investment.

There is, however, some prospect of improved planning and

control of investment in the USSR for two reasons. First, the growth rate of total investment spending has been cut back, and this should ease the central planners' information problems. Second, the State Planning committee, the State Construction Committee and the other central planning bodies concerned are trying to develop a decent database on investment projects. Of the 26,000 construction projects currently under way in the USSR, employing the services of 3,100 construction trusts, only 8,000 are of more than 3 million rubles' value each. These account for 95 per cent of the total value, and the database that is being developed covers only these projects.[51]

If information on projects could in this way be sharply improved, it might be possible not only to monitor their progress more effectively but to insist on the new capital assets being matched with additional labour supplies which have been shifted from older assets withdrawn from use. This matching could be assisted by the 'attestation' (and, where appropriate, abolition) of existing working places proposed for 1984–85.[52] Any self-respecting Sovietologist will be sceptical about the outcome of such endeavours, but there may be a chance of improvement.

CONCLUSION

In general, however, the evidence on labour shortages and labour hoarding reinforces the view that they are part of a more general disorder of inefficient resource use attributable to the centrally administered economic system. The dominant incentives are to hoard labour, not to economise on its use. Labour is therefore inefficiently allocated between old and new equipment; obliged to work at an irregular pace because of hiccups in material supply; strongly tempted to dodge work in order to cope better with the queues in the shops; prone to a combination of cynicism, apathy and larceny in the face of the general muddle imposed by the official workplace environment.

Zaslavskaya points to these phenomena in support of her thesis that 'the main type of worker being formed by the present social mechanism of economic development does not meet the requirements of developed socialism'.[53] I think what she means is that the centralised Soviet economic system makes people lazy and immoral. Whether the centralised economy really adds all that much to the legacy of original sin, I am not sure. But it does seem to keep people unproductive and unprosperous. Decentralisation is probably the only cure. Instead of being corrupted by central control, the Soviet worker could then be corrupted by prosperity, which is more fun.

NOTES

1. This means, roughly speaking, that managers have no reason to fear enterprise failure. The enterprise will always be bailed out of financial difficulties and will only rarely be forced to trim its inputs. *See* Anna-Jutta Pietsch, Ch.10 of this collection.
2. *See* Joseph Berliner, *The Innovation Decision in Soviet Industry*, (Cambridge, MA, 1976).
3. For Hungary this question is considered by Michael Marrese in 'Is Unemployment the Only Answer to Labour Shortage in Hungary?' in Jan Adam (ed.), *Employment Policies in the Soviet Union and Eastern Europe*, (London, 1982), pp.96–123.
4. UN Economic Commission for Europe, *Economic Survey of Europe in 1982*, (New York: UN, 1983), p.94.
5. In Switzerland and (approximately) in Austria full employment still obtains; UN ECE, *op. cit.*, p.25. Something rather fundamental has happened in the Western world, it is true, to end the quarter of a century of full employment after the Second World War. But it is premature to say that modern capitalism cannot return to full employment, and historically inaccurate to say that capitalism and full employment are simply incompatible.
6. The category of so-called 'temporary employees', together with small-firm employers, are outside the 'Japanese employment system', but overall unemployment rates have remained extremely low in the present recession. *See* the internationally comparable unemployment measures regularly given in the *National Institute Economic Review*. Perhaps one should say that Japan has widespread, though by no means complete, job security together with very low levels of unemployment. How far (and in what sense) Japanese unemployment may be understated by conventional unemployment figures, I am not competent to judge. But the 2 to 2.5 per cent rates calculated in the *NIESR* for recent years, since they are adjusted to US definitions, will reflect (unlike the unadjusted UK official figures) more than just the numbers officially registered. That such low rates have a good deal to do with the Japanese employment system is argued by Depler and Regling, who estimate that the 1978 average unemployment rate (adjusted to US definitions) of 2.4 per cent would have been about 6 per cent in the absence of the Japanese employment system (*Finance and Development*, March 1979).
7. *See* Nick Lambert, Ch.15 of this collection.
8. Silvana Malle pointed out (Ch.8 in this volume) that the sheer size of many Soviet employing organisations reduces the likelihood that

redeployment within the organisation will be impossible. Dyker says that slightly more than half the workers made redundant in 'Schchekino'-type productivity deals in 1976–80 were not found jobs in the enterprises in which they were made redundant from their previous jobs; David Dyker, 'Redeployment and Redundancy of Workers Under Andropov' Radio Liberty RL337/83 (7 Sept. 1983). It may well be, however, that most if not all of these workers were *offered* other jobs in their original enterprise, or at any rate in neighbouring enterprises. This 'reduction of staff' is a long-established ritual which is supposed to keep administrative and service staff (cleaners, secretaries, book-keepers) to a minimum. Implementation is often merely a matter of re-classifying people (e.g. book-keepers as stone-cutters) or even reporting that cuts have been made and not making them; checking-up is minimal. *See* B. Nikolaev, 'V shtate—lishnii', *Pravda*, 29 Mar. 1984, p.2.

9. I do not know what the status of cooks and housemaids in private households is. There are a fair number of them in the USSR, but whether one can be legally employed in those capacities by a private person is not clear. The maids who work for resident foreign diplomats are employed by the UPDKh (if not by other agencies) and those who work for Soviet élite households are perhaps provided by the state, like chauffeurs.

10. for example, S. Troitskii, 'Neuyazvimyi tuneyadets', *Pravda*, 4 Aug. 1983, p.3; D. Novoplyanskii, 'Shalyai-valyai', *Pravda*, 3 Aug. 1983, p.2; *idem*, 'Kot Vas'ka–84', *Pravda*, 27 Mar. 1984, p.3. Also much of the 'public discussion' of the draft law on labour collectives; e.g., *Pravda*, 25 April, 26 April and 13 May 1983.

11. Troitskii, referring to an unspecified period of time. Note that this refers only to the number actually arrested.

12. *Ibid.* Apparently the internal passport no longer contains an entry showing place of current employment. Parasites may not have things quite so easy in some regions, however.

13. *Ibid.* and Novoplyanskii, 'Kot Vas'ka–84', *op. cit.* In particular, people who work for the state only two or three months a year are said to be counted as working a full year.

14. *See*, for example, the description of one of the early local experiments requiring all job seeking to be channelled through city labour placement (*trudoustroistvo*) bureaus (in Ufa and Kaluga); *Trud* 29 Jan. 1972, p.2 and 2 Feb. 1972, p.2. This refers to a reduction in average duration of frictional unemployment in these cities, as a result of this experiment, twenty-four to thirteen days. A decade later almost identical figures were given (twenty-four and ten days) for the time taken between jobs in Perm by (a) those seeking a new job independently, and (b) those going through the local bureau; v. Yaborov, 'Kak snizit' tekuchest', *Pravda*, 25 Mar. 1982, p.3; Schroeder, *op. cit.*, p.23 quotes a higher average figure of thirty-one days from *Planovoe khozyaistvo*, 1979, no.10, p.41.

15. *Trud*, 2 Feb. 1972; Novoplyanskii, 'Kot Vas'ka–84', *op. cit.*

16. A. Melent'ev, 'Distsiplina truda', *Pravda* 6 Feb. 1981, p.2.

17. Martin Gilbert, who has made a study of 'refuseniks', estimates that

there were in 1982–84 about 12,000 Jews in the USSR who had lost their jobs as a result of applying for exist visas. (*Birmingham Post* 28 Mar. 1984, p.4; *see also* his *The Jews of Hope* (London: Macmillan, 1984). How many of these are actually unemployed, and how many have got a bad job (stoker or night-watchman) after being pushed out of a good job, is not clear. If all 12,000 refuseniks were unemployed, they would constitute a national unemployment rate of about 0.01 per cent. On the rate of sackings for breaches of labour discipline, I have seen no national statistics. One figure for an individual plant, quoted in a context in which it is unlikely to be untypically high, is for the Lipetsk tractor works: 1.8 per cent of the labour force in 1970 and 1.4 per cent in 1980. L.E. Kunel'skii and B.P. Kutyrev, 'Opyt upravleniya trudovoi distsiplinoi. Itogi anketnogo oprosa', *EKO*, 1983, no.11, pp.18–46, at p.30. For more on the scale of disciplinary dismissals, *see* Nick Lampert, Ch.15 of this collection.

18. For one of many Soviet observations on the importance of this consideration, *see* I. Malmygin, 'Pochemu stanok "otdykhaet"', *Pravda*, 15 Jan. 1984, p.2. Malmygin argues that this is also a factor in overinvestment, because of the rigid plan links between capital stock and the approved complement of staff. It is worth installing more equipment even if you can't find the workers to man it, because management pay is related to numbers of work places (*rabochie mesta*), regardless of whether there are chaps occupying those places. Shchekino advocates have been deploring this for years; *see*, e.g. V Boldyrev in *Pravda*, 26 May 1972, p.2. The quantitative importance of this link, I am advised by Peter Rutland, is hard to assess, for lack of detailed information on the determinants of managers' pay scales.

19. The director of the Kirov synthetic rubber works in Voronezh, having foolishly adopted the Shchekino method, was ordered in 1971 to supply 200 men for construction work. When he claimed that he had no spare labour because he had followed the Shchekino experiment, he was told 'Experiments are your affair. Give us some people!' (*Trud*, 16 Nov. 1971.)

20. Normative net output is in fact based on a (standardised) labour input measure akin to value added. For the decree, *see Ekonomicheskaya gazeta*, 1979, no.32, pp.9–17. For an analysis see P. Hanson, 'Success Indicators Revisited: the July 1979 Soviet Decree on Planning and Management', *Soviet Studies*, vol.XXXV, no.1 (Jan. 1983), pp.1–13.

21. *See* R.P. Dore, *British Factory, Japanese Factory* (London: Allen and Unwin, 1975), and Chs.5–9 of Andrew Shonfield, *In Defence of the Mixed Economy*, Oxford, 1984).

22. For a comparative survey of Japanese and US workers' attitudes towards management, *see* A.N. Whitehill and Shin-ichi Takezawa, 'Workplace Harmony: Another Japanese "Miracle"? *Columbia Journal of World Business*, Fall 1978, pp.24–40.

23. Annual resignations and dismissals as a percentage of the industrial labour force in 1975 are given as 18.9 per cent by Anna-Jutta Pietsch and Heinrich Vogel, 'Displacement by Technological Progress in the USSR' in Jan Adam (ed.), *op. cit.*, pp.145–66, at p.151. In the calculation of a hypothetical frictional unemployment rate given

earlier, I used a 10 per cent turnover rate for the economy as a whole. The Pietsch-Vogel turnover rate with the Schroeder time-between-jobs figure (n.16) would give a frictional unemployment rate of 1.6 per cent.

24. More precisely, it is not built into the relationship as it is in Japan. There may, as in Britain, quite often be strong traditions of loyalty and cooperation in individual enterprises. Dore, *op. cit.*, gives a vivid picture of Anglo-Japanese differences in this respect.

25. Pietsch and Vogel, *op. cit.*, and *see* the chapters in this collection by Sheila Marnie (Ch.12) and Ed Gloeckner (Ch.13). Some particularly forceful recent Soviet articles on this theme are: K. Savichev, '"Zakaz" na spetsialist', *Pravda*, 22 Mar. 1981, p.3; v. Parfenov, 'Inzhenery', *Pravda*, 29 April 1981, p.2; G. Chumakova, 'Paradoks raspredeleniya', *Pravda*, 14 Nov. 1981, p.3; G. Kulagin, 'Rabota vsyakayavazhna', *Pravda*, 27 Dec. 1981, p.2; V. Elyutin, 'Prioritet tvorchestva', *Pravda*, 22 Feb. 1983, p.3.

26. Real GNP in 1981 is estimated to have growth between 1975 and 1981 at 2.2 per cent p.a. in the USSR and 4.7 per cent p.a. in Japan (CIA, *Handbook of Economic Statistics 1982*, p.38).

27. For details, *see* Murray Feshbach, 'Population and Labour Force' in Abram Bergson and Herbert S. Levine (eds.), *The Soviet Economy: Toward the Year 2000* (Winchester, MA, 1983), pp.79–112.

28. Schroeder, *op. cit.*; Feshbach, *op. cit.*; Ann Helgeson, 'Demographic Policy', in Archie Brown and Michael Kaser (eds.), *Soviet Policy for the 1980s*, (London, 1982), pp.118–45 and Ann Helgeson's chapter in this volume (Ch.9).

29. *See* the chapter by Silvana Malle in this collection (Ch.8).

30. P. Hanson, *Trade and Technology in Soviet-Western Relations* (London: Macmillan, 1981), Ch.11. This conclusion comes from thirteen plants for which the comparison could be made.

31. *Times* 16 Dec. 1981, p.26, for example, on production of Ford Escorts at Halewood and Saarbrucken.

32. *Op. cit.*, p.3.

33. In the discussion of the Feshbach paper, Bergson and Levine, *op. cit.*, pp.430–31.

34. This is my interpretation, not Schwalberg's.

35. $Q = Ae^{\ell t} L^{\propto} K^{1-\propto}$ where Q = output, L = labour inputs, K = capital inputs, ℓ is a measure of 'total factor productivity' and $\propto$ is an imputed 'factor share' in output for labour and $1 - \propto$ the imputed 'factor share' for capital. The factor shares are fixed weights for a given year.

36. CIA, *op. cit*, p.72.

37. M.L. Weitzman, 'Industrial Production' in Bergson and Levine, *op. cit.*, pp.178–91. The CIA measure of industrial output is of a hybrid character, and is not precisely a value added measure. The point to note here is that it is not the same as the official Soviet gross industrial output series. The Weitzman calculations cited here are for 1950–78 and do not cover the further slowdown after 1978.

38. Herbert S. Levine, Daniel L. Bond, Charles Movit and Elizabeth Ann Goldstein, *The Causes and Implications of the Sharp Deterioration in*

Soviet Economic Performance (Washington DC: Wharton Econometric Forecasting Associates, 1983). Levine *et. al.* emphasise the simultaneity of this extra slowdown with the cut-back in planned investment growth, and the fact that it is the residual (total factor productivity growth) which falls so sharply. But the residual necessarily takes the strain of the slowdown when it is calculated using fixed weights for factor inputs (i.e., when elasticities of output with respect to both labour and capital inputs are fixed *a priori*). The Levine *et. al.* analysis has something in common with K.K. Val'tukh, 'Investitsionnyi protsess i intensifikatsiya proizvodstva' *Eko* 1982, no.3, pp.4–31.

39. In the first issue each year of *Ekonomicheskaya gazeta* (henceforth *Ekon. gaz.*) on the pack page.

40. *Ekon. gaz.*, 1979, no.19, p.2; and 1982, no.18, p.4.

41. The average actual work-time per weeks in Soviet industry in 1973 and 1974 was reported as 40.6 hours when the average standard work-week was 40.7 hours. *Vestnik statistiki*, 1975, no.5, p.45. It also appears, rather curiously, from Soviet writings on output and work-time that planners do not set monthly plans in such a way as to allow for variations in standard work-time.

42. *Narodnoe khozyaistvo SSSR v 1982 godu* (henceforth *Narkhoz. . .*), p.372. The standard work-week was the same in all the years considered here.

43. On the many influences on the TFP residual other than 'technological progress', *see* Abram Bergson, 'Technological Progress' in Bergson and Levine, *op. cit.*, pp.34–79; *also* Hanson, 'Brezhnev's Economic Legacy', paper presented at NATO Economics Directorate Colloquium, Brussels, April 1984. In the present estimates, moreover, it is important to bear in mind that the output measure is the official Soviet index of gross industrial output, so that current material inputs constitute another independent variable.

44. E. Gorbunov, 'Effektivnost' vlozhenii, *Pravda*, 1 Dec. 1983, p.2. *See also* Malmygin, *op. cit.* and V. Parfenov and V. Cherkassov, 'Rabochie mesta i lyudy', *Pravda*, 9 Mar. 1984, p.2. New regulations for the 'attestation of new work places have, after long preparation, been introduced. See *Ekon. gaz.*, 1984, no.20, pp.11–14.

45. Soviet data show retirements of capital stock in 1983 as only 2.1 per cent of end-1981 capital assets for the economy as a whole. *Narkhoz 82*, p.48.

46. I am grateful to Joseph Porket for raising this issue.

47. Stephen Shenfield, 'Why Does Sampling Play Such a Secondary Role in Soviet Statistics?', CREES Discussion Paper RC/B18, University of Birmingham, 1982.

48. I am indebted to Peter Rutland for discussion of this.

49. The ratio of total machine-hours (or sometimes man-hours) planned to be worked during the 24-hour period to the number worked in the most active shift. Full three-shift working would have a shift coefficient of 3.0; pure single-shift working would have a shift coefficient of 1.0.

50. I ignore here the possibility that the different measures are so defined as to be mutually inconsistent and produce meaningless results. The

survey being a TsSU survey, this cannot be ruled out. It should also be noted that shift coefficients in machine-building have tended slowly downwards in an earlier period, from 1.55 in 1959 to 1.42 in 1975. *See* Vladimir Kontarovich, 'Capital–Labour Substitution and Soviet Growth Slowdown', working paper, University of Pennsylvania, 1984.

51. S. Bulgakov (in charge of developing a unified investment planning system in USSR Gosplan), 'Nachinaetsya s plana', *Pravda*, 7 Sept. 1983, p.2.

52. Yu. P. Batalin (chairman of the USSR State Committee for Labour and Social Problems), Attestatsiya rabochikh mest', *Ekon. gaz.*, 1984, no.10, p.5. Detailed guidelines on working-place attestation were published in *Ekon. gaz.*, 1984, no.20, pp.11–14.

53. Tatyana Zaslavskaya, 'Doklad o neobkhodimosti bolee uglublennogo izucheniya v SSSR sotsial'nogo mekhanizma razvitiya ekonomiki', Moscow seminar paper reportedly presented in April 1983. RFE-RL Arkhiv Samizdata AS 5042, vypusk 35/83 (26 Aug. 1983), p.29; translated as 'The Novosibirsk Report', *Survey*, vol.28, no.1 (Spring 1984), pp.88–109.

7 Systemic Aspects of Employment and Investment in Soviet-type Economies

D.M. NUTI*

The purpose of this paper is that of identifying and discussing those features of employment and investment in Soviet-type economies that are system-specific; that is, due to socialist planning rather than to the necessary system-free relationships between economic variables in any economy.

A priori reasoning might suggest that system-specific features are absent or weak. There is a dual relationship between capital investment and the employment of labour: current investment provides both a component of current *demand* requiring the employment of labour on existing capital stock, and the *supply* of a component of the future stock of equipment necessary to employ future labour. *Supply* aspects of investment and employment—which have been thoroughly investigated in the theory of production and of economic growth and are no longer controversial—do not appear to have a systemic content. The literature is rich with theoretical and empirical studies virtually indistinguishable for both capitalist and socialist systems. Production functions, output elasticities with respect to factors, technical progress residuals have been theorised and computed *ad nauseam* for both systems; Kalecki's model of socialist growth (which is the best theoretical effort of its kind) is nothing but the supply side of an ordinary policy-orientated growth model (i.e. with investment subject to the policy-maker's behavioural function rather than that of aggregate investors), complete with its extensive and intensive phases. A major reason for this coincidence of approaches might be the association of supply relationships with the long run, when overall constraints might be expected to dominate systemic

* European University Institute, Florence.

features. Short-term *demand* aspects of investment and employment, on the contrary, can be deemed to be systemic because of socialist methods of investment planning and allocation of labour as opposed to capitalist markets; in the case of capitalism they are also controversial, as witnessed by the Keynesian–monetarist debates. However, it turns out that these specific systemic features of socialism, far from requiring the development of a specific theory, fit old-fashioned bourgeois theory much better than the capitalist system itself: investment planning is supposed to do what capitalist markets should do (i.e. coordinate present and future claims on consumption) according to general equilibrium theory but do not do because they are incomplete; saving and investment decisions are unified in the same central agent, and the very distinction between the demand and supply aspect of investment therefore disappears because current investment is planned and undertaken exclusively for the provision of future plant to employ labour and generate consumption. It would seem that capitalism, not socialism, needs the spelling out of its own systemic features that depart from the standard textbook.

Even the direct observation of the most spectacular difference between modern capitalist and socialist systems (i.e. mass unemployment versus full employment of labour) does not contradict the theoretical coincidence of systems. This difference can and should be properly regarded not as a necessary systemic feature but as a difference in economic policy. It is true that it is sometimes difficult to distinguish between a persistent policy stance taken by a system and a specific systemic feature; in particular, one should remember Kalecki's warnings about the obstacles to full employment policies in the capitalist economy, and the class disciplining role of unemployment; but it is still useful to distinguish between policies and systems. Any economy undertaking demand management, with a strictly observed wages policy restraining real wages, the enforcement of labour mobility (regardless of the desired location or of the full utilisation of acquired skills) and the insulation from international trade and finance can achieve full employment of labour (whether at this full employment workers as a class would obtain higher total real wages is another matter). If real wages are kept low enough, full employment might also be consistent with an open economy, at least most of the time. Even if there is not enough equipment for all, after the demechanisation of multiple shifts, work sharing and employment subsidies will overcome that constraint. In capitalist countries, close to full employment was obtained by Nazi Germany by a combination of corporatism, repression and macro-economic policies which were Keynesian *ante litteram*; today it is obtained in Japan by feudal means, Austria by neocorporatism; tomorrow unemployment might fall drastically in Great Britain under a Labour government committed to protectionism or trade planning, and willing to make the political concessions necessary for workers to agree to retrain and move around for lower real wages. Conversely, it is perfectly possible for labour unemployment to arise in a reformed Soviet economy at last decentralised and more open to international markets. It still remains to be shown that full employment is a *systemic* issue.

Reflection and closer scrutiny, however, confirm that there are systemic features of investment and employment in Soviet-type economies, both in their demand and supply aspects, due to departures of reality from the socialist economy model or to gaps in that model, and that those systemic features affect significantly both the interpretation of facts and the evaluation of policies. A number of tentative suggestions about these systemic features are grouped below under the following headings: overaccumulation; labour shortage and production functions. Some conclusions are drawn about the theoretical and practical relevance of these systemic features.

OVERACCUMULATION

Soviet-type economies differ from the text book model of socialist economy conceived as a general equilibrium model of a giant firm in two important respects vis-à-vis investment. First, they are *sequential*; that is, investment decisions are taken not once-and-for-all but recurrently, as in Hicks' temporary equilibrium rather than as in the Arrow-Debreu general equilibrium approach, thereby raising problems of expectations, dynamic adjustment, and therefore of modelling of investment behaviour. Second, they are *multilevel*; that is, even if investment decisions are centralised, an influence is exercised by lower levels through the manipulation of information and participation in a dialogue with the centre. Both features open the possibility of investment being subject to behavioural regularities of its own, in spite of its nominal role of a policy variable in central planning.

It is widely accepted that there is a distinct bias towards

accumulation and overaccumulation in the Soviet-type economy, which is the main feature of its investment behaviour; while dynamic adjustment to recurring overinvestment takes the form of investment cycles through the pattern of starts and completion of projects.[1]

There are many reasons for the accumulation bias of the Soviet-type economy. First, both at the macro and the micro level the same urge to accumulate typical of the capitalist system is present, but without the checks and constraints of the capitalist system (such as stock market valuation, takeover bids, bankruptcy discipline, and so on); moreover, pressure for investment is exercised also at the local and the ministry level. Second, overoptimistic expectations about labour productivity raise investment requirements for the creation of new jobs over actual requirements. Third, in the course of communications and interactions between the various agents (the Party, Gosplan, ministries, firms associations and firms) strategies are developed that result in overaccumulation tendencies. Higher levels impose deliberately overambitious production and investment tasks in order to mobilise reserves concealed by lower levels; lower levels insure themselves against the risk of underfulfilment by bidding for more plant; investment is made to look more attractive that it actually is so that investors can 'hike themselves onto the plan' and later be in a more favourable position to negotiate completion. High investment targets and systematic overfulfilment are a primary systemic feature of the Soviet-type economy.

As long as labour reserves are available to man new plant, drawn from the urbanisation process, the growth in active population and natural demographic growth, this accumulation bias is a source of economic growth—provided other constraints such as foreign currency or other bottlenecks do not prevent the utilisation of investment. Accumulation may be excessive with respect to the preferences the population would have expressed through a market or a political process if given the chance; or with respect to the preferences of the leadership, who might have preferred a different trade-off between consumption and investment in the pattern of plan fulfilment and overfulfilment, or with respect to the internal or external sources of finance; but all these definitions of overaccumulation are by and large subjective and controversial, and in any case accumulation has a positive influence on income (though not necessarily on consumption levels). If however—as it seems to have been the case in the

USSR—more accumulation takes place than can be manned by the workforce, then this is an unambiguous signal of a damaging systemic bias towards *over*accumulation.

A number of theoretical and policy implications follow from the existence of overaccumulation in Soviet-type economies:

First, it puts full employment of labour in a more sober perspective. The unemployment of 'dead' labour (in Marxian parlance) congealed in capital equipment is no better than the unemployment of 'live' labour on the dole, from the viewpoint of systemic achievement.

Second, together with the systemic underprovision of consumption goods relatively to wage payments, overaccumulation provides an environment of endemic excess demand in which neither central planning nor markets can function properly. Central planning was originally understood as a way of preventing imbalances, not as a permanent administration of imbalances. Markets can only work when goods can be bought and sold at market prices, and there can be no question of reforms until the systemic commitment to price stability is dropped. It was never a feature of the original socialist design that socialism should be a world of excess demand and queueing, and it is grotesque that this should have become the case.

Third, it is dubious whether economic decentralisation would be sufficient to remove the overaccumulation bias, and whether in that case it would not overshoot the mark towards the capitalist-style underinvestment and labour unemployment. All reform schemes from Lange to date are surprisingly lacking in their dealing with investment decisions.

LABOUR SHORTAGE

It is essential to distinguish between a number of alternative concepts which are all aspects of labour shortage but have very significant differences and systemic implications.

There is labour shortage relative to existing capital equipment; this is nothing but the mirror image of overaccumulation; it is a systemic phenomenon but not a separate phenomenon from overaccumulation. There is also labour shortage as an aspect of generalised factor-shortage relative to demand; this is a consequence of systemic excess demand which may be present even in the absence of overaccumulation. The first notion implies the absence of opportunities for substituting equipment for labour; the second implies the existence of substitutability of labour for other inputs. Both labels are statements about factor substitutability, and it might be useful to recall that there may very well be substitutability between capital and labour *ex ante* (i.e. before resources are committed to a specific technical form) but not necessarily *ex post*. When technical progress is embodied in machines of different vintages another form of capital–labour substitutability is obtained by scrapping or not scrapping older machines, but premature scrapping of equipment (with respect to the planned lifetime on the basis of which the original investment decision was made) is just another form of labour shortage and overinvestment.

There is labour shortage in the sense of demographic slowdown towards stagnation leading to a 'manpower problem'[2]. The so-called manpower problem is more likely to be a blessing in disguise. Of course, demographic slowdown is bound to reduce overall income growth rates, with which both CIA and Soviet leaders are obsessed, but while overall size and growth might have some, though debatable, importance for defence, the economics and politics of growth are better served by growth rates of income *per capita*, and this would only be affected by demographic slowdown under fairly strong assumptions. A manpower problem would arise if the flexibility in the regional and sectoral structure of employment afforded by employment growth was paramount and could not be replaced by Shchekino-type measures, which would appear to be designed primarily to promote precisely that kind of flexibility; or, if the provision of a costly public good, such as external security, was a fixed overhead cost which could be advantageously spread over a larger population; or, if there was a Verdoorn-type link between productivity and employment growth. But there does not appear to be any evidence of this kind of factor. Obviously, *unexpected* demographic decline will hurt a 'labour shortage' economy more than a non-'labour shortage' one, but the decline *is* expected, and there is no reason to believe that an overaccumulating system would systematically overshoot more with a stagnant than with a growing labour force.

'Labour shortage' makes labour hoarding by firms and absenteeism by workers more costly to the economy (by making labour more productive than the going wage). The elimination of hoarding or absenteism would have the favourable effects of any one-and-for-all productivity increase, but would not have a re-equilibrating effect unless they were unexpected. Also, their effect can be easily overplayed; some hoarding has positive effects on production flexibility, and neither hoarding nor absenteeism affect growth *rates*, as opposed to *levels*.

'Full employment' of labour does not correspond to 'labour shortage', which is 'over-full' employment and involves a disequilibrium, while full employment is—in a strict sense, if not in common parlance with reference to Soviet-type economies, an equilibrium notion. Anyway, one should distinguish whether full employment goes with or without labour reserves in the sense mentioned above, of labour which can be made available readily, without premature scrapping of equipment and without losses of output much higher than the wages of redeployed workers, from declining employment sectors to growing employment ones and from old to new machines. Clearly 'full employment' with 70 per cent of employment in agriculture, and every able-bodied person regimented into multiple shifts on scanty available capital at a productivity lower than the wage rate is a very different economic phenomenon from 'full employment' at under 20 per cent of agricultural employment (and still underequipped agriculture), with multiple shifts reduced to those where they are technically necessary, abundant capital and labour productivity higher than the wage rate. Such is the difference between 1931 and 1981 in the USSR, and this cannot be neglected. Even if there had not been any excess of aggregate demand, or any excess of capital equipment, at some point probably in the early sixties the Soviet economy began to exhaust labour reserves in a meaningful sense, and this—rather than the aggravating circumstances of imbalances in the supply of consumption goods and capital per man—is the central feature of employment and investment in the Soviet economy (even earlier in other East European economies).

In a market economy the approach of exhaustion of labour reserves, even somewhat before getting anywhere near full employment, manifests itself with real wage increases, inflation, profit squeeze and a reduction of the share of investment. These are all forms of self-regulating mechanisms, which may sometimes generate turbulence and instability but by and large generate some automatic feedback. There is no doubt that a socialist economy should also make some moves in the same direction. Even if real wage trends remained unchanged the drying up of labour reserves should be signalled to firms by a payroll tax (wage drift was there already in the mid-thirties and cannot be relied upon to speed up sufficiently when labour reserves are exhausted). Inflation is there but in a compressed form. Profit rates fall because of capital waste, but the profit share is maintained and the share of investment actually increases sometimes (in the Soviet Union from 28 per cent of material product in 1966–70 to 30 per cent in 1971–75 and 31 per cent in 1976–80), while there is no reason to assume that future consumption is such an inferior good as to warrant an increasing share of current expenditure when its price (i.e. the incremental capital–output ratio) increases. This lack of response of investment and employment policies to changing underlying circumstances in the structure of the economy—which are openly and blatantly visible and therefore do not raise any of the old-fashioned problems of information gathering and processing under central planning—is a crucial and worrying systemic feature of the Soviet-type economy, much more so than the more widely debated instances of micro-economic failures and waste.

PRODUCTION FUNCTIONS

Much of the discussion of employment and investment in Soviet-type economies is conducted in terms of production functions, linking the value of output to the quantity of production factors, and more often the value of output per man to the value of capital per man in individual sectors or in the whole economy, with a time factor standing for technical progress. Assumptions about the nature of technical progress allow us to estimate elasticities of output with respect to factors, and assumptions about elasticities lead to estimates of technical progress.

As long as these are intended as exercises to test the consistency and plausibility of one's conjectures, these are harmless exercises. There are a number of established criticisms in capital theory that should lead one to take the results of these exercises with more than a pinch of salt (capital malleability, neutrality of technical progress, arbitrariness of constance of elasticity of substitution, consistency between factor prices used to price capital and output and factor prices generated by the competitive solution, marginal product pricing, and so on). All these reservations hold with reference to the Soviet-type economy, but there are also additional *systemic* criticisms that can be levied against the use of such an approach.

Basically production functions are only partly the expression of technological, or engineering, relationships between inputs and output. They also implicitly require a competitive pricing of inputs and outputs (with reference to *somebody*'s preferences, whether the planner's or those expressed through markets) and the optimising of technical choice by firms given those prices. In the Soviet-type economy most inputs and outputs are underpriced, but some are more underpriced than others. Capital goods are more underpriced than consumption goods from the viewpoint of cost and less underpriced from the viewpoint of demand. Labour is underpriced with respect to capital goods, as witnessed by the relative capital abundance and labour scarcity. Technical choice is often erratic, but in so far as it conforms to cost minimising criteria it will take a technical form less capital-intensive than consistent with the overall rate of investment and appropriate to the availability of labour. If capital was malleable, this inefficient and inappropriate choice would be easily rectified after the event; but experience shows that capital is highly specific, especially in modern technology; underequipped labour and unused capacity is the observable result. (In a capitalist economy capacity is also underutilised because of demand factors; this raises difficulties with the empirical use of production functions but does not lead to underequipment of labour given actual relative factor prices.)

At a policy level, this confirms the needs for conveying to investors the exhaustion of labour reserves by means of either higher wages or a payroll tax. At an empirical level, this undercapitalisation of labour coexisting with underutilisation of capacity undermines standard propositions about productivity and substitutability trends in the Soviet Union and predictions about its ability to sustain growth, all based on empirical production functions. The observed fall in capital productivity might be due to the increasing importance of this undercapitalisation and underutilisation rather than to an actual worsening of opportunities open to Soviet planners. Slow labour productivity growth might be the result of the underequipment and the continuation of extensive growth (i.e. without the benefit of technology corresponding to the actual investment per man if this investment were to be of the kind appropriate to the amount of labour available and fully utilised). Growth prospects for the Soviet economy (and for its East European replicas) would appear to be both better and worse than envisaged by production function analysts: better, because more efficient technical choice reflecting actual labour scarcity might mobilise unsuspected reserves; worse, because not even economic reform, without a major redistributive shift towards labour or the revival of fiscal policy, can bring about a technical choice more appropriate to labour balances, and because there is no systemic feature preventing socialist leaders from reacting to external imbalance with brutal domestic deflation (as witnessed by Eastern performance in the early 1980s).

NOTES

1. Bauer, T., 'Investment cycles in planned economies', *Acta Oeconomica*, vol. 21, no. 3, pp.243–60.
2. Hanson P., see this collection, ch.6. Schroeder, G., 'Managing labour shortages in the Soviet Union' in J. Adam (ed.) *Employment Policies in the Soviet Union and Eastern Europe*, London, 1982.

8 Heterogeneity of the Soviet Labour Market as a Limit to a more Efficient Utilisation of Manpower

SILVANA MALLE*

The phenomenon of labour shortage is generally analysed in aggregate terms, although Soviet sources provide clear evidence of partial disequilibria. Labour turnover does not affect all branches, enterprises, sex, age and educated groups to the same degree, let alone regional and territorial areas. Partial disequilibria seem to arise from both imperfect planning and the stochastic behaviour of labour supply, which planning techniques seem unable to defeat.[1] Priority criteria introduce exogenous elements of differentiation, and physical indicators are unsuitable to reflect the endogenous heterogeneity of labour demand and supply.

This paper is based on the assumption that an understanding of the factors lying behind labour shortage may be helped by a disaggregation of micro-economic labour behaviour. It is limited to the industrial field and focuses on those aspects of industrial relations, such as hiring, training, promotion prospects, workers' displacement and earning differentials, which allow a distinction to be made between primary and secondary labour markets.[2]

The purpose of this paper is to show that the heterogeneity of the Soviet labour market is an important obstacle to the attainment of aggregate planned equilibrium and is an autonomous factor in the decreasing efficiency of production.

HETEROGENEOUS LABOUR MARKETS

In the Soviet-type planned economy all enterprises have a built-in

* Associated professor in Comparative Economic Systems at the Faculty of Economics and Commerce of Verona University, Italy. The research on this paper is financed in part by a grant from the Italian CNR, no. CT81-0371.10.

interest in hoarding material and labour resources.[3] But each enterprise's potential employment faces different constraints. Enterprises are heterogenous from the point of view of their relative endowment in technology, budget means, fringe benefits and socio-cultural environment. They do not have the same potential labour supply which depends on different social aspirations, needs and skills. The labour market is, therefore, characterised by a number of organisations separated by prices and allocative decisions adopted by planning organs. Goals and means are allocated in different proportions according to central priorities. Policy discrimination establishes more or less favourable conditions for employed labour and may add further advantages and disadvantages to the nature, location and relative position of each enterprise. Each organisation tends to behave as an internal labour market. This means that the main bulk of employed labour is expected to remain within the given organisation and to improve its position by being promoted to higher posts. Jobs are graded and evaluated in order to categorise labour in specific wage ratings. In hiring, preference is given to young workers educated in schools attached to the organisation. Managers are promoted or demoted according to reliability criteria. Their interests condition the behaviour of the enterprise.

The heterogeneity of labour markets sustained by the planning system is in itself the primary cause of *tekuchest'*, i.e. unplanned turnover which includes notices (quits) by workers and disciplinary dismissals [below the word turnover on its own always means unplanned turnover], which each organisation tries to curb. In an excess labour-demand economy, however, the success of one enterprise in maintaining a stable or expanding workforce is bound to conflict with parallel efforts of other enterprises. Thus, high turnover in some markets may reflect excessive job security in other markets and be stimulated by the latter. The distinction between primary labour markets and secondary labour markets may be used as a tool to assess the direction of labour flows and the relative capacity of each labour market to consolidate or improve its position. This distinction may apply to an association of enterprises, factories, plants and workshops within branches, which as a whole may be placed in a better or worse position within the range of central priorities.

As long as primary labour markets keep expanding, there may not be a barrier to entry, although a relative barrier may be represented by each enterprise's preference for a certain combination of skill-age-sex. Job security in managerial posts may become a powerful obstacle to entry of young, highly educated manpower, especially if expansion is checked by planning decisions. Obstacles to labour mobility in the primary labour market may thus be reflected in high turnover within the secondary labour market of those sections of the workforce which offer skills in excess of primary labour market demand.

According to aggregate data, industrial turnover accounts for one-third of total labour turnover. Clothing, sugar, gas, woodworking, leather and shoes and the building-material industry have turnover rates which are between 10 and 30 per cent above the average. The highest rates of turnover are found in the food and timber industries.[4] Industrial branches with a high turnover are characterised by seasonal factors, low capital intensive techniques and a low level of mechanisation/automation. In 1981 only 3.7 per cent of the enterprises statistically reported in the timber, wood-working, cellulose and paper industry, and 5.4 per cent of the enterprises in the light industry were fully mechanised/ automated enterprises.[5] Below-average turnover characterises the leading branches of the Soviet model of industrialisation, metallurgy, engineering and coal industry, which happen to be concentrated largely in the European part of the Soviet Union. This territory is also the area with the most aging population. Turnover is 30 per cent below average in the Moscow, Leningrad, Tula, Vladimir, Gor'ki, Yaroslavl *oblasts*. Higher than average turnover characterises the autonomous republics of the USSR.

Average mobility per year is 25 per cent above what is considered the normal level.[6] Differences in territorial demographic trends, industrial development and culture should be considered in separating heterogeneous labour markets. The relation between organised and individual mobility is 1:4 in general, but 1:9 on a territorial basis.[7] However, endogenous systemic factors, on which this paper concentrates, provide a more stimulating approach to heterogeneous labour markets. Among these factors, a crucial role in explaining labour turnover within and across industrial branches is the relative access to goods and services through employment. The availability of flats, kindergartens and canteens, holidays in rest houses and pensions, specialised and higher-education, cultural and sporting facilities, repair and shopping centers depends on the type and scale of the enterprise. Given that 50.4 per cent of the average Soviet budget is still spent on food and 39.8 per cent on non-food consumer goods,[8] both of which are in short supply, the degree of access to fringe benefits has a significant effect on workers' preferences. These benefits are rationed to consumers according to the degree of priority of the organisation where they are employed.[9] Correlations between access to fringe benefits and turnover have been found by sample research (Table 8.1).

Table 8.1: *Labour turnover according to scale of enterprises in* Minlegpishchmash *(machine building for light and food industry) in 1973–75*

Enterprise scale (no. of workers)	1973–75 average turnover per year (as % of the total workforce)	Number of services provided to workers
below 250	40.2	1–2
251–500	26.9	2–3
501–1,000	21.7	3–5
1,001–2,000	20.9	4–7
2,001–5,000	17.4	6–8
5,001–10,000	13.7	9–12
above 10,000	7.9	12–15
Average for the ministry	19–20	

Source: A. Gal'tsov, 'Ukreplenie predpriyatii-vazhnii faktor snizheniya tekuchesti kadrov', *Sotsialisticheskii trud*, 1977, no.1, p.33.

Although information of this sort is difficult to procure and cannot lead to generalisations, it supports the hypothesis that labour turnover reflects the systemic heterogeneity of the labour markets and the different leverage that each organisation has on employment.

HETEROGENEOUS LABOUR MARKETS AND HIRING

Soviet enterprises hire 75 per cent of the workforce at the gate.[10] Although direct hiring is interpreted as a primary cause for labour turnover and increasing attention is paid to organised job placement,[11] no consistent evidence suggests that the latter would reduce turnover. The disproportion between the jobs listed in industrial handbooks (6,800) and those acquired in vocational schools (PTU), (1,400),[12] hints at how skill balances are hardly attainable through organised job placement. Misallocation of labour may, indeed, provoke increases in turnover.[13] The obligatory placement of young graduates is often circumvented by informal channels and expediency.[14] The rate of turnover among young graduates assigned to production is very high during their first three years of employment.[15] Different technological and financial endowments seem to affect the capacity of each organisation to screen and retain the new entrants.[16] Primary labour markets are not hostile to direct hiring in so far as it provides an opportunity to check the actual skills, capacity and personal qualities of new entrants. Secondary labour markets, on the contrary, have an interest in organized job placement, because high turnover shifts the emphasis of labour demand to quantity rather than quality of labour. Enterprises with high rates of turnover are, in fact, the major customers of job placement services.[17]

The policy of job appointment is also indicative of heterogeneous labour market behaviour. Some enterprises resist the obligation to place new entrants in jobs pertaining to their official skills and assign them a lower skill-rating (*razryad*).[18] In other cases, the assigned *razryad* is higher than the skills required to perform the job.[19] Between 1979 and 1982 the average *razryad* increased more slowly (from 4.07 to 4.13) in branches adopting an 8 *razryady* scale than in branches rated on a 6 *razryady* scale (from 3.42 to 3.53). The average *razryad* decreased by thirteen decimal points in the metal-working and engineering branch rated on the 8 *razryady* scale.[20] One possible cause for the inverted trend in this major branch (which could be considered a primary labour market because of the greater possibility of promotion) may have been an extraordinary number of dismissals of older workers, accompanied by hiring of new entrants in lower *razryady* due to rapid technological restructuring. Part of the freed workforce may have been displaced to lower-rated jobs in maintenance and repair.

The rapid concentration around the average *razryad* seems to be due to two types of imbalances: excess demand for skilled and unskilled manual labour, and excess supply of educated new entrants. These phenomena are the result not only of improvements in general education and the retirement of older manual workers but also of the slow process of renewal and modernisation of plants. In eleven ministries of engineering, obsolete technology, which in 1967 represented 16.2 per cent of the total technical endowment, had increased by 1981 to 30.6 per cent.[21] Between

1970 and 1981 the rate of increase in new capital investment had slowed down (Table 8.2).

Table 8.2: *Entry and exit of industrial production basic funds (as a percentage of total funds at the end of the year, in enterprises with an autonomous budget)*

	1970 entry	1970 exit	1975 entry	1975 exit	1980 entry	1980 exit	1981 entry	1981 exit
Total industry	11.9	1.8	8.8	1.6	8.1	1.4	7.3	1.3
Engineering and metal working industry	13.9	1.4	10.2	1.2	9.6	1.2	8.7	1.1

Source: Akhmedzhanou T.B., 'Voprosy intensifikatsii ispol'zovaniya rabochikh mest' v promyshlennosti', *Finansy SSSR*, 1983, no.6, p.13.

New investment essentially concerns the production process. Supply and storage of raw materials, capital and current repair, packaging, transport and loading have remained, by and large, untouched by modernisation.[22] About 50 per cent of industrial manpower is employed in auxiliary jobs, more than 13 million do unskilled jobs.[23] An increasing imbalance between the skills on offer and the skills required has developed. Between 1940 and 1980 the number of specialists with higher and middle specialist education related to industrial jobs had increased 23.3 times, while the number of engineering technical personnel (ITRs) employed in industry had increased five times. Of those with higher education, 40.7 per cent are engineers; they represent 4.37 per cent of total industrial employment.[24] According to financial experts there should be one specialist with higher education for every three to four specialists with middle-grade specialist education, and for every eight to nine blue-collar workers. Sample research shows an excessive proportion of ITRs: 15.1 per cent of total industrial employment compared to 79.5 per cent blue-collar workers and 5.2 per cent clerical workers.[25]

This aggregate imbalance may have aggravated the heterogeneity of the labour market. Large-scale enterprises, which have their own vocational schools (PTUs) and often higher education facilities, may hire more skilled and qualified labour in lower-paid auxiliary jobs, which the new entrants accept in order to have access to the benefits offered by primary labour markets.[26] The concentration of educational institutions in large towns with a better socio-cultural environment favours a territorial imbalance of skill distribution. Between 1970 and 1979 the number of people with higher, incomplete higher, and average specialist education doing manual labour increased from 4.9 to 7.9 per cent. In Moscow, between 5 and 10 per cent of the graduates of higher educational institutions (VUZy) and technical colleges (*tekhnikumy*) are employed in jobs not requiring a specialist education.[27] At the same time, secondary labour markets experience shortages and instability among educated new entrants. Detailed research into the timber and wood-working industry shows that turnover is directly related to level of education.[28] New plants built in remote regions with poor environmental benefits are often inactive because of a shortage of specialists.[29] Inefficiency may grow in both labour markets. Specialised labour appointed to lower jobs in the primary labour markets, where promotion prospects are jeopardised by the saturation of the most prestigious posts, may become dissatisfied and in some cases conflicts may arise. Turnover in the secondary labour markets may prevent the consolidation of motivated manpower and result in poor performance indicators, on which the possibility of expansion depends.

HETEROGENEOUS LABOUR MARKETS, TRAINING AND QUALIFICATION

Each year about 6 million workers learn a new profession and more than 20 million study to improve their qualifications.[30] More than 70 per cent of the new entrants are trained on the job by the enterprises.[31] However, the quality of training varies considerably. It depends on available facilities and managerial interests. Training premises are allocated to enterprises by the ministries according to their scale.[32] Associations of enterprises and large-scale factories have started having their own centers for training in new skills (*professiya*).[33] Large-scale enterprises in the export and defence industry, where the demand for quality products is more binding, have an interest in improving their labour skills. Leading enterprises, such as the S. Ordzhonikize computer and engineering factories (located in Minsk and Podol'sk respectively) train workers for the time considered adequate to master their skills. The car factories in Gor'ki and Volgograd adopt tests to check the adaptability of new entrants to available jobs.[34] In most factories, however, one to two months training in a narrow skill is adopted and often used formally to assign a higher *razryad*, which is considered necessary by management to slow down labour turnover.[35] The lack of interest in the quality of output means that there is little incentive to improve training. In secondary labour markets, management is interested in appointing workers to their jobs as soon as possible to ensure the continuation of the production process.

A more subtle discrimination is detectable in training for specialised professions requiring higher education. Workers may improve their knowledge either by attending day courses in higher educational institutions and technical colleges (*tekhnikumy*) while on leave from their jobs, or by registering for evening and correspondence courses. Law protects the right to study in terms of supplementary leave and a guaranteed monthly wage.[36] However, Leningrad evening students complain that management does not lend its support to study either by granting day-leave for examinations, or in making shift duty more flexible. Management is hostile to workers studying because it disrupts production rhythm and programmes and because a 'too-developed young man may give trouble'.[37] High turnover among educated staff in secondary labour markets is not likely to stimulate a benevolent attitude by management towards workers studying, if their mobility may potentially increase.[38] Nor is management in primary labour markets particularly interested in autonomous workers' initiatives in improving education, if managerial posts are becoming saturated. Where technology requires stricter rhythms of production, disruption caused by study leave may, in fact, be feared by management. In primary labour markets, therefore, management tries to exert direct control over access to education. The cases of the Leningrad metal plant and the Moscow 'Likhachev' automobile plant suggest that only a selected number of reliable workers are granted access to paid further education in the fields designated by the management to prepare them for managerial functions.[39] Government policy seems to favour an educational policy which relieves the state budget of the burden of higher education and at the same time increases labour supply. By keeping the number of admissions to VUZy stable during the eleventh five year plan and allowing some increase in evening and correspondence study, the workforce has been increased by 400,000 units a year.[40] This policy seems shortsighted. An increasing number of graduates in evening and corresponding courses, the standard of which is notoriously defective, may lower the general level of education without curbing youngsters' expectations and may even affect the cultural level of the forthcoming generation. The heterogeneity of the labour market may increase, as may inefficiency in the secondary labour markets due to the combined effects of low productivity and low discipline, while the selection of candidates for management posts within the protected primary labour markets may not grant the supremacy of intelligence and creativeness over diligence and conformism which the recent appeals for 'entrepreneurship' in production would require.

HETEROGENEOUS LABOUR MARKETS AND PROMOTION PROSPECTS

Graduates from higher educational institutions and technical colleges have the right to be placed by their employer organisations in jobs and at levels related to their qualification.[41] These regulations may explain workers' demand for education both in secondary and primary labour markets, where it would be hard for outsiders to be appointed to high positions. To reach the highest *razryady* and technical and executive positions, young people may be willing to perform less skilled jobs in less attractive plants and workshops and bear the cost of their education until graduation allows them to apply for better qualified jobs within the same organisation.[42] Demand for education is a symptom of demand for promotion. If upward mobility is checked by the limitation of available posts, a horizontal occupational mobility may be sought. Although there are no comprehensive figures, it is thought that occupational mobility is high and is mostly an unplanned phenomenon.[43] The manifestation of occupational mobility may give some insight into the different behaviour of primary and secondary labour markets. A survey recently conducted among the enterprises of the Altai Krai and Novosibirsk confirms that inter-firm turnover is higher when turnover within the firm is low. Similar findings had been obtained from a sample of textile factories in the Moscow area in 1971–72.[44] Both studies suggest that when managers try to check internal mobility, labour tends to leave the organisation. It is then possible that small- and average-scale firms in secondary labour markets offering lower promotion prospects have higher turnover rates than large-scale enterprises in primary labour markets which may 'internalise' turnover by displacing workers to other occupations within the organisation. To keep promotion prospects open, primary labour markets must continue to expand. They will use their lobbying capacity to create new plants. They may urge concentration. But they may also create fictitious posts. There are increasing numbers of senior engineers, senior specialists and chiefs of section and bureau in large-scale enterprises. This procedure may be more successful in overcrowding managerial-technical posts than in production jobs, where technology demands stricter labour norms. However, even in this field enterprise autonomy in labour organisation may be used to create new posts.[45] The post of 'brigadier' – when brigades may include between five and ten members and the post of foreman has not been abolished – may also be seen as an expedient to widen promotion prospects with increasing production capacity. If new technology requires new skills, the primary labour market may avoid dismissal of older workers by displacing them to auxiliary plants or lower clerical jobs. In this way retraining may be avoided through a combination of superfluous posts and inner displacements which serve essentially to protect senior staff.[46] The built-in conservatism of the organisations may increase. Promotion rules based on seniority and on job experience may become a major obstacle in replacing senior staff with more innovative personnel. By increasing the hierarchy of posts, new entrants face longer waits for promotion. They may resent subordination to less-educated staff trained on the job. Inefficiency may increase.[47]

However, new forms of labour organisation, such as 'combining jobs', defined by *Goskomtrud*'s instructions as the 'performance by a worker, together with his primary job established by the labour contract, of supplementary work belonging to another profession [function]'[48] may help to reduce the dissatisfaction with work and mitigate the burden of labour hierarchy. Combining jobs may lead to codification of new complex jobs and introduce elements of flexibility into labour organisation. The success of this form of labour organisation will depend on the use made of it and on the actual possibilities for adopting it. It could lead to redundancies and possibly the redistribution of skilled labour from primary into secondary labour markets if some basic indicators of performance favouring the hoarding of labour reserves were changed.[49] But it could also be used to conceal the real need for manual unskilled labour which skilled workers may be asked to perform.[50]

HETEROGENEOUS LABOUR MARKETS AND LABOUR LAW ON DISPLACEMENT

Labour law may be an obstacle to new forms of organisation, depending on the degree of protection offered to labour and on its application by the courts.

According to a ruling of the Supreme Court of the RSFSR, 'combining jobs' is to be categorised as displacement requiring the worker's consent only when a substantial increase in the volume of work is involved. Displacement to another job as such is not defined by law. By the ruling of the courts, displacement requires the worker's consent if it implies the change of any of the three components of the labour contract: content, place or material conditions.[51] However, there are no rules on the articulation of consent. The courts' ruling suggests that it must be voluntary (not extorted) and clear (although it could be tacit). The worker should be informed about the new working conditions.[52] These regulations seem to leave much room for management's discretion. Primary labour markets may offer their employees better protection. The ZIL production association and the Moscow 'Frezer' plant issue booklets where detailed accounts of individual work performance, responsibilities and adherence to technological discipline are reported.[53] However, workers' preference for primary labour markets gives management a leverage that secondary labour markets do not have. In the case of combining jobs it is the management who decides whether the change in volume of work is insubstantial and therefore does not require the worker's agreement. In some cases, workers have been displaced to another plant within the same organisation without their consent, on the grounds that the new job represents promotion.[54] Since there is no agreement on what an enterprise actually consists of, the management of a trust uniting several enterprises within a given area could displace workers between enterprises without violating the law on dismissal. Cases of dismissed workers being returned to their former organisation, but to another job, by the courts[56] suggest that older workers may accept demotion to lower occupations so that they do not lose their claims to housing, pension benefits and other advantages related to seniority. These cases also suggest that the greater the leverage of the management over labour, the greater the possibilities for management control over labour organisation. Large-scale enterprises in primary labour markets may internalise turnover, avoid open redundancies and show better performance indicators than secondary labour markets, which are limited by their scale and poor benefits.

HETEROGENEOUS LABOUR MARKETS AND EARNING DIFFERENTIALS

In Soviet studies of turnover the amount of attention paid to earning differentials is usually negligible. This may, however, be due to inaccurate research methods.[57] Centrally determined wage differentials may be insufficient to evaluate workers' responses to earning potential since the latter includes both bonuses and income earned in extra-job activities and opportunities. Press debate on 'unearned' income as a source of labour indiscipline suggests that management tolerance of extra-job sources of income is inversely related to its leverage over labour.[58] Some economists claim that overt economic differentials should be preferred to concealed ones.[59] The process of wage adjustment carried out by planners in the 1970s shows the development of a conflicting mechanism of central impulses and decentralised feedbacks from the heterogeneous labour markets. The central trend towards greater uniformity in wage determination rules[60]— which has led to the reduction of the schemes of skills scale differentials (*tarifnye setki*) from 10 to 3,[61] to the gradual increase of minimum wages by branches and to single skill-wage rates of similar occupations across branches—may account for the reduction of the decile ratio between 1956 and 1976 from 1:8 to 1:4.[62] But this process seems to have been resisted from below. Some research points to an increasing inequality of earnings in the 1970s.[63] Different wages for similar jobs across branches even within single towns persist.[64] In 1972 it was established that the ratio between maximum and minimum wage (*diapazon*) in each skill scheme should be 1.56 for enterprises belonging to the 6 *razryady* scale and 2.1 for the enterprises in the 8 *razryady* scale.[65] However, in 1979 the actual minimum–maximum wage ratio was already higher. It was 1.71 in the average for time-wage workers, and it reached 2.02 in the engineering, cellulose and paper, wood-working industries; 2.1 in the textile industry and 2.2 in the oil industry.[66]

The heterogeneous labour markets may resist central wage guidelines in several ways. Management assigns a *razryad* to each job. The adoption of the coefficient of personal contribution

(KTU) to evaluate each worker's labour effort may even nullify central wage differentials.[67] The fragmentation of indicators of performance in brigades, as compared to global success indicators applying to the enterprise, increases the potential for decentralised wage differentials unrelated to final output. By breaking down the annual plan into monthly targets and underrating initial targets, management may artificially increase the bonus part of piece-wages (55 per cent of workers are still on the piece-work system),[68] particularly in the branches of wood-working, building-materials, light and textile and food-processing industries where the pace of technological change is slower. Piece-wage workers are mainly 'production' workers. Auxiliary labour employed in maintenance and repair and other activities providing back-up for the production process is paid according to the time-wage scheme. Although confined to the 'non productive' category by the planning system based on volume indicators, these workers also have access to bonuses related to increases in productivity. Excess demand for such labour, which established wage rates do not reflect, induce managers to bid up their wage offers.[69] In secondary labour markets this behaviour results in higher rates of turnover among machine repair workers. However, some research suggests also that turnover is higher among workers employed in 'non-profile' branches, than in 'profile' branches.[70] This may indicate that secondary labour markets may not bid up their offers enough to compensate for the attraction that primary labour market jobs, especially in engineering, exercise over skilled workers. The engineering and metal processing industry may, in fact, grant up to 20 per cent extra pay, provided that it works on 'progressive, scientifically-based norms'.[71] This sum would be higher than the average material incentive fund (MIF) per one worker, which in 1980 was 181.8 rubles; that is, less than 9 per cent of the average monthly wage in industry.[72] Funds allotted to material incentives by branches determine relative branch advantages, and this conceals even higher discrimination among enterprises. In 1975 bonuses increased the average wage by 4.9 per cent in the timber and wood-working industry, by 6.4 per cent in machine building for the light and food industry, by 12 per cent in the industry of precision instruments and automation equipment and by 13.4 per cent in the medical industry.[73] But workers paid on the so-called VAZ-scheme, which has been applied in high-priority industry, represent only 2.6 per cent of engineering and metal-working workers, 1.5 per cent of electrotechnical, 0.3 per cent of machine-tool, 0.8 per cent of precision instruments, 0.7 per cent of tractor-agricultural engineering and 25 per cent of automobile industry workers.[74]

Earning differentials among managerial staff may also differ from the centrally established ones, depending on the opportunities and policy of distribution of bonuses. Managerial wage differentials should depend on the position of their enterprise within the branch grouping, related to indicators of scale and priority.[75] However, on average the bonus on ITR wages is 25 per cent with peaks of 30 to 40 per cent in some jobs.[76] Decisions concerning whether, when, to whom and what kind of bonuses to assign come from the management.[77] Some enterprises increase ITR bonuses by decreasing other bonuses paid out of the MIF. Other enterprises reduce their bonuses in order to increase the annual premiums to other workers.[78] The funds assigned to socialist emulation are in general insignificant. But leading factories, such as the Tula combine plant, the Krasnoyarskii cellulose paper combine, and so on, have assigned 10 per cent of the MIF for this purpose. Other leading factories have excluded some of their plants from this reward, using the norms on labour discipline.[79] In some cases, the funds assigned to work and activities which come under the category of fringe benefits exceed the total bonuses paid to workers.[80] The bulk of enterprises, however, do not exclude any workers from bonuses. In 1962, 70 per cent of workers received bonuses; in 1982, the figure was 90 per cent.[81]

The highly diversified practices in micro-manipulation of earning differentials permit only some cautious hypotheses on different heterogeneous labour market behaviour. Primary labour markets which enjoy a privileged position in planning decisions and have more leverage over labour are more respectful of central wage guidelines. They may avoid labour turnover by enlarging the range of fringe benefits available to workers and by enhancing those performance indicators which allow them to retain their privileged position. In the primary labour markets, earning differentials between ITR and blue-collar workers may be higher than the average, thus justifying the competition among educated youngsters for entry into this market, even accepting positions where initial earnings are relatively low. The adoption of more sophisticated techniques of job evaluation together with job redesigning, may help to keep blue-collar workers' earning differentials more related to productivity indicators.

In secondary labour markets, earning differentials between ITR and blue-collar workers tend to level out. In 1981 their ratio was 1:1.23 for industry as a whole.[82] The policy of keeping productivity norms low in order to enhance the size of bonuses, together with turnover being related to earning differentials for similar jobs but unrelated to productivity differentials, push up the unit cost of labour. If most of the consumer goods and food-processing enterprises are in secondary labour markets, as seems to be the case, a wage-pushed inflation, detectable in the non-state market, may be the outcome of heterogeneous labour market behaviour.

CONCLUSION

All Soviet enterprises have an inherent interest in expanding employment, but they do not have equal possibilities in attaining this goal. Labour markets are heterogeneous both on the side of labour demand and supply. Each organisation acts as an internal labour market. However, leverage over labour is uneven. Primary labour markets and secondary labour markets may be distinguished according to their position in central priorities and their capacity of consolidating or improving it. The rate of turnover may be taken, *ceteris paribus*, as an indicator of the comparative advantages of being employed in the primary or secondary labour markets. Workers in the primary labour markets resist mobility into the secondary labour markets, while new entrants allocated to the latter try to move into the primary labour markets, and the more skilled and educated among them may be successful in their attempts. Consequently, primary labour markets tend to reach saturation point in some skills and specialisation before secondary labour markets. The barrier to entry into some jobs may be considered proportional to job security of the already employed. The management in primary labour markets may use their leverage over labour for a better screening of new entrants and also, if necessary, to persuade them to accept less-skilled occupations. *Ceteris paribus*, the primary labour markets may employ more skilled and educated manpower, but not necessarily in jobs requiring their skills or specialisations. There may be, therefore, a tendency to employ more skilled and specialised labour than needed; underutilisation of it and disaffection towards work may increase if promotion prospects diminish. Primary labour markets may try to reduce these sources of inefficiency by lobbying for continuous expansion and by internal job-redesigning. Neither solution, however, can avoid increasing labour costs.

Secondary labour markets are confined to a poor socio-cultural environment, lower fringe benefits and poor promotion prospects. The higher rates of turnover among new entrants induce managers to favour more restrictive legislation on job placement and short, poor quality training. Increased workers' education is feared because it may lead to higher turnover. Excess demand for manual and auxiliary labour sustained by obsolete technology forces management to adopt a bonus policy comparatively more favourable to blue-collar workers and to tolerate extra job sources of income. Decentralised wage increases unrelated to productivity may result in increasing unit labour costs and wage-push inflation in the consumer goods market.

NOTES

1. *See* N.F. Fedorenko, Iu.V Ovsienko and N.Ia. Petrakov, 'Planomernost' i problemy sovershenstvovaniya khozyaistvennogo mekhanizma upravleniya', *Ekonomika i matematicheskie metody*, 1983, no.3, p.401.
2. The term 'labour market' seems justified also in the Soviet economy, because labour is not directly allocated to production. Moreover, in the current situation management seems to enjoy considerable freedom in modifying centrally determined wage differentials.
3. *See* J. Kornai, *Economics of Shortage*, North Holland, vol.A., 1980.
4. V.I. Markov, *Oplata truda v sisteme upravleniya ekonomiki razvitogo sotsializma* (Moscow, 1980), p.145. See also *Zanyatost' naseleniya: izuchenie i regulirovanie* (Moscow, 1983), pp.54–64.
5. *Narodnoe khozyaistvo SSSR v 1982*, (Moscow, 1983), p.96, 109, personal calculations.
6. Markov, *op. cit.*, pp.146–7, I.S. Maslova, 'Sovershenstvovanie mekhanizma pereraspredeleniya rabochei sily'. *Voprosy ekonomiki*, 1982, no.7, p.53.
7. Maslova, *loc. cit.*, p.52.
8. O.P. Saenko, 'Byudzhet sovetskoi semya', *Znanie: ekonomika*, 1983, no.1, p.24.
9. Z.I. Pruts, R.M. Sultanova and M.I. Talalai, *Sozdanie postoyannykh kadrov na predpriyatiyakh* (Moscow, 1980), p.34, 49.
10. V. Yabokov, 'Kak snizit' tekuchest'', *Pravda*, 25 Mar. 1982; 85 per cent of the workers find another job before resigning, especially in large towns where large-scale factories are concentrated.
11. *See* A.E. Kotlyar and M.I. Talalai, 'Puty sokrashcheniya tekuchesti kadrov', *Voprosy ekonomiki*, 1981, no.5, p.35; A. Helgeson, 'Finding

Work in the Soviet Economy. Employment Agencies For First-Time Job Seekers', unpublished paper presented at NASEES Conference 1984.

12. V.A. Sidorov, 'Effektivnost' truda i kachestvo podgotovki rabochikh kadrov', *EKO*, 1981, no.1, p.162.

13. Maslova, *loc. cit.*, p.57.

14. M. Matthews, *Education in the Soviet Union: Policies and Institutions since Stalin* (London: 1982), p.72; S.E. Wimbush and D. Ponomareff, 'Alternatives for Mobilizing Soviet Central Asia Labour: Outmigration and Regional Development', unpublished paper, (Santa Monica, 1979), p.13..

15. L.E. Kunel'skii *Zarabotnaia plata i stimulirovanie truda* (Moscow, 1981), p.42; N. Rogovskii 'Tekhnicheskii progress—osnova povysheniya proizvoditel'nosti truda', *Planovoe khoziaistvo*, 1982, no.2, p.34.

16. See L.N. Stroimtsov, *Sovershenstvovanie raboty s kadram na predpriyatii*, (Moscow, 1977), pp.4–13, concerning *Dneprovsk engineering plant*'s endowment of laboratories for sociological research on professional selection, and of vocational schools and screening of new entrants through exams.

17. Maslova, *loc. cit.*, p.57.

18. Established by law in 1973.

19. See A.E. Kotlyar and M.I. Talalai, *Molodezh' prikhodit na proizvodstvo*, (Moscow, 1978), pp.31–32; Kunel'skii, *op. cit.*, p.150; T.V. Ryabushkin, 'Pokazateli sotsial'nogo razvitiya rabochego klassa', *Sotsiologicheskie issledovaniya*, 1980, no.4, p.21.

20. *Vestnik statistiki*, 1980, no.6, p.63; 1983, no.6, p.60, 62.

21. V. Radaev, 'Mera truda i glavnyi faktor ee razvitiya', *Planovoe khozyaistvo*, 1983, no.6, p.105.

22. See V. Silin and A. Sukhov, 'Intensifikatsiya—reshayushchii faktor ekonomicheskogo rosta', *Planovoe khozyaistvo*, 1983, no.5, p.105; Yu. Demin, 'Ruchnoi trud—na plechi machin', *Kommunist*, 1981, no.11, pp.24–8.

23. See E.R. Sarukhanov, *Sotsial'no ekonomicheskie problemy upravleniya rabochei siloi pri sotsializme* (Leningrad, 1981), pp.182–3; D. Shtefanich, 'Voprosy planirovaniya proizvoditel'nosti truda', *Planovoe khozyaistvo*, 1982, no.7, p.88.

24. S.A. Kugel', 'Kvalifikatsiya i real'naya deyatel'nost' inzhenera', *Sotsiologicheskie issledovaniya*, 1983, no.1, p.92; A. Shuruev, 'Voprosy planirovaniya podgotovki spetsialistov dlya narodnogo khozyaistva', *Planovoe khozyaistvo*, 1982, no.8, p.96.

25. T.B. Akhmedzhanov and T.N. Sukhoverkhova, 'Analiz effektivnosti ispol'zovaniya trudovykh resursov', *Finansy SSSR*, 1984, no.4, p.66.

26. Cf. A.I. Stavtzeva, O.S. Khoriakova *Trudovoi dogovor'* (Moscow, 1983), p.85; L.E. Kunel'skii, *op. cit.*, p.151.

27. *Vestnik statistiki*, 1983, no.11, pp.66–80. There are higher concentrations in trade and communal catering, chemical industry, sea transport and metallurgy, as well as in the most developed republics. On this phenomenon *see also* A.J. Pietsch and H. Vogel, 'Displacement by technological progress in the USSR', in J. Adams (ed.) *Employment Policies in the Soviet Union and Eastern Europe*, (London, Macmillan,

1982), pp.159–60, and L.P. Korolev, *Trudovye resursy i ikh ispol'zo- vanie* (Moscow, 1981), p.54; M.N. Rutkevich, 'Sblizhenie rabochego klassa i inzhenerno—tekhnicheskoi intelligentsii', *Sotsiologicheskie issledovaniya*, 1980, no.4, p.29.

28. M.Ia. Loiberg, *Stabilizatsiya proizvodstvennykh kollektivov v lesnoi i derevo-obrabatyvayushchei promyshlennosti* (Moscow, 1982), p.85–6.

29. S. Saltybaev and A. Zuikov, 'Planovoe obespechenie puskovykh ob'ektov kadrami v Khazakhskoi SSSR', *Planovoe khozyaistvo*, 1983, no.12, p.90; R. Tikidzhiev, 'Voprosy sbalansirovannosti vosproizvod- stva osnovykh fondov i trudovykh resursov', *Planovoe khozyaistvo*, 1981, no.12, p.45; G. Yastrebtsov, 'Usloviya truda', *Pravda*, 27 Mar. 1983.

30. *Sobranie postanovlenii pravitel'stva SSSR*, 1979, no.17, art.113; R.K. Ivanova, *Pererastanie sotsialisticheskogo truda v kommunisticheskii* (Moscow, 1983), pp.204–5. The impressive figures on improving qualification are likely to conceal much formalism. Soviet workers have, in fact, not only a subjective right to improve their skills but also a duty stated by law, the infringement of which may bring about negative juridical consequences up to dismissal; See E.V. Magnitskaia and A.S. Pashkov, *Raspredelenie trudovykh resursov, (Pravovye voprosy)* (Moscow, 1980), p.55.

31. L.A. Moiseev, *Zakon peremeny truda v sotsialisticheskom proizvod- stve*, Izd.vo Moskovskogo Universiteta, 1976, p.69; and B.G. Rubin, *Vosproizvodstvo rabochei sily vysshei kvalifikatsii*, Izd.vo Rostovs- kogo Universiteta, 1975, pp.94–5.

32. *See* Saltybaev and Zuikov, *loc. cit.*, p.92.

33. Ivanova, *op. cit.*, p.129.

34. *See* Kotlyar and Talalai, *op. cit.*, 1978, pp.25–7. On testing psycho- physiological requisites of new entrants to some skilled job, *see also* Strimtsov, *op. cit.*, pp.17–18.

35. *See* N.V. Anishina and I.N. Evseeva, 'Vysvobozhdenie rabochey sily i ulushenie ee ispol'zovaniya', *Organizatsiya i planirovanie otraslei narodonogo khozyaistva*, 1981, no.64, p.57.

36. E.I. Voilenko, 'L'goty dlya obuchaiushchikhsya bez otryva ot proizvodstva', *Vestnik vyshei shkoly*, 1983, no.11, pp.57–8.

37. 'Molodezh' i trud', *EKO*, 1983, no.8, pp.112–13. *See also* S.F. Minakova, 'Zaochnoe i vechernee studenstvo: sposob zhizhni i sotsial'nye effekty', *EKO*, 1983, no.6, p.66; V.I. Sin'kov, 'Konflikty v trudovom kollektive', *Sotsiologicheskie issledovaniya*, 1982, no.2, pp.17–18; A. Vlasov, 'A Worker Is a Lofty Title', *CDSP*, 1983, no.40, pp.8–9.

38. *See* N.A. Aitov, *Tekhnicheskii progress i dvizhenie rabochikh kadrov* (Moscow, 1972), p.65.

39. K.A. Osipov, 'Ekonomicheskaya i sotsial'naya effektivnost' podgo- tovki inzhenerov zavodami-vtuzami', *Sotsiologicheskie issledovaniya*, 1983, no.1, pp.106–8.

40. I.G. Reznik, 'Kakoi forme obucheniya otdat' predpochenie', *EKO*, 1983, no.6, p.83.

41. Stavtzeva and Khoryakova, *op. cit.*, p.91.

42. In the Rostov coal basin 40 per cent of the workers who are studying

are employed in repair or clerical jobs (V.A. Chupanov, *Sovremennye sovetskie rabochie*, Moscow, 1980, p.112). In the Gor'ki *oblast'*, 28.6 per cent of the 2nd *razryad* workers attend evening *tekhnikumy* and 17.1 per cent evening VUZy (Ryabushkin, *loc. cit.*, p.23).

43. *See* N.V. Nemchenko, 'Mobil'nost' trudovykh resursov', *Vestnik Moskovskogo Universiteta*, 1974, no.1, p.69, 72; Pietsch and Vogel, *op. cit.*, pp.146–51.

44. *See* E.G. Antosenkov and I.A. Shishkina, *Sotsial'no ekonomicheskie problemy truda na promyshlennom predpriyatii*, Novosibirsk, 1979, pp.119–20; V.I. Mikhailovskaya, 'Vnutrizavodskaya tekuchest' i ee rol' zakreplenii kadrov', *Izvestiya Sibirskogo Otdeleniya AN SSSR*, 1982, no.1, p.24; I.S. Maslova, *Ekonomicheskie voprosy pereraspredeleniya rabochei sily pri sotsializme*, (Moscow, 1976), pp.91–2.

45. *See* S.I. Shkurko, 'O povyshenii stimuliruyushchei roli tarifov i okladov v zarabotnoi plata', *Planovoe khozyaistvo*, 1983, no.8, p.77; O. Novozhilov, 'Kak auknetsia. . .', *EKO*, 1984, no.5, p.137, on extra-pay for mastering a new skill as a means to increase, in fact, the number of *razryady* from 6 to 12. It has been adopted at the Volga automobile factory..

46. *See* N.A. Grishchenko and O.M. Nikandrov, 'Rost teknicheskogo stroeniya sotsialisitcheskogo proizvodstva i vysvobozhdenie rabochei sily', in *Sotsial'no ekonomicheskie problemy razvitiya pervoi proizvoditel'noi sily sotsialisticheskogo obshchestva* (Leningrad, 1978), pp.65–6; *Problemy povysheniya effektivnosti ispol'zovaniya trudovykh resursov v SSSR. Nauchno-analiticheskii obzor*, (Moscow, 1981), p.44.

47. *See* G.V. Dvoretskaya, A.Ia. Krushel'nitska and V.P. Moskalenko, *Organizatsiya oplaty i stimulirovanie truda v promyshlennosti* (Kiev, 1979), pp.78–9; I.S. Maslennikov, 'Trudovoi kollektiv i sovetskaya politicheskaya sistema', *Sovetskoe gosudarstvo i pravo*, 1983, no.1, pp.118, 121; F.E. Udalov, 'V odnoi dolzhnosti ne bolee 7 let', *EKO*, 1983, no.12, p.133; V.N. Ivanov, *Trudovoi kollektiv sub'ekt sotsial'nogo upravleniya*, (Moscow, 1980), pp.134–7.

48. *Byulleten'*, Gosudarstvennyi komitet po trudu i sotsial'nym voprosam, 1982, no.8, p.3.

49. Enterprises which reduce employment by mixing jobs have the right to remain within the same branch grouping to which they belong, thus leaving managerial earnings unaffected (*Byulleten'*, Gosudarstvennyi komitet po trudu i sotsial'nym voprosam', 1983, no.8, p.5); but managers of leading factories still claim to have an interest in hoarding labour reserves related to planning indicators (*see*, 'Nuzhna reshitel'naya perestroika', *EKO*, 1983, no.8, p.32).

50. *See* D. Karpukhin, 'O sootnoshenii rosta proizvoditel'nosti truda i zarabotnoi platy', *Planovoe khozyaistvo*, 1983, no.10, p.91.

51. *See* V.I. Egorov, 'Yuridicheskie garantii prava na trud rabochikh i sluzhashchikh', *Sovetskoe gosudarstvo i pravo*, 1983, no.8, p.43; L.Iu. Bugrov, 'Perevod na druguyu rabotu', *Sovetskoe gosudarstvo i pravo*, 1983, no.8, p.77; Statzeva and Khoryakova, *op. cit.*, p.68.

52. Bugrov, *op. cit.*, p.80.

53. V. Glazyrin and I. Vereshchaka, 'Yuridicheskaia sluzhba pre-

dpriyatiya i ukreplenie trudovoi ditsipliny', *Khozyaistvo i pravo*, 1983, no.4, p.58.

54. Statzeva and Khoryakova, *op. cit.*, p.72.
55. *Ibid.*, pp.95–7.
56. *Ibid.*, pp.72–3.
57. *See* I.M. Popova and V.B. Moin, 'Zarabotnaya plata kak sotsial'naya tsennost'', *Sotsiologicheskie issledovaniya*, 1983, no.2, pp.103–9; N.V. Andreekova, 'Aktual'nye problemy upravleniya sotsial'nymi protsessami na promyshlennom predpriyatii', *Sotsiologicheskie issledovaniya*, 1980, no.1, pp.19–20.
58. *Pravda*, 8 Jan. 1981; 3 Oct. 1983; and for a critical view, *see* V.M. Rutgaizer, 'Chelovek truda v sfere raspredeleniya i potrebleniya', *EKO*, 1981, no.9, pp.53–62. For a thorough review of illegal income sources *see* G. Grossman, 'Notes on the illegal private economy and corruption', *A Compendium of Papers Submitted to the Joint Economic Committee Congress of the United States*, (Washington: 1979), vol.1, pp.835–54.
59. G. Popov, 'O ruble zarabotannom', *Pravda*, 25 May 1980.
60. *See* A. McAuley, *Economic Welfare in the Soviet Union* (London: Allen and Unwin, 1977), pp.202–4.
61. Kunel'skii, *op. cit.*, 1981, p.27.
62. *Ibid.*, p.122.
63. *See* M. Ellman, 'A Note on the Distribution of Earnings in the USSR Under Brezhnev', *Slavic Review*, December 1980, p.670.
64. N.A. Vasilenko, A.N. Steklova and N.A. Arakelian, 'Fond zarabotnoi platy i effektivnost' proizvodstva', *Finansy SSSR*, 1983, no.6, p.16; N. Rogovskii, 'Novoe v planirovanii truda', *Sotsialisticheskii trud*, 1980, no.2, p.15.
65. McAuley, *op. cit.*, p.202.
66. L. Keifets, 'Gosudarstvennoe regulirovanie zarabotnoi platy', *Voprosy ekonomiki*, 1983, no.6, pp.37–8.
67. *See* G.T. Kulikov, 'Kollektivnye (brigadnye) formy organizatsii truda v promyshlennosti', *Organizatsiya i planirovanie otraslei narodnogo khozyaistva*, 1980, no.61, p.24; I. Zheleznov, 'Pooshchrenie za konechnye resultaty v khozraschetnykh brigadakh', *Sotsialisticheskii trud*, 1981, no.4, p.84; 'Brigada na proizvodstve: segodnya i zavtra (kruglyi stol)', *EKO*, 1981, no.10, p.54.
68. *Vestnik statistiki*, 1983, no.6, p.63.
69. *See* Shkurko, *op. cit.*, pp.76–77.
70. *Formirovanie i stabilizatsiya kvalifitsirovannykh kadrov promyshlennosti i stroitel'stvo* (Novosibirsk, 1982), pp.204–5.
71. L.E. Kunel'skii 'Povyshenie stimuliruyushchei roli oplati truda', *EKO*, no.3, p.12.
72. *See* V.T. Parasochka, 'Fondy pooshchreniya predpriyatii i proizvodstvennykh ob'edinenii', *Finansy SSSR*, 1983, no.1, p.20.
73. S.I. Shkurko, *Stimulirovanie kachestva i effektivnosti proizvodsta* (Moscow, 1977), p.231.
74. *Vestnik statistiki*, 1983, no.6, pp.63–8. On the advantages enjoyed by workers on VAZ-scheme, *see* G.Ya. Rakitskaya and A.N. Shokin, 'Preobrazovaniya v sfere truda v 80-e gody', *Znanie: ekonomika*,

1984, no.2, pp.30–1.

75. E.K. Vasilev and L.M. Chistiakova, *Effektivnost' oplaty upravlencheskogo truda i effektivnost' proizvodstva* (Moscow, 1972), pp.44–59.

76. Shkurko, *op. cit.*, 1983, p.75.

77. A.A. Fatuev, *Voznagrazhdenie za trud po sovetskomu trudovomu pravu* (Moscow, 1977), pp.31–44.

78. Shkurko, *Stimulirovanie kachestva i effektivnosti proizvodstva, op. cit.*, pp. 206, 223.

79. *See* I. Aniukhovskii and V. Morosova, 'Vashnoe uslovie uspekha', *Khozyaistvo i pravo*, 1983, no.5, p.20; and 'Nuzhna sosnatel'naya rabochaya' ditsiplina, *Khozyaistvo i pravo*, 1983, no.3, pp.5–7.

80. *See* Shkurko, *op. cit.*, 1977, p.225.

81. Karpukhin, *op. cit.*, p.91.

82. See *Narodnoe khozyaistvo SSSR v 1982*, (Moscow, 1983), p.370.

PART III

Socio-Economic Problems

9 Geographical Mobility—Its Implications for Employment

ANN HELGESON*

Full employment, 'the maximum satisfaction of the demand for jobs by the able-bodied population,'[1] must be realised in the places in which people live. Jobs and people are located in discrete places. Both are geographically mobile, but the determinants and constraints to mobility differ between the two categories. This chapter will outline the salient migration trends in the period between the censuses of 1959, 1970 and 1979 in the light of some generalisations about employment policy. The results of migration during 1959–79, as well as some other demographic factors which vary by region, will then be examined in the context of anticipated problems for employment in the 1980s and 1990s.

First, it seems useful to look at some engrained Soviet attitudes toward population movement, which inform any examination of policy measures designed to constrain or facilitate migration.

MIGRATION IN A PLANNED ECONOMY: ATTITUDES AND POLICIES

There is a tendency to assume that the determinants of population migration are, if not coincident with, then at least not conflicting with the determinants of the geography of workplaces.[2] It is true that much migration is job-related and some of this proceeds along the lines drawn on the planners' mental maps. But there are all sorts of non-employment-related motivations which inspire Soviet population movement and immobility. As a result there have been 'irrational' migration trends, judged by the criteria of the planners,

* Centre for Russian and East European Studies, University of Birmingham.

145

especially after the loosening up of movement controls in the post-Stalin years. Some of these will be outlined below.

Along with the assumption that migration and regional labour demand both change in harmony (a component of the socialist 'law' of population), two policy principles have developed since the 1930s to assist the inevitability of this harmony. In using the term policy principles I refer not to stated tactics or even strategies to achieve a desired goal, but rather to normative statements of how things should work. These norms are part of a larger and firmly implanted metaphor of Soviet society as a well-oiled machine, the mechanism of which must be understood if the machine is to be manipulated toward the desired goal. The labour and migration component of this well-oiled machine would have the work force responding to the pushing and pulling of levers representing migration incentives or constraints by moving to places where labour is needed, or staying where they are if their labour is most effectively used there.

There are two policy principles, nowhere explicitly stated but implicit, as I hope to show, in more concrete policy measures taken from the early 1930s:

(1) People should be constrained from changing their place of residence spontaneously or independently, whether their moves are related to employment or not.

(2) That migration necessary to provide labour for expanding employment and regional development should be coordinated and channelled by state agencies.

The first principle developed early in the 1930s in response to the mass mobility which resulted from the 'revolution from above' of those years. Collectivisation and industrialisation sent huge numbers of people pouring into the cities to look for their places in the new order. The high levels of labour turnover in those years—a result of food shortages, the search for better pay and conditions, and the absence of the habits of industrial discipline—was economically dysfunctional as well. Rural-urban migration at this time was more intense than any observed up to then in the history of world industrialisation, and the resulting urban growth induced great pressure on the development of urban residential infrastructure in a very hard-pressed economy. Spontaneous movement was looked upon unfavourably at this time and a series of measures seeking to dam the rural-urban (and inter-urban) flood was devised.

The beginning of the era of central planning and the construction of industrial enterprises in previously undeveloped cities and regions necessitated a large volume of migration and the settlement of whole new towns. This migration was to be planned and organised. The construction workers and future metal-workers of Magnitogorsk, for example, would be recruited from the ranks of the collective farmers and moved at state expense from their former places of residence to the Urals. Until the recruiters arrived, everyone was to stay put.

Perhaps the most obvious manifestation of the first principle is the Internal Passport System, which began to operate in 1933.[3] By making residence permits (*propiski*) compulsory in all towns and 'urban-type' settlements, thus creating an administrative lever to control inter-urban migration and, more significantly, denying internal passports (and the consequent possibilities of migration) to the entire collective farm population, spontaneous migration was severely discouraged. Other less obvious measures of this period also facilitated the immobilisation of the population. Incentives were connected to length of employment in a given enterprise. Social security benefits, such as they were at the time, were reduced if the continuous employment record (*stazh*) was broken by job-changing. A series of measures, culminating in the well-known 1940 decree making it a criminal offence to quit a job without permission, froze more and more workers to their current employment and allowed the compulsory transfer of others.[4]

The second principle is exemplified in several organised channels of migration which were created in the 1930s and still exist today. Most important among them are Orgnabor (organised recruitment), agricultural resettlement, the compulsory placement of university and technical college graduates, and the so-called 'social appeals' (*obshchestvennye prizyvy*) organised by the Komsomol and other 'social' organisations.[5]

These and other institutions which emerged to realise the two principles of population movement never actually worked all that efficiently. There have always been thousands (perhaps millions) of people who have not had their residence permits in order but were still hired by hard-pressed personnel departments without the strictly necessary local *propiska*. There have probably been equally large numbers of urban dwellers who did not have passports at all. Incentives offered to stay put were often a reality only on paper and there was not much to lose from reductions in already extremely low pension and disability benefits from the social security system. The state migration channels seem to have been chaotic in their organsiation and in many cases exacerbated the problem of excess mobility.[6] Complaints in the press about Orgnabor recruiters promising the world to recruits who had already signed contracts with other recruiters and who would anyway cross the paths of recruits coming in exactly the opposite direction, were common.

There was no desperate need for the state migration channels to operate all that efficiently in these early years and the failure to stem spontaneous movements only caused problems to those responsible for low-priority things like city planning, urban transport, housing and cinema construction. There were few problems with a shortage of potential workers in the rural reservoir, although there were shortages in skilled specialities. The huge numbers pouring into the cities were absorbed into employ- ment easily enough, especially since labour could be substituted for capital. The well-known labour-intensive predelictions of Soviet industry that are listed in the literature on today's labour shortage began to develop.[7]

Despite the obvious faults in the operation of the 'well-oiled machine', the ideal developed and prospered in the mind if nowhere else. This was assisted by much in the economic literature which described a normative economic mechanism as if it actually existed and also by the fascination exerted by the possible existence of the world's first centrally planned economy. The chaos and tragedy of market economies in the 1930s only served to make the ideal of a 'well-oiled mechanism' that much more appealing.

The period beginning in about the mid-1950s saw the relaxation of many of the controls and the retreat into obscurity of many of the organised migration channels. The passport system seems not to have prevented the migration to the cities of something on the order of twenty five million rural people during 1956–70. The 1940 statute which had immobilised many was repealed in 1956, although most Soviet writers agree that the penalties for illegal job-changing were not enforced after about 1951. The regulations on calculating *stazh* (continuous employment) and the reduction of social security benefits were loosened up in 1960 so that a person's *stazh* would not be interrupted by job-changing as long as the period spent between jobs was less than a month. The migration channels, although they continued to operate, were placing a very small proportion of workers.

I once thought of the two principles described above as a useful way to generalise policies of the past. In my work on inter-regional migration during the 1960s I wrote of the relaxations of control and the reassertion of the legitimacy of individually motivated and executed migration.[8] Admittedly, the specialists still talked of appeals to patriotism eliciting migration to Siberia and a kind of unconscious understanding on the part of workers of where they were needed. But increasingly the academic study of migration (which had largely ceased in the period from 1930 to 1960) concerned itself with the explanation of the results of millions moving where they pleased.

The 1960s was a period of steady and increasing growth of the labour force and there was little worry about labour shortages on the whole, although there were some problems in unattractive regions like Siberia and the North (which is where the serious empirical research into migration began[9]). There was a considerable amount of slack in the labour economy so that 'irrational' migrations could be withstood while new enterprises could still be built and manned in the growing economy.

But as the urban population continued to grow by migration, the rural reservoir was draining. Urban birthrates were declining also at this time and the overall labour shortage to be experienced in the 1980s began to become clear to the reemerging demographic profession.[10] The problem slowly dawned on the labour economists. By the mid-1970s even the political leadership was referring to looming labour problems.[11]

In the meantime the well-oiled machine image was reawakening in the minds. With the expected labour shortages a mechanism was needed more than ever to assure that labour movements coincided with labour needs. The unfortunate notion developed that it was necessary only to tinker with the machine, oil the old levers and perhaps give it some new ones.

A recent article on the employment system (*trudoustroystvo*) by an authority on contemporary labour issues proposes a reform of the system that explicitly echoes the two mobility principles discussed above:

The further development of the employment system will allow improved labour redistribution along the following lines:
  (1) The minimisation of the volume of job-changing.
  (2) The rationalisation of the geography of labour mobility
  (3) A greater coincidence between the skills and composition of job-changers and the jobs they move to.
  (4) Minimisation of the period spent between jobs.[12]

The old principles have indeed reasserted themselves. Residential stability is now encouraged by a new set of incentives tied to length of service in one enterprise, including housing benefits, extra vacation time.[13] Frequent job-changers are penalised by loss of *stazh* if they change jobs more than once in the course of a year as a result of a major decree on labour discipline at the end of 1979.[14] The period between jobs allowed before the interruption of *stazh* was reduced to three weeks in 1983.[15] The 1979 decree extended the period of notice that must be given to employers before quitting from two weeks to one month. This was further increased to two months in the 1983 measures. Those who have been transferred to lower-paying work for up to three months as a result of internal infringements of labour discipline cannot give notice of their intention to leave until the expiry of the disciplinary period.

At the same time the upgrading, reorganisation and renaming of the State Committee on Labour and Social Questions (GOSKOM-TRUD) in 1978 resulted in the revitalisation of the old state migration channels.[16] There is much talk of new channels, although nothing has yet emerged, with the exception of the first published decree outlining the procedures for the compulsory placement of graduates of technical schools (PTU's).

MIGRATION TRENDS 1959–1979

Data and Methods for the Study of Soviet Migration

In theory the Soviet Union should have some of the best migration statistics in the world. Whenever any Soviet citizen changes their place of residence it is necessary to have the residence permit (*propiska*) stamped in the citizen's internal passport. The *propiska* procedure involves filling in forms at both origin and destination. The data on these forms are processed by the statistical organs.[17] Before 1975 a few migration tables on the economic-region scale based on passport system data appeared in *Vestnik Statistiki*, but none of the passport data are currently published. Soviet migration research after the publication of the 1970 census results did not yield any all-Union series of migration estimates on a meaningful scale, being limited in most cases to estimates of net migration for the nineteen economic regions.[18] One western monograph on interregional migration during this period is also unfortunately limited to the economic region scale.[19] To my knowledge no comprehensive series of net migration estimates at the more detailed, oblast, level for that period has ever been published.

There are several tried and trusted methods for producing net migration estimates based on census population totals for regions in the absence of any direct question in the census about migration. All are based on methods of estimating the expected natural change in the region (that is, births and deaths), comparing this expected regional population with the actual observed regional population at the end of the intercensal period and calling the residual 'net migration'. I have selected a census survival rate method, primarily because it eliminated the distorting effect of error in estimating oblast-level birth rates which vary over a very broad range in the USSR, and because it allowed the calculation of net migration for ten-year age groups. Methodological details and the complete set of net migration estimates for 168 regions (in general, oblasts), eight ten-year age groups, separately for rural, urban and total population can be found in my unpublished thesis.[20]

The published results of the 1979 census did not include data on the age structure of the population which means that estimates like those described for 1959–70 are impossible.[21] Other 'residual' methods of estimating intercensal net migration are also rendered impossible by the cessation of publication of oblast-level births and deaths (or rates derived from these), and the absence of a life table applicable to 1979. For the whole period 1970–79 we can only see total population change by oblast, which is influenced more by natural increase than by migration. (See Map 3). So the materials below are much more detailed for the 1960s than for the 1970s.

Population redistribution 1959–70

The results of migration to and from 168 regions are illustrated on Maps 1 and 2. The maps show what was done with the newly possible opportunities for independent migration after the mid-1950s. Three striking facts emerge from these maps and the calculations lying behind them:

(1) A southward drift of the Soviet population with a broad belt of out-migration in the north extending from the western border of the USSR nearly to the Pacific between latitudes 50° and 60° North; and a concentration, south of this belt, of oblasts which experienced net in-migration.[22]

(2) The enormous and isolated growth by migration of Moscow

Oblast and secondary concentrations of in-migrants to other large European metropolitan regions (Leningrad, Kiev, Minsk, the Baltic Republics).

(3) The relative unimportance of the eastern regions in the overall population redistribution. While there may have been a great deal of movement into and out of Siberia over the period the net result is nearly insignificant. There are some outlying regions which experienced some success— especially the Khanty-Mansiisk region where the oil developments of the 1960s were taking place, and some in the Far East—in general we observe the absence of any major net movement in or out of the eastern regions.

None of these observations from the maps can be said to conform to the official view of how the Soviet population should have been changing at this time. The southward movements tended to exacerbate a situation of surplus labour in regions like the North Caucasus and Central Asia. In addition to growth by migration these regions were also growing rapidly by natural increase. Industrial employment was not expanding rapidly in these largely agricultural regions and indices like kolkhoz man/ days worked per year were actually decreasing as the agricultural population grew.

The northern out-migration belt, on the other hand, is precisely where the largest concentrations of industry were located, and where the labour shortages of the 1980s would hit the hardest. The isolated growth of the largest cities within this northern region has been deplored and fought since the 1930s with *propiska* limitations and decrees prohibiting the siting of new enterprises or even the expansion of existing ones in the largest cities.[23] In 1981 the list of cities with such restrictions was extended.

The massive move to the east envisioned by Khrushchev and his successors simply did not materialise, although as I shall show below, there was limited success in enticing the younger members of society to the east, if only temporarily.

If the net migration estimates for each of the 168 regions on Maps 1 and 2 are summed forming large amalgamated regions then we can begin to see the broader patterns. Some information is lost due to the cancellation of movement within these amalgamated regions, but some very useful rough estimates of population redistribution on the all-Union scale are obtained.

When we split the entire country into a series of two-region systems we can even cite the direction of movements with

Table 9.1: *Net population redistribution, 1959–1970*[1]

From	To	Net Migration (000's)
Western USSR	Eastern USSR[2]	174
Northern USSR	Southern USSR[3]	3,133
RSFSR	Rest of USSR	2,147
Rest of USSR	Central Asia & Kazakhstan	1,178
Siberia and the Far East	Rest of USSR	1,003
Rest of USSR	Regions containing a republic capital[4]	3,234
Rest of USSR	Moscow, Leningrad, Kiev and Minsk Obs.	2,051

Notes:

1. This table illustrates only a few of the possible amalgamations of 168 oblasts into a bi-regional scheme.
2. Eastern USSR includes Central Asia, Kazakhstan, Siberia and the Far East.
3. Southern USSR includes the Ukraine, Moldavia, the Caucasian Republics, Central Asia and Kazakhstan, the North Caucasus Economic Region and Volgograd, Astrakhan and Kalmyk regions.
4. Including Leningrad Oblast.

Source: A. Helgeson, 'Soviet Internal Migration and Its Regulation Since Stalin', unpublished PhD thesis, Berkeley, 1978, p.70.

confidence.[24] Table 9.1 illustrates several ways of splitting the USSR into two-region systems of this kind. Thus, when the country is split roughly into a northern and a southern region we observe a net southward movement of about 3.1 million. The east-west exchange, in comparison, is exceedingly small—about 174,000 to the east. If we take Central Asia and Kazakhstan out of the eastern 'half' and put it back in with the rest of the country we find a net migration out of Siberia and the Far East of over a million. Similarly, if we split the country into a Central Asian/ Kazakh region and the rest of the country lumped together we observe a net move to Central Asia/Kazakhstan of over a million. The Russian republic can be seen to have lost 2.1 million to the other regions of the country.

The age, sex and skill composition of the migrant populations is as important as the total numbers of migrants. The census data do not allow the correlation of sex and skill characteristics with migration, but we can see some very interesting patterns in the distribution of the ages of the migrants. The overall age structure in inter-oblast migration and rural-urban migration is shown in Tables 9.2 and 9.3. As is to be expected, migration is heavily

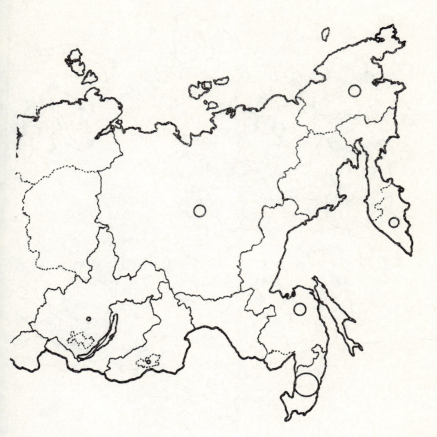

Map 1: Net in-migration USSR 1959–70
(Circles proportional to total net in-migration)

Source: A. Helgeson, 'Soviet Internal Migration and its Regulation Since Stalin',
PhD thesis, University of California, Berkeley, 1978.

Map 2: Net out-migration USSR 1959–70
(Circles proportional to total net out-migration)

Source: A. Helgeson, 'Soviet Internal Migration and its Regulation Since Stalin',
PhD thesis, University of California, Berkeley, 1978.

Table 9.2: *Age structure of inter-regional migrants, 1959–70*

Age in 1970	Net Migrants	% of all Net Migrants
10–19	1,929,128	23.8
20–29	2,556,550	31.6
30–39	1,604,745	19.8
40–49	911,914	11.3
50–59	473,968	5.9
60–69	404,743	5.0
70–79	210,651	2.6
10–79	8,091,699	100.0

Table 9.3: *Age structure of rural-urban migrants 1959–70*

Age in 1970	Net Migrants	% of all Rural-Urban Net Migrants
10–19	5,958,765	30.7
20–29	6,306,639	32.5
30–39	3,275,777	16.9
40–49	1,823,375	9.4
50–59	902,004	4.6
60–69	683,815	3.5
70–79	415,134	2.3
10–79	19,401,509	99.9

concentrated in the younger ages. Nearly two-thirds of rural-urban migrants were under the age of thirty at the end of the period and well over half of the inter-oblast migrants were of this age. Over three-fourths of the net migrants in both cases were under the age of forty.

While the largest numbers of net migrants were in the younger age groups, the highest migration rates are also observed among the young. Table 9.4 shows the relation of the number of net migrants in each age group to the total population at that age. Since net migration represents the balance of in- and out-migrants we can only guess at the number of actual moves made by each of the age groups. It seems likely that there were more moves cancelling each other among the younger groups. If we assume that there were six actual moves for every one net inter-regional migrant,[25] the average for all age groups, then nearly half of the 20–29 age group made inter-oblast moves during 1959–70.

The regional pattern of net migration in the 20–29 age group is

Table 9.4: *Net migration rates for ten-year cohorts*

Age in 1970	Average Cohort Size 1959–70	Inter-Regional Migrants as % of Average Cohort Size
10–19	47,722,296	4.0
20–29	31,569,868	8.1
30–39	38,061,774	4.2
40–49	31,373,156	2.9
50–59	22,199,543	1.5
60–69	18,619,049	2.2
70–79	10,222,985	2.1

Source: A. Helgeson, 'Soviet Internal Migration and Its Regulation Since Stalin', PhD Thesis, Berkeley, 1978, p.73.

very much different from the patterns observed in the cases of the older age groups. The 20–29 age cohort is found to be moving towards regions of out-migration by older migrants. In the Urals, for example, which lost huge numbers of older migrants and was suffering already from labour shortages as a result, the 20–29 age group gained considerably as a result of net in-migration: In Sverdlovsk oblast 24,000 net in-migrants in the 20–29 cohort crossed the paths of ten times as many out-migrants in the other age groups. In Chelyabinsk oblast there was little or no net movement in the 20–29 group, but heavy out-migration among the other age groups.

In the North Caucasus, where surplus labour was building up as a result of both in-migration and natural population growth, the 20–29 age group actually experienced net out-migration in Krasnodar kray and held about even in Stavropol.

In many Siberian oblasts which lost net migrants as a whole there were gains in the 20–29 cohort (Krasnoyarsk, Tomsk, Irkutsk) or significantly smaller losses (Novosibirsk, Omsk). In many of the Far Eastern oblasts overall net in-migration is almost wholly attributable to the balancing effect of a large volume of in-migration by the 20–29 group (Maritime kray, Khabarovsk, Kamchatka).

Table 9.5 shows the age structure of migration to the amalgamated regions in Table 9.1. Particularly notable here is the relative unimportance of the 20–29 group in the north-south drift of the population, and the large number of young people—especially those in their 20s—migrating eastward and rescuing what would otherwise have been a net westward movement of population as a

Table 9.5: *Age structure of net migration 1959–70 between aggregated regions in Table 9.1 (thousands)*

Eastern USSR[1]			Siberia & Far East		
10–19	+28	2.3%	10–19	−355	23.0%
20–29	+554	45.7%	20–29	+270	17.5%
30–39	+111	9.2%	30–39	−227	14.7%
40–49	−271	22.4%	40–49	−308	20.0%
50–59	−97	8.0%	50–59	−185	12.0%
60–69	−52	4.3%	60–69	−149	9.7%
70–79	−98	8.1%	70–79	−48	3.1%
10–79	+174		10–79	−1,003	

Southern USSR[2]			15 Regions containing Republic capitals + Leningrad Oblast		
10–19	+985	31.4%	10–19	+919	28.4%
20–29	+124	4.0%	20–29	+1,054	32.6%
30–39	+823	26.3%	30–39	+602	18.6%
40–49	+475	15.2%	40–49	+288	8.9%
50–59	+363	11.6%	50–59	+183	5.7%
60–69	+316	10.1%	60–69	+129	4.0%
70–79	+47	1.5%	70–79	+59	1.8%
10–79	+3,133		10–79	+3,234	

RSFSR			Moscow, Leningrad, Kiev & Minsk Obs.		
10–19	−700	32.6%	10–19	+525	25.6%
20–29	−29	1.4%	20–29	+815	39.7%
30–39	−569	26.5%	30–39	+345	16.8%
40–49	−272	12.7%	40–49	+191	9.3%
50–59	−298	13.9%	50–59	+77	3.7%
60–69	−254	11.8%	60–69	+56	2.7%
70–79	−25	1.3%	70–79	+43	2.1%
10–79	−2,147		10–79	+2,051	

Central Asia & Kazakhstan					
10–19	+383	30.0%			
20–29	+284	22.2%			
30–39	+338	26.4%			
40–49	+37	2.9%			
50–59	+89	7.0%			
60–69	+97	7.6%			
70–79	−50	3.9%			
10–79	+1,178				

Note: For each region the left column is age of the net migrants in 1970, the centre

whole. In Siberia and the Far East the 20–29 group was the only one to show a net in-migration.

The movement to the republican capitals, and especially to the four European capitals, is also dominated by the 20–29 group, although these movements are not against the stream as in the case of eastward migration. A third of the net migrants to capital cities are people in their twenties and forty per cent of migrants to the four European capitals were in the 20–29 cohort. But four 'capital' regions showed either very small gains relative to other age groups (Moldavia and Lithuania) or substantial losses in the 20–29 group (Georgia and Azerbaydzhan).

Migration during 1970–79

As outlined above, we are on much shakier ground when we try to generalise about migration in the 1970s. Sadly we are not able to follow up the interesting age group patterns observed for the 1960s. With the exception of one table of migration results from the 1979 census, which is treated below, we are thrown back on the reports of Soviet research in trying to uncover migration trends during 1970–79. It is hoped that the 'socio-demographic survey' of five per cent of the Soviet population which was done in January 1985 will yield more data to shed light on migration trends and changes in the composition of the labour force.[26]

There is one published table from the 1979 census that contains data on migration.[27] (See Table 9.6). The extended census questionnaire given to every fourth household asks about length of residence in that place (*naselenniy punkt*). The first part of the question asks if the person has ever lived in another place. The tabulation of replies to this question which were published give us the number of lifetime migrants (the standard demographic term for people who have changed their place of residence at least once during their lifetime) sub-divided by republic and broken down further into rural and urban population.

The highest proportion of lifetime migrants is predictably to be

column is the number (000s) of net migrants to or from the region to/from all other parts of the USSR, the right column is the proportion of that age group in all net migration change in the region.
1. See note 2 Table 9.1.
2. See note 3 Table 9.1.

Source: A. Helgeson, 'Soviet Internal Migration and Its Regulation Since Stalin', unpublished PhD thesis, Berkeley, 1978.

found among the urban populations of the Baltic republics and the lowest proportion among rural inhabitants in Central Asia and the Caucasus. This neatly demonstrates the correlation of proportion of lifetime migrants with other factors characterising levels of development in Soviet regions. For republican populations as a whole (that is, both urban and rural) the range is from 62.3 per cent lifetime migrants in Estonia to 22.3 per cent in Uzbekistan.

The table goes on to present the tabulated results of the question which asks each lifetime migrant to state the year that s/he moved to their current place of residence. These results demonstrate that the variations in migration behaviour *among* lifetime migrants in the fifteen republics is not nearly so great as the republican variation in proportion of lifetime migrants. It can be seen that between thirty and forty per cent of lifetime migrants, regardless of republic or rural/urban residence, have moved in the last five years.

The real republican differences, then, are in the proportion of people who have *ever* moved. Once the first move has been made a person moves into a less regionally differentiated category of lifetime migrants.

With the exception of this one table of census migration results we must obtain our information from Soviet secondary sources.[28] Much of the published material on migration during 1970–79 is poorly documented so we have to take the reported results on faith. The following are commonly reported trends from the 1970s:

(1) After about 1975 rural out-migration in the RSFSR began to slacken.

(2) Beginning in the early 1970s there was a slowdown in the southward movement of the population. Currently all the economic regions in the south of the country are experiencing net out-migration, with the single exception of the North Caucasus.

(3) There is now net migration growth in Siberia and the Far East, with notable successes in West Siberia.

(4) Mobility rates among the Central Asian populations have increased faster than among the traditionally more mobile European nationalities. (This can be confirmed in Table 9.6).

(5) The most active group for migration comprised those between the ages of sixteen and twenty-four.

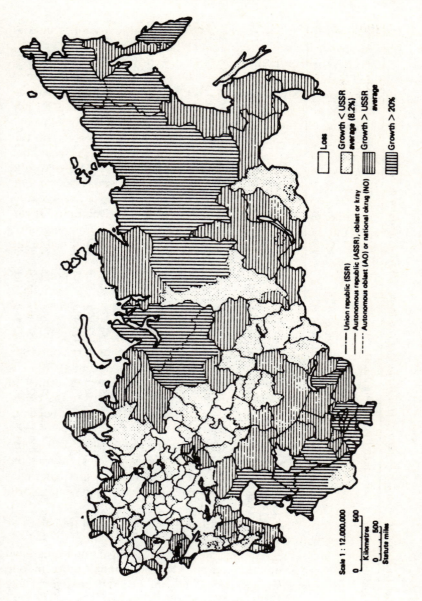

Map 3: Population growth rates 1970–79

Source: A. Helgeson in A. Brown and M. Kaser (eds), *Soviet policy for the 1980s*, London, 1982, p.130.

Table 9.6: *Duration of residence at current (1979) place of residence: USSR and union republics*

Total Population		of which those living at current residence:				Duration at current place of residence of those not living in place of birth per cent						
		Since Birth	%	Not since Birth	%	<2 yrs	2–6 yrs	6–9 yrs	10–14 yrs	15–19 yrs	20–24 yrs	>25 yrs
USSR												
Urban + Rural	262,084,654	138,562,446	52.9	123,522,208	47.1	16.3	18.2	13.0	11.5	10.5	8.3	22.2
Urban	162,442,608	70,646,213	43.5	91,796,395	56.5	15.4	17.7	12.9	11.6	10.8	8.3	23.3
Rural	99,642,046	67,916,233	68.2	31,725,813	31.8	19.0	19.6	13.4	11.0	9.7	8.1	19.2
RSFSR												
Urban + Rural	137,409,921	63,401,059	46.1	74,008,862	53.9	16.2	18.1	12.7	11.1	10.2	8.1	23.6
Urban	94,942,296	38,734,100	40.8	56,208,196	59.2	15.1	17.4	12.5	11.2	10.4	8.2	25.2
Rural	42,467,625	24,666,959	58.1	17,800,666	41.9	19.8	20.1	13.4	10.8	9.4	8.0	18.5
Ukrainian SSR												
Urban + Rural	49,609,333	27,908,907	56.3	21,700,426	43.7	15.0	17.1	12.7	11.8	11.1	9.0	23.3
Urban	30,168,937	13,453,730	44.6	16,715,207	55.4	14.5	16.9	12.9	12.1	11.5	9.1	23.0
Rural	19,440,396	14,455,177	74.4	4,985,219	25.6	16.7	17.5	12.4	10.8	9.8	8.4	24.4
Belorussian SSR												
Urban + Rural	9,532,516	5,276,041	55.3	4,256,475	44.7	17.1	19.0	14.0	12.9	10.4	7.9	18.7
Urban	5,234,295	2,101,300	40.1	3,132,995	59.9	16.9	19.1	14.5	13.6	10.7	7.8	17.4
Rural	4,298,221	3,174,741	73.9	1,123,480	26.1	17.9	18.7	12.7	10.8	9.5	8.0	22.4
Uzbek SSR												
Urban + Rural	15,389,307	11,963,664	77.7	3,425,643	22.3	20.8	20.9	14.2	12.4	9.3	6.7	15.7
Urban	6,281,636	3,929,173	62.6	2,352,463	37.4	20.8	20.1	13.8	12.8	9.6	6.7	16.2
Rural	9,107,671	8,034,491	88.2	1,073,180	11.8	20.9	22.7	15.2	11.4	8.6	6.6	14.6

Kazakh SSR											
Urban + Rural	14,684,283	7,190,201	49.0	51.0	19.1	20.4	14.8	12.5	12.3	8.2	12.7
Urban	7,855,220	3,160,062	40.2	59.8	18.2	20.0	14.8	12.8	12.5	8.2	13.5
Rural	6,829,063	4,030,139	59.0	41.0	20.6	21.0	14.7	12.0	12.2	8.3	11.2
Georgian SSR											
Urban + Rural	4,993,182	3,330,173	66.7	33.3	10.9	14.6	11.4	11.0	11.7	9.9	30.5
Urban	2,548,667	1,488,864	58.4	41.6	11.8	16.2	12.3	11.6	12.1	9.6	26.4
Rural	2,444,515	1,841,309	75.3	24.7	9.4	11.6	10.0	10.0	11.0	10.3	37.7
Azerbaydzhan SSR											
Urban + Rural	6,026,515	4,627,508	76.8	23.2	17.0	19.2	12.8	12.3	11.7	7.7	19.3
Urban	3,169,962	2,031,947	64.1	35.9	17.5	19.8	12.8	12.5	11.8	7.3	18.3
Rural	2,856,553	2,595,561	90.9	9.1	14.8	16.6	12.4	11.6	11.4	9.8	23.4
Lithuanian SSR											
Urban + Rural	3,391,490	1,510,575	44.5	55.5	16.9	19.8	14.7	12.4	10.4	7.5	18.3
Urban	2,034,879	742,912	36.5	63.5	15.9	19.0	14.7	13.2	11.0	8.0	18.2
Rural	1,356,611	767,663	56.6	43.4	19.1	21.6	14.4	10.9	9.0	6.4	18.6
Moldavian SSR											
Urban + Rural	3,949,756	2,652,703	67.2	32.8	20.1	20.8	13.7	11.7	9.7	8.2	15.8
Urban	1,532,924	644,044	42.0	58.0	20.1	21.2	14.3	12.5	10.1	7.7	14.1
Rural	2,416,832	2,008,659	83.1	16.9	20.0	19.9	12.6	10.1	8.7	9.1	19.6
Latvian SSR											
Urban + Rural	2,502,816	990,370	39.6	60.4	14.6	17.8	12.6	11.7	11.2	8.4	23.7
Urban	1,697,026	630,417	37.1	62.9	12.8	16.6	12.1	11.9	11.8	8.8	26.0
Rural	805,790	359,953	44.7	55.3	18.7	20.6	14.0	11.3	9.7	7.6	18.1

Table 9.6: Duration of residence at current (1979) place of residence: USSR and union republics (continued)

Total Population		of which those living at current residence:				Duration at current place of residence of those not living in place of birth per cent						
		Since Birth	%	Not since Birth	%	<2 yrs	2–6 yrs	6–9 yrs	10–14 yrs	15–19 yrs	20–24 yrs	>25 yrs
Kirghizian SSR												
Urban + Rural	3,522,832	2,258,780	64.1	1,264,052	35.9	21.1	20.0	14.2	12.3	10.8	7.2	14.4
Urban	1,384,761	590,199	43.8	758,562	56.2	20.3	19.2	14.1	12.6	11.3	7.4	15.1
Rural	2,174,071	1,668,581	76.7	505,490	23.3	22.2	21.3	14.3	11.7	10.0	6.9	13.6
Tadzhik SSR												
Urban + Rural	3,806,220	2,725,525	71.6	1,080,695	28.4	17.1	18.9	14.5	11.9	9.9	8.6	19.1
Urban	1,315,827	715,450	54.4	600,377	45.6	18.7	19.0	14.1	11.5	10.5	8.3	17.9
Rural	2,490,393	2,010,075	80.7	480,318	19.3	15.2	18.8	14.9	12.5	9.0	9.0	20.6
Armenian SSR												
Urban + Rural	3,037,259	2,143,595	70.6	893,664	29.4	14.3	17.1	14.6	12.8	11.5	7.7	22.0
Urban	1,985,679	1,276,856	64.3	798,823	35.7	14.4	17.6	15.2	12.9	11.4	7.2	21.3
Rural	1,051,580	886,739	82.4	184,841	17.6	13.6	15.4	12.1	12.5	12.0	9.7	24.7
Turkmen SSR												
Urban + Rural	2,764,748	2,030,599	73.4	734,149	26.6	18.7	20.7	14.8	11.5	10.6	6.7	17.0
Urban	1,309,673	775,629	59.2	534,044	40.8	19.4	20.7	14.4	10.7	10.3	6.8	17.7
Rural	1,455,075	1,254,970	86.2	200,105	13.8	16.9	20.9	15.9	13.4	11.3	6.5	15.1
Estonian SSR												
Urban + Rural	1,464,476	552,746	37.7	911,730	62.3	13.8	15.7	12.0	11.2	11.2	9.5	26.6
Urban	1,016,826	371,530	36.5	645,296	63.5	11.4	13.8	11.4	11.1	12.2	10.4	29.7
Rural	447,650	181,216	40.5	266,434	59.5	19.6	20.3	13.5	11.4	9.0	7.2	19.0

Source: Vestnik Statistiki, No.7, 1982, pp.77–79.

MIGRATION AND ITS IMPLICATIONS FOR EMPLOYMENT

The details about migration in the previous sections lead to some implications for employment. We can pinpoint future employment problems and, to a limited extent, problem regions, and anticipate some possible policy measures in the realm of labour mobility. I do this by looking at what we might loosely call 'determinants' of migration and by extrapolating patterns observed in the past on to the population structure of the near future.

Determinants of overall levels of migration

1. Age structure of the population. Everywhere in the world young adults participate most actively in migration. This was certainly the case in the Soviet Union in the 1960s and seems to have been in the 1970s. So the proportion of young adults in the population as a whole and in particular regions will influence overall levels of migration as well as the dynamics of labour force growth. Table 9.7 shows the anticipated effects on republican labour-age population, in the absence of migration, of the size of the generation entering the labour ages in the latter half of the 1980s and the size of the generation retiring at that time. The regional differentiation shown in this table reflects the high and low natural increase rates characteristic of the Central Asian/Caucasian and Slavic/Baltic regions, respectively, in the 1960s. The labour force 'entrants' who were aged 0–4 in 1970 are also in the extremely mobile ages in the 1980s. They will have come into the 20–29 cohort, which moved in such a distinctively 'rational' manner in the 1960s.

Especially among the young adult populations in the Western and Slavic regions where this cohort will be a small one we might anticipate not only less migration but, as a result, a much less pronounced overall 'rationality' in migration patterns, if the age patterns of migration in the 1960s are stable. Specifically the problems of labour supply in Siberia and the North may become more acute.

Older migrants tended to move southwards in the 1960s, although we are told that this pattern was not so distinct in the 1970s. So we might expect further out-migration from the RSFSR in the latter 1980s by, curiously, exactly the same people that were moving to Siberia twenty years previously. Below I will explain why I think it is precisely these older people who are being wooed

Table 9.7: *Age groups projected as entering and leaving labour-age during the 12th Five Year Plan (1986–90)*

Republic	Size of age group in 1970 census 0–4	(thousands) 40–44	0–4 as percentage of 40–44
RSFSR	9,318.6	10.940.3	85
Latvia	160.2	181.7	88
Ukraine	3,442.0	3,881.3	89
Estonia	96.1	103.8	93
Belorussia	742.1	687.5	108
Georgia	432.5	364.5	119
Lithuania	267.5	225.6	119
Moldavia	337.6	239.1	141
Armenia	288.0	168.8	171
Kazakhstan	1,545.3	849.1	182
Kirghizia	413.0	180.7	229
Azerbaydzhan	743.7	289.6	257
Turkmenia	348.0	115.5	301
Uzbekistan	1,882.0	622.7	302
Tadzhikistan	493.2	153.0	322
USSR	20,509.0	19,003.1	108

Source: V.I. Perevedentsev, 'Sotsial'no-demograficheskaya situatsiya i vstuplenie molodezhi v trudovuyu zhizn'', *Rabochiy klass i sovremenniy mir*, No.2, 1980, p.90.

by offers of material incentives to stay where they are.

But what of the large numbers of young adults coming into the working ages in the Central Asian and Caucasian republics? Can we expect them to. provide the labour needed in Siberian extractive industries in the 1980s? This is, of course, a hotly debated question,[29] to which I address some comments in the next section.

2. Migration history of the population. The one published table on migration from the 1979 census confirms an intuitively attractive notion about the importance of individual migration histories. It is the first move that makes the difference. After a person has changed their place of residence once, it is that much easier to do it again. This is particularly significant from the southern regions, which have been undergoing a process of modernisation, a time when traditionally the population begins to become more mobile. The first move out of the warm embrace of the traditional Islamic culture in Central Asia will open wide horizons and make it difficult to return for the very large young adult generation in the region. One Soviet sociologist found that of the young people he surveyed in Central Asia 42.2–48 per cent of them would be willing to go outside their republics, temporarily, in order to obtain education and professional qualifications.[30] If they went, that first move would transfer them into the more mobile category of those who had made the first move. This is not just a statistical reclassification. Their lives, their aspirations and their mobility patterns will be transformed.

3. *The relative scarcity of labour.* In a situation of overall labour shortage there are job advertisements everywhere. Opportunities to improve one's situation by job-changing without the necessity of moving elsewhere are facilitated. In the absence of any (more) control on job-changing we would expect labour turnover levels within regions to increase. Some of the reports of migration in the 1970s confirm this indirectly by citing a decrease in the levels of *inter*-regional migration and an increase in *intra*-regional movements,[31] which seems to fit reasonably into the notion of ubiquitous labour demand.

Of course, the relative scarcity of labour is related to labour utilisation policy. Any change in this, as the enforcement of the 'limits' to the size of enterprise labour forces introduced in 1979, the introduction of labour-saving technology and other measures, will affect the total number of jobs available and their location. It is not the purpose here to say anything new about labour utilisation, except to note that such measures as are being taken do not seem to be regionally differentiated. Just as much effort seems to be going into the abolition of less productive manual labour in Central Asia as in the more labour-deficit regions like, for example, the Urals.

4. *Institutional constraints to migration and official channels of migration.* Here we should look again at the two 'principles' of population movement proposed earlier. While the effect of policy measures based on these two principles was weakest during the 1960s at a time of labour force growth and the general loosening of controls at that time, I expect the old migration principles to reassert themselves in the 1980s and 1990s. I expect, on the one hand, that spontaneous mobility will again be discouraged, resulting in a decrease in rates of migration. Some of the measures introduced during the last several years which are intended to have this effect have already been discussed. On the other hand, the renewed interest in the state migration channels may have an offsetting effect and *increase* migration rates among young people.

But, as in the earliest years, we must not overestimate the efficacy of these policy measures. Especially in this area of Soviet economy policy, measures say more about intentions than about what might confidently be expected.

Determinants of migration destinations

It is implied in the previous section, using what we know about the future age structure of the populations in various regions and the migration proclivities of the different age groups, that certain migration paths are more likely than others. Similarly, other factors which influence the overall levels of migration also influence their directions. The relative scarcity of labour has a distinct regional dimension. Migration histories build up mental maps of good and bad places to live. Institutional constraints and official migration channels can be slanted in accordance with regional labour needs.

1. Regional development goals and job siting. Obviously the location of jobs and the siting of new jobs is a factor influencing migration decisions. No one will move to a place where s/he cannot find a job. But in a situation of overall labour shortage jobs can be found virtually everywhere, so this factor is weakened. The assembly of work forces for new enterprises, especially those in developing regions, is made very difficult in these circumstances. Simply siting jobs will not ensure that they are filled.

This is a particularly vexing problem for the 1980s. The development and expansion of extractive industries in the eastern regions must have a labour force. There was limited success, at a time of fairly rapid labour force growth, in attracting oil workers to West Siberia in the 1960s, although much of that migration turned out to be temporary and out-migrants had to be constantly replaced. In conditions of even more rapid labour force growth in the latter half of the 1970s there was limited success in attracting construction workers for the Baikal-Amur Mainline railway (BAM). Research published in 1980 suggests that about a third of these came to the region through the 'Komsomol appeal' channel, another ten per cent via Orgnabor, graduate distribution, special distributions of demobilised soldiers, and another thirty per cent in the transfer of entire construction brigades and trusts from other regions of the country. Only about a fourth of the work force came under their own steam, indicating that the state migration channels are playing an important role at least in this prestige enterprise.

The BAM is now officially finished. The 'golden spike' was driven into place late in 1984 and the labour problems in the developing BAM zone are taking on a different character.[32] Even if many of the construction workers remain in the region to work in the newly-developing extractive industries there will be a constantly increasing demand for labour in the region.

Another problem region in the developing energy complex of the eastern regions is the Kansk-Achinsk coal basin, strung out along the 'old' Trans-Siberian railway. Coal mined using open-pit methods here is the cheapest to be found in the Soviet Union and the intention is that mining here should be stepped up. This region will be competing with the BAM zone for dwindling numbers of young migrants, as will the far northern regions of the West Siberian gas-producing zone.

2. Residential preferences. In a situation of labour shortage and employment possibilities everywhere the non-employment-related attractions of places can be more influential in individual migration decisions. The attractions of the more southerly regions of the country for the migrants of the 1960s was as much related to residential amenity as to job availability. The attractiveness of the less severe climate of places like the North Caucasus, which continues to grow by migration, or the Crimea, the southern parts of the Ukraine or Central Asia, for the Russians cannot be overstressed. Food supply in these southern regions is also considerably better than in the northern half of the country.

In the 1960s the migrants in the north-south channel were in the ages over thirty, those who had established families (there were a lot of children in the stream) and professions. They moved independently, outside of the state migration channels. This was a decidedly 'irrational' migration stream and recent comments like those of Kotlyar cited above about reducing unnecessary job-changing are addressed to these and other migrants. As we have seen, new controls to prevent excess labour turnover have been introduced and a new series of incentives to long employment in one enterprise.

The incentives to long service in one enterprise seem to me to be very important to the age groups over thirty in the labour force. Although this chapter is not the place for a long discussion of the changing sources of consumer goods and services in the Soviet economy, the subject deserves a brief mention. In addition to the explicit state measures providing such incentives as extra vacation time to long-serving employees of an enterprise, many of the other sources of consumer well-being are now being provided through the agencies of places of work. An increasing proportion of housing, child care centres, and even polyclinics and retail shopping outlets are under the control of enterprises. To the extent that all these goods and services are in short supply, some means of rationing them has to be devised. One of the criteria in housing allocation for example, or places in nurseries, might very well be on the basis of length of *stazh* in the enterprise. Family living standards are very important to the older age groups and the arguments for remaining in place would seem to be very powerful for them.

3. *Official channels and incentives to move to particular places.* Built into the new statutes on the organised migration channels like Orgnabor, the distribution of graduates and others are regional biases in favour of regions undergoing economic development and those with labour deficits. We have seen earlier that a much larger proportion than average of the BAM construction workers were recruited through one organised channel or the other. (The usual proportion cited of hirings outside the state channels is on the order of eighty-five per cent). I think this is likely to be the case for other economic activities in Siberia and the North.

The great majority of the migrants in the state channels are in the young adult ages: sixty-three per cent of Orgnabor recruits in one large sample,[33] most graduates of educational institutions, nearly all Komsomol members and those demobilised from the Army. Numerically, by far the most important group of young participants in the state migration channels comprise young people being placed in their first jobs upon graduation from various sorts of educational establishments.[34] It is important to note that all these channels of placement involve little or no choice on the part of those placed and that built into the series of new statutes on these channels is a bias in favour of the eastern regions. Those placed are required to remain in these jobs for period varying from one to three years.

So, while the incentives to stay put would seem to be directed at the older age groups, the dominant concern of the organised migration channels will be the movement of young members of the labour force.

4. *The importance of rural living conditions for the volume of rural-urban migration in the near future.* Rural regions have always born the brunt of irrational migration trends. In times and regions of labour shortage in urban occupations the rural reservoir was tapped with little regard for the labour supply situation in agriculture. The slowing of rural out-migration in the 1970s

observed by many Soviet scholars may be more related to the ample labour supply situation in the towns than to a preference to remain in the countryside. Now that labour shortages are acute in most northern and western cities, we might expect greater pressure on rural out-migration, with consequent losses to the agricultural labour supply.

CONCLUSIONS

The determinants of migration do not completely mesh with the determinants of the geography of jobs. There is some wishful thinking that they do or that tinkering with existing policies might be able to engineer the appropriate migration trends. If the reports of migration in the 1970s have a basis in fact then some of the irrational migrations of the 1960s have been partially reversed. But there was a good deal of slack in the labour economy of the 1970s.

The shortages of the 1980s are caused both by the smaller numbers of young adults coming into the labour force and by the tendencies in the existing economic mechanism for enterprises to hire more labour than they need. The shortages of the 1980s and the need for migrants in developing regions and new enterprises must be met. The small numbers in the young and most mobile groups will make this increasingly problematic in the next two decades. More than ever it is necessary that the machine should work, but at the moment the machine is little more than a figment of the imagination. Levers which never worked all that well are simply being polished and oiled.

NOTES

1. A. Kotlyar, 'Polnaya zanyatost' i sbalansirovannost' faktorov sotsialisticheskogo proizvodstva', *Voprosy ekonomiki*, No. 7, 1983, p.106.
2. *See*, for example, Ye.V. Kasimovskiy, (ed.), *Trudovye resursy-formirovanie i ispol'zovanie*, (Moscow, 1975), pp.15–18.
3. Ann Helgeson, 'The Soviet Internal Passport System—A Case Study of Institutional Control of Population Movement', University of Essex, Economics Department, Discussion Paper No.126 (March 1979).
4. *See* Solomon M. Schwarz, *Labour in the Soviet Union* (London, 1953) for details of these measures.

5. Ann Helgeson, 'Perevod vs, perekhod—Prospects for a Soviet Population Distribution Policy', unpublished NASEES conference paper, 1979, pp.7–28.
6. John Barber, 'The Organised Recruitment of Manual Labour for Soviet Industry 1931–40', unpublished NASEES conference paper, June 1982.
7. *See* Philip Hanson, Ch.6 in this collection.
8. Ann Helgeson, 'Soviet Internal Migration and Its Regulation Since Stalin', PhD thesis, (Berkeley, 1978) Ch.3 and appendices.
9. Eg V.I. Perevedentsev, *Sovremennaya migratsiya naseleniya zapadnoy Sibiri*, Novosibirsk, 1965. T.I. Zaslavskaya, (ed.), *Migratsiya Sel'skogo Naseleniya*, (Moscow, 1970).
10. Ann Helgeson, 'Demographic Policy' in Archie Brown and Michael Kaser (eds), *Soviet Policy for the 1980s*, (London, 1982), pp.118–45.
11. *See*, among other places, *Trud*, 24 February, 1981, p.4.
12. A. Kotlyar, 'Sistema trudoustroystva v SSSR', *Ekonomicheskye nauki*, No.3, 1984, p.58.
13. 'O dal'neyshem ukreplenii trudovoy distsipliny i sokrashchenii tekuchesti kadrov v narodnom khozyaystve, *Sobranie postanovlenii pravitel'stva SSSR*, No.3, 1980, article 17.
14. *Ibid,*
15. Pravda, 7 August, 1983.
16. Some recent decrees on organised migration channels: (1) re: distribution of graduates—*Byulleten' Minvuza*, No.10, 1980, pp.25–36; (2) re: distribution of PTU graduates—*Professional'no-tekhnicheskoe obrazovanie*, No.7, 1983, pp.18–19; (3) re: agricultural re-settlement—*Byulleten' goskomtruda*, No.10, 1979. Goskomtrud is now known as the State Committee on Labour and Social Questions.
17. Helgson, *op. cit.*, 'The Soviet Internal. . . .'
18. *See*, for example V.I. Perevedentsev, *Metody izucheniya migratsii naseleniya*, Moscow, 1975, p.58 and B.S. Khorev and V.M. Moiseeko, (eds.), *Migratsionnaya podvizhnost' naseleniya v SSSR* (Moscow, 1974), pp.80–1.
19. Peter Grandstaff, *Interregional Migration in the USSR* (Raleigh, 1980).
20. Helgeson, *op. cit.*, 1978, 'Soviet Internal Migration. . . .'
21. The compilation of all published results from the 1979 census can be found in: *Chislennost' i sostav naseleniya SSSR*, (Moscow, 1984).
22. Curiously, the boundary between the northern and southern regions in the European part of the country is roughly coincident with a line separating the glaciated northern territories with the less chaotic mature river valleys of southern European Russia (i.e. the more productive agricultural regions).
23. B.S. Khorev, 'Aktual'nye nauchno-prikladnye problemy ogranicheniya rosta krupnykh gorodov v SSSR', *Ekonomicheskye Nauki*, No.3, 1984, pp.60–8.
24. Since the USSR is assumed to be a closed system to international migration, then in a two regional system, of course, the in-migration in one region is net out-migration from the other.

25. Which is reasonable assuming the same gross: net migration ratio as in 1968–69. See Helgeson, 1978, pp.337–8.

26. An interview in *Sovetskaya Rossiya*, 3 January, 1985 with the head of the Central Statistical Administration indicates that one of the major areas of interest to be covered by the survey is that of labour resources.

27. *Vestnik statistiki*, Vol.7, 1982, pp.77–9. *Vsesoyuznaya perepis' naseleniya—vsenarodnnoye delo* (Moscow, 1978), pp.27 and 63.

28. L.L. Rybakovsky, 'O migratsii naseleniya v SSSR, *'Sotsiologicheskye issledovaniya*, No.4, 1981, pp.7–14. *Naseleniya SSSR—spravochnik* (Moscow, 1983). D.I. Valentey, (ed.), *Rasselenie i demograficheskie protsessi* (Moscow, 1983). A. Topilin, 'Programmo-tselevoy podkhod k regulirovaniyu migratsii', in *Kuda i zachem edut lyudi* (Moscow, 1979). V.I. Perevedentsev, 'Migratsiya naseleniya i razvitie selskokhozyaystvennogo proizvodstva', *Sotsiologicheskie issledovaniya*, No.1, 1983, pp.54–61.

29. *See*, for example, M. Feshbach 'Prospects for Out-migration from Central Asia and Kazakhstan in the Next Decade' in US Congress—Joint Economic Committee, *Soviet Economy in a Time of Change*, Vol.1, Washington, D.C., 1979 and A. Sheehy, 'Prospects for Early Out-migration of Rural Central Asians Remain Bleak', *Radio Liberty Research* 360/83, 28 September 1983.

30. *See* D.I. Zyuzin, 'Prichini Nizkoy Mobil'nosti korennogo naseleniya respublik Sredney Azii', *Sotsiologicheskiye issledovaniya*, No.1, 1983, 109–17.

31. L.L. Rybakovsky, 1981, *op. cit.*

32. *Pravda*, 2 October, 1984, p.1.

33. Yu. Matveev in A.Z. Maykov (ed.), *Migratsiya naseleniya RSFSR* (Moscow, 1973), p.73.

34. For further details *see*: A. Helgeson, 'Finding Work in the Soviet Economy: Employment Agencies for First-Time Job Seekers', *Business Graduate*, Autumn 1984.

10 Shortage of Labour and Motivation Problems of Soviet Workers

ANNA-JUTTA PIETSCH*

Whereas for capitalist countries unemployment has been the subject of many different theories, the opposite is true of the problem of labour shortage in socialist countries. An attempt was made to investigate this question in the 1920s in the Soviet Union.[1] But this was short-lived and today in the Soviet Union there has been no theoretical attempt to explain this phenomenon, although there is much literature describing shortages of labour within the factory and on the labour market.

In this situation many Western social scientists have found it promising to look at the theory of shortage developed by Kornai.[2] It is not a theory dealing particularly with labour shortage, but treats the phenomenon of shortage in a general way. According to Kornai's theory, shortage is an inherent factor of central planning affecting alla sectors of the economy. Summarising his theory for the needs of this paper, one can say at the most obvious level that he sees the reason for shortage in the excessive demand of socialist enterprises for resources. This demand, he states, is insatiable in principle, even if production is organised in a reasonably efficient way and prices are set adequately, which of course is not always the case. With insatiable demand and finite production, shortage must occur sooner or later because demand meets a definite limit, which Kornai calls 'resource constraint'. He sees the reason for this insatiable demand by socialist enterprises in the absence of a 'budget constraint'. Whereas the demand of capitalist firms for goods and services is limited by their budget, socialist enterprises have various possibilities to expand it. This can happen during the planning process, when firms compete for resources, and it can happen afterwards, when firms declare themselves to be unable to

* Research Associate, Osteuropa-Institut, Munich.

fulfil the plan without additional resources. Moreover, they apply for tax exemption, additional credits, subsidies or higher prices for their goods. The motives behind this behaviour vary. One is their endeavour to minimise the effort to fulfil the plan. Another reason is the strong expansion drive socialist economies have developed at all levels of the planning and executing bureaucracy. Everybody wants to see his branch, his firm, his division grow. This expansion drive is also well known to bureaucratic institutions in capitalist countries in the form of Parkinson's Law. But, if it becomes universal, it ends up by blocking itself because it exceeds the existing resources. Then chronically stochastic shortage is the result.

Kornai's theory is quite comprehensive, but some questions remain unanswered. He has not considered the quantitative aspect of his theory. So one cannot make any prediction about the scale of the expansion drive of the firms and on what its scale depends. In the following we will consider Soviet labour policy in the light of Kornai's theory of shortage and, at the same time, we will see if we can learn something about the quantitative aspects of excessive demand of enterprises for labour.

THE EXHAUSTION OF LABOUR RESOURCES

According to Kornai's theory, the expansion drive of firms is not blocked by budget considerations, and this leads to excessive demand for all sorts of resources, including labour. A look at the empirical data of the employment sector shows that until 1970 the demand for labour did not meet a physical-resource constraint on the labour market. There was no open unemployment, and the additional manpower given by demographic growth could be absorbed in the economy.

Table 10.1 shows how demographic growth has fluctuated due to the effects of the war. The generation entering the labour force in the 1960s were the children of the generation born during the war. Their successors in the 1970s were children of the generation born in the 1950s, when war was over. Since then, however, the birth rate has fallen and has led to an extremely small growth-rate of working-age population in the 1980s.

Shortage of labour cannot be explained simply by a reduction in demographic growth. This becomes quite clear when one considers that it was surprisingly felt to an ever greater extent during the

10.1: *Increase in Soviet population of working age 1960–2000*

Period	Decadal rate of growth (per cent)
1960–70	9.21
1970–80	18.34
1980–90	3.83
1990–2000	4.88

Note: Males 16 to 59 years, females 16 to 54 years.

Source: A. McAuley and A. Helgeson, 'Soviet Labour Supply and Manpower Utilization 1960–2000', unpublished paper, 1978, p.5a.

1970s, in a period of large population increase. But once labour shortage exists, it will of course be aggravated by the dramatic reduction in demographic growth, such as is being experienced in the 1980s.

Table 10.2 shows the development of the participation rate; that is, the number of employed people in the social sector (state enterprises and collective farms) divided by population 16 to 54–59 years of age. As one can see, this rate increased continuously until 1970. Since that year the participation rate has remained more or less the same, with a small decline from 80.84 per cent in 1970 to 80.52 per cent in 1979. This decline can be explained by labour market situation in Central Asia, which we will discuss later.

Table 10.2: *Development of Soviet participation rates*

	1950	1960	1970	1975	1979
Population of working age (000's)	103.363	119.381	130.003	143.023	152.443
Employees in the social sector (000's)	68.020	84.332	105.095	115.477	122.747
Participation rates (per cent)	65.80	70.64	80.84	80.74	80.52

Sources: Occupational data: *Nar.Khoz.* Population of working age: Census results, and G. Baldwin, *Population Projections by Age and Sex*, (Washington, D.C. 1979).

The participation rate in the above table is very high in comparison with Western countries. In West Germany the corresponding quota was 62.5 per cent in 1982.[3] This difference is not due simply to unemployment in West Germany. If the unemployed people were included, the quota would increase to 66.9 per cent. The growth of the participation rate is due to two factors: the first one is the reduction of private agriculture, the second is the decrease in the number of women occupied only in the household.

Table 10.3 shows the development of private agriculture as far as manpower is concerned. As a potential resource of labour force for the social sector, only people occupied exclusively in private agriculture can be considered. Here the workforce is predominantly female, as the table makes clear. As a resource for an additional labour force in the 1980s, it is practically exhausted.

Table 10.3: *People working exclusively in private agriculture*

	1959 (000's)	1970 (000's)	1979 (000's)
Persons working exclusively in private agriculture	5,036	1,824	564
Of which women	4,822	1,662	539

Sources: Census results: 1959, *Itogi vsesoyuznoi perepisi naseleniya 1959 goda SSSR* p.99; 1970, *Itogi vsesoyuznoi perepisi naseleniya 1970 goda*, vol.5, p.146; 1979, *Vestnik statistiki* 9, 1981, p.79.

The second and more abundant source of labour-force growth in the social sector has been women occupied in private households. Table 10.4 shows that there has been a significant increase in the female participation rate, especially between 1950 and 1970. It is also much higher than in Western countries. In West Germany the female participation rate was 47.2 per cent in 1982.[4] In the Soviet Union the participation rate for women between 20 and 40 years of age, the time of child-birth and care, is also very high. In 1970 it reached 85.1 per cent for women of between 20 and 29 years of age and 91.2 per cent for women between 30 and 39 years old.[5]

Table 10.4: *Soviet female participation rates*

	1950	1960	1970	1975	1979
Women employed in the social sector (per 1,000)	33.532	40.084	54.300	59.931	64.233
Participation rate (per cent)	59.9	62.7	81.6	82.1	83.1

Sources: Participation rates 1960–75, A. McAuley, *Women's Work and Wages in the Soviet Union* (London, 1981), p.37; 1950 and 1979, own calculations based on *Nar.Khoz. SSSR* of relevant years.

McAuley has called this participation rate excessive. It has caused a dramatic fall in the birth rate. It is difficult for Soviet women, as elsewhere, to combine profession and family work. One reason is the unequal division of labour in the household between men and women. The other reason is the fact that child-care institutions are not sufficient in quantity and quality. Mothers complain that children often get ill and develop more slowly because they do not get the attention they need.[6] The government has responded to the decline in the birth rate and the complaints of the women by introducing a baby year in 1981.[7] This will certainly resolve some of the women's problems, but it will also reduce the participation rate to some extent.

The reasons for the high female participation rates are to be found, on the one hand, in the state's women's emancipation programme. It was propounded for years that women could achieve an equal position in society only by integrating themselves in the labour force. This programme meant that efforts were made to guarantee equal education for women and men, and women are thus prepared for work from the start. On the other hand, women claim that they are working primarily for financial reasons.[8] This, however, does not explain completely the high participation rates. Salaries were much smaller in 1950 (on average 64.2 roubles) than in 1982 (172.5 roubles),[9] but despite this, women stayed at home in this period. This does not mean that nowadays Soviet women work because of consumeristic attitudes. The living standard is still very modest compared with Western countries. But it shows that the living standards towards which people aspire is not an absolute but a social category. If it becomes usual for women to be employed, the family income thus made possible becomes the aspiration level for others.[10] In this respect women's nominal wages are not decisive. In the Soviet Union women's wages are lower than those of men.[11] If the woman takes on a job, this suddenly increases the family's budget by more than 50 per cent. This increase is more important than the fact that her salary is less than that of her husband.

Since the reserves of labour have been exhausted, great efforts have been undertaken to employ old-age pensioners. The proportion of old-age pensioners with permanent jobs decreased between 1959 and 1970. In 1959, 68.0 per cent of men between 60 and 69 years of age continued to work, whereas in 1970 only 29.3 per cent did so. The proportion of women who continued to work also declined. In 1959 it was 40 per cent for the age group of 55–59 years and only 23.5 per cent in 1970.[12] This was due to the material assistance given to the pensioners. In 1964 old-age pensions for kolkhoz members were also introduced. But this decrease was only temporary. In 1979, 7.5 million recipients of old-age, invalidity and other pensions had a permanent job, compared with 6.2 million in 1959.[13] It is not expected that this proportion will increase.

The use of foreign labour (*Gastarbeiter*) is not considered to be a solution. There are some 50,000 such workers, which represents a very small proportion of the Soviet labour force. They do not come individually but together with their firms, hired to execute special projects in the Soviet Union.[14] Recently there have been some hints that the length of work-time is a point of discussion in the Soviet Union. Chernenko alluded to this possibility in his speech to the workers of the metallurgical plant 'Serp i molot' in Moscow.[15] This would be a further step in the direction of extensive growth. One may doubt, however, whether it will be effective.

So far we have considered the supply side of the labour market. With respect to the demand side one can show that Soviet firms have managed successfully to expand their labour force beyond the plan during the whole period (see Table 10.5). This table shows planned and actual rates of growth of Soviet employment. Actual growth rates are much higher than the planned figures, especially between 1950 and 1966. Later the discrepancy becomes smaller because the resources of additional workers diminished. Thus these figures show that one of the factors influencing the rhythm of expansion is the abundance of additional resources.

Table 10.5: *Planned and actual growth rates of Soviet employment (per cent)*

Period	Industry		State Sector	
	Plan	Actual	Plan	Actual
1951–55	2.5	4.2	2.8	4.6
1956–60	1.9	5.1	–	5.1
1959–65	2.9	4.5	2.9	4.6
1966–70	2.1	2.8	–	–
1971–75	1.1	1.4	1.0	1.7
1976–80	0.7	–	–	–

Source: 1951–75: J. Adam, *Wage Control and Inflation in the Soviet Bloc Countries* (New York, 1979), p.50. 1976–80: *Economic Survey of Europe 1976*, Part II, S. 71.

At the same time it becomes clear that there was no conflict of interests between planning authorities and firms in principle, but only about the dimension of growth. As Adam showed in his study of wage control and inflation, the authorities were able to control wages per capita very rigidly.[16] So one can assume that they would have been able to do so also with respect to the wage-fund. But as planning authorities are in favour of expanding employment, they did not impede the firms' expansive behaviour until it hit the resource constraint. In the case of labour, the resource constraint is not identical with the absolute exhaustion of potential labour. It is not feasible for 100 per cent of the able-bodied population to be actually employed. The absorption process reaches a point where it cannot be expanded any more. This is what Kornai calls the 'tolerance limit of employment'.[17]

In Figure 2 the absorption process of reserve labour is summarised once more. The horizontal axis represents time. On the vertical axis the share of potential reserve labour in total population of working age is measured. It is the total labour force of working age minus the employed population. The figure shows that potential reserve labour was relatively high in the 1950s. It continuously went down until reaching the 'tolerance limit'. This seems to have happened in the 1970s. The mobilisation of the able-bodied population seems complete. The participation rate has now more or less stabilised. The tolerance limit separates the mobilisable from the non-mobilisable reserves. The latter represent about 20 per cent of the population of working age. They consist of students, housewives, military persons, people doing private agriculture, artisans, artists and people not able to work because of illness, and frictional unemployment caused by labour turnover.[18] The above figure also gives a more exact meaning to the problem of the transition from the extensive to the intensive type of growth, which is often discussed in Soviet literature. From the moment absorption of reserve labour reached the tolerance limit (i.e. more or less in 1970), the possibilities of extensive growth were exhausted, if one does not take the prolongation of labour time as a realistic proposition.

This general tendency is, however, not true for all Soviet regions. Central Asia shows a quite different picture. Central Asia experienced in the 1970s rapid growth of the population of working age (50.06 per cent for 1970–80), and quite a high growth rate is predicted for the 1980s (32.94 per cent for 1980–90).[19] One would expect that the additional labour force would have been

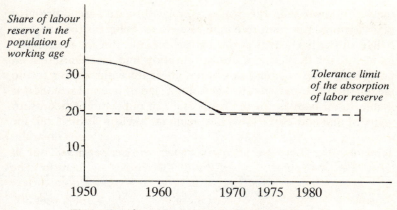

Figure 2: *Absorption process of reserve labour*

Source: Table 16 and J. Kornai, *Economics of Shortage*, (Amsterdam, 1981), vol.1, p.258.

eagerly absorbed because it occurred in a period of overall labour shortage in the industrial centres of the Soviet Union, in Siberia and even in the countryside of the Russian republic. But this was not the case. Asian people were not willing to migrate, mainly for cultural reasons. This led to a decline in the participation rates between 1970 and 1979 (Table 10.6).

Table 10.6: *Development of participation rates in Kazakhstan and Central Asia*

Republic	1970	1975	1979
Soviet Union	80.84	80.74	80.52
Kazakhstan	74.32	73.60	71.70
Kirgizia	72.75	70.60	67.80
Uzbekistan	71.78	68.40	64.30
Turkmenia	72.70	72.90	70.80
Tadzhikistan	66.80	64.80	62.70

Sources: Occupational data: *Nar.Khoz.* Population data: 1970, *Itogi vsesoyuznoi perepisi naseleniya 1970 goda* Vol.II p.13; 1975 and 1979, G.S. Baldwin, *Population Projections by age and sex*, Bureau of the Census Washington, 1979, p.17.

The data in this table also show that participation rates in 1970 were already much lower than the Soviet average. This, of course, should not be interpreted as open unemployment. Central Asia still has a different and more traditional social structure. Families and birth rates are high, and female participation rates are therefore lower than the Soviet average. Private agriculture also plays a more important role than elsewhere. Whereas the absolute height of the participation rates is not an indicator for unemployment but for the level of industrialisation and modernisation of different Soviet regions, this is not the case with respect to the decline in participation rates. It is not a sign of unemployment if it is due to an increase in the proportion of pupils and students 16 years of age and older. This has been analysed in Table 10.7.

Table 10.7: *Pupils and students in day-schools, 16 Years of age and over, in the Central Asian republics and in Kazakhstan.*

| Republic | 1970 | | 1979 | |
	000s	Per cent of the population of working age	000s	Per cent of the population of working age
USSR	6,437	5.5	8,223	5.7
Kazakhstan	333	5.1	478	6.3
Kirgizia	65	4.9	91	5.7
Uzbekistan	252	5.1	386	5.2
Turkmenia	41	4.3	57	4.3
Tadzhikistan	61	5.0	77	4.4

Sources: Nar.Khoz. of the Republics in question. Number of pupils in vocational-technical day-schools, own estimates. For more details *see:* A.-J. Pietsch, R. Uffhausen, *Arbeitskraftepotential und Migrationsverhalten in den Zentralasiatischen Republiken und Kazakhstan*, in *Osteuropa-Wirtschaft* (1984), 1.

With the exception of Tadzhikistan, considerable effort has been made to raise the educational level of Central Asia's youth. This is especially important if one considers the large number of children and youngsters of school age. But the increase in the number of pupils and students in the relevant age group can only partly explain the decline in participation rates. The same can be said of the increase in the proportion of army recruits. There is also a demographic reason for this. Following Feshbach's estimate that 80 per cent of the age group 18 to 20 years are in the armed forces, their proportion in relation to the total population rises when the numbers in these age groups are higher. That this has been the case can be seen in Table 10.8.

In Table 10.9 the combined effect of the higher proportions of students, pupils and soldiers on the employment situation is examined. This is done by adding the number of pupils, students and recruits, as shown in Tables 10.7 and 10.8, to the number of employed persons in the social sector. It turns out that this does

Table 10.8: *Recruits in the Central Asian Republics and in Kazakhstan in 1970 and 1979.*

Republic	000s	1970 Per cent of the population of working age	000s	1979 Per cent of the population of working age
Central Asia	274	3.2	479	3.7
Kazakhstan	207	3.2	290	3.5

Sources: Own calculations based on estimates of M. Feshbach, 'Prospects of Outmigration from Central Asia and Kazakhstan in the Next Decade, in, Joint Economic Committee (ed.), *Soviet Economy in a Time of Change* (Washington, 1979), and M. Feshbach and S. Rapawy, Population and Manpower Trends and Policies, U.S. Department of Commerce, unpublished manuscript, May 1976, p.26.

not stabilise participation rates. As it is not feasible that private agriculture, though expanding in Central Asia, has absorbed much of the additional labour force, a certain degree of unemployment must have come into existence. This is also confirmed in the Soviet literature. In *Planovoe Khozyaistvo*, for instance, it is stated that young people have problems finding work especially in the towns.[20] Starting from the hypotheses that in 1970 there was no unemployment, and discounting the effects of a higher proportion of pupils, students and recruits, unemployment in Central Asia can be estimated to be 4 per cent.

Table 10.9: *Proportion of annual average of employed persons, plus pupils and students aged 16 years and older plus recruits (per cent of total population of working age)*

	1970	1979
Central Asia	79.49	74.06
Kazakhstan	82.65	80.82

Sources: See Tables 20–22.

How does this fit in with Kornai's theory? Is it in contradiction to it? We see that the process of absorbing additional labour, shown for the Soviet Union in Figure 1, has been interrupted in Central Asia. But this was not due to a slackening of the expansion drive of the firms, nor to more rigid budget control. It is caused by an extraordinary growth in population and by the unwillingness of Asian people to move to other regions of the USSR. This reduced mobility has its reasons mostly in cultural barriers, which,

however, will not be unsurmountable, if one takes into consideration that unemployed people in the Soviet Union do not get any
state subsidies. For some time parents will help their unemployed
children, but they cannot do this in the long run. Therefore, there
will probably be a certain degree of temporary out-migration of
younger people. However, in the light of Kornai's theory, one
should ask why the expansion drive of the enterprises was not
strong enough to integrate the additional manpower. Obviously
there is a budget constraint in some cases even before the resource
constraint is reached.

This probably has to do with some sort of self-restriction. My
hypothesis is that the expansion drive of a given period depends on
what level of expansion beyond plan has been achieved in the
previous period and on the possibilities to find untapped resources. But this hypothesis needs further investigation. It would
have been interesting to see if expansion of employment beyond
the plan has increased now that there are additional resources and
if enterprises have changed their hoarding behaviour. But this
cannot be done for lack of data.

Another question to be asked is why Soviet planners did not
take measures to create more work places in Central Asia. The
demographic situation and unwillingness of Asian people to move
from their native regions were known a long time ago.

SHORTAGE OF LABOUR AND 'UNEMPLOYMENT ON THE JOB'

Kornai's theory does not only help to explain the process of
absorption of reserve labour by the expansion drive at all levels of
the economic bureaucracy but also the slack inside the factories,
which accompanies shortage on the labour market. Kornai has
called it 'unemployment on the job'.[21] Slack in the use of labour
inside the factories can be permanent or temporary. Shortage
induces the firms to hoard labour. It is an act of prudence for the
firm to keep superfluous labour because of the losses caused by
turnover and because sooner or later the firm may expand, and the
superfluous labour will then be needed. This is often criticised in
the Soviet literature. Displacement of workers because of technical progress is often combined with expansion of the enterprise so
that high proportions of displaced workers get a new job in the
same enterprise and only a small proportion is released onto the

labour market. Aitov, who investigated displacement by technical progress in the Bashkir region, indicated that this proportion was 20 per cent.[22] Shchekino's results were similar. A tendency to hoard is also induced by the central allocation of labour. If superfluous labour were to be released, the lower number of staff would be prescribed in the next plan as an obligatory quota.

The second effect of shortage is temporary idleness of labour in the factories. It takes the form of intra-shift down-time caused by bottlenecks of labour itself (e.g. when workers indispensable for the collective activity have not come to work), or by bottlenecks of other sources (e.g. when materials have not arrived, parts are missing or machinery breaks down). Because such events are frequent occurrences in Soviet factories, a greater reserve army of workers is needed inside the factory. This is necessary to compensate for down-time after the required materials arrive and in order to produce the missing parts themselves. McAuley and Helgeson have shown that more people are employed in this 'back-yard' production than in the enterprises specialising in these products.[23]

Other reasons for enterprises keeping the labour they need only temporarily is the need to send workers to the harvest campaigns or to help in local projects such as the building of hospitals, schools, kindergartens, and so on. Working 'in bursts and starts' not only leads to lower efficiency, it also has a more negative effect on the attitude of workers towards their work.

DEFICITS OF LABOUR ORGANISATION AND MOTIVATION PROBLEMS

It is well known in Western countries that shortage in the labour market worsens workers' discipline and increases their bargaining power for higher wages. It creates the possibility for heightened labour turnover and absenteeism. This is the case because one of the most severe threats for workers, the fear of losing their work, disappears. As a result, under conditions of labour shortage, dissatisfaction among workers with working conditions and payment manifests itself more openly. Workers in such a situation not only use their bargaining power to increase their wages but also to reduce their work effort.[24] This problem has become especially acute in the Soviet Union because of some recent social developments.

In 1983 and 1984 the results of some empirical sociological investigations were published.[25] In the 1970s large-scale surveys of industrial workers' attitudes towards their work, executed in the 1960s, were repeated. These studies show that Soviet workers, especially the younger ones, have built up a new value system. Whereas workers in the 1960s ranked the content of work highest, workers in the 1970s had a more instrumental attitude towards work. They are more interested in financial reward for their work, concentrate their activities more on private life than on the public sphere and have many more complaints about working conditions, and especially about 'bursts and starts' in the use of their working time, than the workers now forty years of age and older. This change of attitude has, on the one hand, to do with the fact that organisational problems increase under the conditions of chronic shortage. On the other hand, it has to do with a modification in the social composition and age structure of the Soviet working class. The workers of forty years of age and older were brought up during the war or in the immediate post-war period. The hardship of this time had a long-lasting influence on them. It was up to each individual to improve things. So workers took their own initiatives to keep production going. Their motivation can be compared in some respect to that of the generation in West European countries during the reconstruction period, although there have always been complaints about the low discipline of the Soviet workers. But problems of discipline have undoutedly increased with young workers. The reason for their different attitude towards work, in the view of Yadov and his colleagues who were responsible for a large part of this empirical sociological research, lies in the better standard of living and in the high level of education of younger workers. These two elements make younger workers more demanding with regard to work conditions, organisation of their work and payment.

SUMMARY

Soviet employment has been examined in the light of Kornai's theory of shortage. It has been shown that Soviet employment expanded steadily in the period after the Second World War, absorbing not only growth of the labour force but also integrating social groups working in private agriculture or in the household. This process exceeded planned figures, especially when labour resources were abundant. The process led to a shortage of labour, which was felt more intensively in the 1970s but which already existed during the whole period. This happened because, after a period when the demand of the factories sometimes hit a social barrier (the willingness of women to enter the labour force), it began to met a physical barrier in the 1970s. Since then participation rates have reached maximum level and have not increased any further.

The course of the absorption process of additional labour resources in the Soviet Union provides empirical evidence for Kornai's theory. As he shows, shortage of the factors of production as well as of goods in centrally planned social systems is due to the excessive demand of the enterprises not responsible for their costs.

When one looks at the quantitative aspects of the process, the Soviet example shows that it depends on the volume of additional resources and the commitment of the planning authorities to expand production. On the other hand, this process does not guarantee full employment. The Central Asian republics, which have experienced an explosion of population in working age since the seventies, are finding it difficult to absorb the additional manpower. This has led to a decline in participation rates, which is a sign of unemployment, since one cannot assume that the whole decline was compensated by a corresponding increase in private agriculture. This shows that the expansion drive of the enterprises is a very steady one. It cannot be doubled or tripled within a short time. It is regulated by some sort of self-regulation which may depend on the level of expansion realised in the previous period.

The second part of the paper dealt with the consequences of chronic shortage of manpower for labour organisations, the use of the labour force within the firms and on the motivation of the labour force. As Soviet sources show, the younger generation of workers is less willing to tolerate organisational shortcomings in factory life than their elder colleagues. A generation more critical than that born during the war and shortly after it is confronted with a reality characterised by organisational shortcomings in industrial production, which are intensified under conditions of labour shortage. Shortage of labour, on the other hand, gives them a strong position on the labour market. This enables them to demonstrate their discontent. This demonstration takes the form of reduced work effort and discipline, which in turn aggravates the problem of labour shortage.

NOTES

1. L.N. Kritsman, 'Geroicheskyi period velikoi russkoi revolyutsii (opyt analiza t.-n. Voennogo kommunizma)', *Vestnik kommunistichskoi Akademii*, 1926, no.9; V.V. Novzhilov, 'Nedostatok tovarov', *Vestnik finansov*, 1926, no.2.
2. J. Kornai, *Economics of Shortage* (Amsterdam, New York, Oxford, 1980).
3. *Statist. Jahrbuch der Bundesrepublik Deutschland 1983* (Wiesbaden, 1983), pp.96 110.
4. *Ibid.*
5. A. McAuley, *Women's Work and Wages in the Soviet Union* (London, 1981), p.36.
6. *Ibid.*, p.99.
7. *Materialy XXV s'ezda KPSS* (Moscow, 1981), pp.137, 178.
8. H. Wiegmann, 'Die Situation der berufstatigen Frau in der Sowjetunion', in W. Gumpel (ed.), *Arbeits– und Sozialpolitik in der Sowjetunion* (Munich, Vienna 1976), p.61.
9. *Narodnoe khozyaistvo SSSR*, 1982.
10. See Kornai, *op. cit.*, p.393.
11. See McAuley, *op. cit.*, p.11.
12. McAuley, *op. cit.*, p.36.
13. J.L. Porket, 'The Shortage, Use and Reserves of Labour in the Soviet Union', in *Osteuropa-Wirtschaft*, 1984, no.1, p.10.
14. *Ibid.*, p.60.
15. *Pravda*, 30 April 1984.
16. J. Adam, *Wage Control and Inflation in the Soviet Bloc Countries* (New York, 1979), p.50.
17. Kornai, *op. cit.*, p.258.
18. Porket has estimated frictional unemployment to be between 1 and 2 per cent: see J.L. Porket, 'The Shortage, Use and Reserve of Labour in the Soviet Union', in *Osteuropa-Wirtschaft*, 1984, no.1, p.17.
19. See A.-J. Pietsch and R. Uffhausen, 'Arbeitskraftepotential und Migrationsverhalten in den zentralasiatischen Republiken und Kasachstan', in *Osteuropa-Wirtschaft*, 1984, no.1, p.26.
20. A. Bachurin, 'Problemy uluchsheniya ispol'zovaniya trudovykh resursov', in *Planovoe khozyaistvo*, 1982, no.1, p.25.
21. Kornai, *op. cit.*, p.254.
22. N.A. Aitov, *Tekhnicheskii progress i dvizhenie rabochikh kadrov* (Moscow, 1972), p.25.
23. A. McAuley and A. Helgeson, 'Soviet Labour Supply and Manpower Utilization', 1960–2000, unpublished manuscript, 1978, p.34.
24. See Ch.F. Sabel and D. Stark, 'Planning Politics and Shop Floor Power: Hidden Forms of Bargaining in Social-Imposed State-Socialist Societies', in *Politics and Society*, vol.11, no.4, 1982. p.439.
25. See the survey article of V.A. Yadov, 'Otnoshenie k trudu: Konseptual' naya model' i tendentsii', in: *Sotsiologicheskie issledovaniya*, 1983, no.3, p.50; M. Lewin, 'Jugend und Arbeit, Interview mit W.A. Jadov, A.N. Alexejew und W.J. Schtscherbakow', in *Sowjetwissenschaft–Gesellschaftswissenschaftliche Beitrage*, 1984, no.1, p.35.

11 Productivity Campaigns in Soviet Industry

PETER RUTLAND*

The aim of this chapter is to review the processes of policy formulation and implementation on the subject of labour productivity in Soviet industry. We are dealing here with the use to which labour resources are put *within* the plant.

Most studies of the labour process in the West are based upon a detailed investigation of the behaviour and attitudes of workers and managers on the shop floor. Limitations on Westerner access to industrial establishments rule out such an approach in the USSR. The detailed studies carried out by Soviet sociologists are only published in heavily censored form, and the data which are made available are orientated towards the specific problem which is the subject of their investigation. Despite there being the occasional book-length study of individual plants, there are few which could be described as 'case studies' in the usual sense.[1]

Thus one is obliged for the purposes of investigation to adopt a 'top down' approach, to view the labour process as an area in which the central planners struggle to impose certain policies and achieve certain targets. It goes without saying that such a 'managerialist' approach has severe intellectual limitations. Apart from curtailing one's capacity to explore the interests and attitudes of the workers themselves, it also involves unwarranted assumptions about the existence of these all-knowing central authorities, setting priorities for the development of the nation's economy. However, it is within these limitations that Soviet academics and journalists are obliged to work, and if we are to try to make sense

* From 1985, University of York, Texas, Austin. The research for this paper was greatly facilitated by a visit to the Togliatti Engineering–Economics Institute in Leningrad in October 1984 under the auspices of the British Council.

of and learn from their publications, we must temporarily suspend our critical judgement and accept this paradigm for the purposes of investigation.

THE FORMULATION OF THE PROBLEM

Most Soviet economic policy revolves around the straightforward issue of the growth and development of the Soviet economy, concentrating on data for the output of the various industries, usually measured in physical terms (tonnes of coal, millions of shoes, and so on). But Soviet policy-makers also find themselves engaged in a struggle to raise labour productivity. This is an imperative which political and economic leaders the world over are aware of to a greater or lesser extent, but Soviet leaders would seem to accord a degree of prominence to the productivity issue not found in other systems and to mount administrative and political campaigns on this subject on a scale which could only be envisaged in a command economy of the Soviet type. Questions of unemployment, the balance of payments, inflation, poverty and living standards but rarely find their way onto the public Soviet policy agenda. There can be little doubt that these issues *are* discussed behind closed doors, but they are tangential to the economic campaigns which draw in the mass of Soviet workers and officials who are not privy to the hidden discussions.

The sources available to Western scholars may not be the whole truth about Soviet policy-making, but they are at least a sizeable chunk of the truth. One should not assume that there must be a vast alternative economic strategy being passed down through clandestine party channels. Emigrés have alerted us to the prevalence of corruption, false reporting and manipulation of product quality, but this does not (yet) add up to the displacement of the official plan mechanisms. No doubt the party itself does monitor certain variables and tries to impose policy priorities which diverge from those in the public arena. But the organisational resources of the CPSU are limited—much more limited, it can be argued, than is conventionally assumed in the West—and are concentrated on ideological organisational and political tasks rather than strictly economic affairs. These are still overwhelmingly the province of ministerial and factory officials.

To return to the theme of labour productivity, whence comes this concern with productivity in the minds of Soviet planners?

One can trace it right back to Marx's vision of socialism as an economic system which would be more efficient than capitalism. Soviet leaders still feel under some sort of ideological (cum nationalistic) obligation to 'catch up and overtake' the advanced capitalist economies; for example, the main Soviet statistical, handbook still exhaustively compares US and Soviet performance across the whole range of economic indicators.[2]

However, there is also a powerful pragmatic rationale for concentrating on the productivity indicator—Soviet leaders above all expect growth from their economy, and productivity is a vital source of such growth. Labour supply had continued to expand at some 1.6 per cent per annum through the 1960s and 1970s as a result of strenuous campaigns to recruit additional workers,[3] but this growth alone is insufficient to generate the desired rate of growth of national income.

How do Soviet policy-makers perceive the issue of productivity? We should not fall into the trap of assuming that the problem is formulated in terms roughly comparable to those found here in the West. The present author finds little evidence to support the view that Soviet industrial organisation responds to the same over-arching technical logic as is to be found in capitalist industry, despite the fact that one can identify certain discrete areas of convergence. Soviet policy-makers' attitudes towards productivity must therefore be treated *sui generis*. They can be grouped around the following three themes: economic theory (the 'objective' dimension); ways of stimulating the workforce (the 'subjective' dimension); and the immanent organisational logic of the system.

PRODUCTIVITY AND SOVIET ECONOMIC THEORY[4]

It is difficult to underestimate the extent to which Soviet industrialists and planners are reared in an intellectual environment different to our own. Basic economic concepts such as opportunity cost and the laws of supply and demand are not taught in Soviet economic polytechnics. (This is not to deny that there is a small band of economic specialists well versed in Western economic techniques.) Their approach remains rooted to a remarkable degree in the classical economics of Karl Marx.

Thus Soviet economists approach the question of productivity primarily from the point of view of the efficiency with which labour resources are utilised, labour (as opposed to capital) being seen as the source of all economic wealth. The practical implications of this theoretical commitment are complex and to some extent contradictory, particularly when it comes to the implications for investment policy. They draw from Marx the idea that automation and mechanisation are the decisive factors in reducing the 'socially necessary labour expenditure'. This view can be traced up from Lenin's fascination with the electrification plan, through Stalin's injunction to 'master technology' during the first five-year plan, to the 'scientific-technical revolution' of the 1960s. Its most concrete manifestation is the very high rate of accumulation of capital which has been sustained throughout the Soviet era, at a rate roughly 40 per cent higher than in the OECD countries.[5]

However, this programme of investment and automation has not produced the desired results, for the means of production thus created have not been efficiently utilised. The causes lie in the highly centralised system of plan targets, the absence of incentives for the efficient use of resources at plant level, and so on. The piling up of investment completely outran the supply of manpower on the labour market, with the result that by 1983 over 10 per cent of work places were standing idle.[6] Capital productivity is a category which Soviet economists have been reluctant to recognise as legitimate, and received little direct attention in the past.[7] As a result, indices of capital use have shown a steady decline since the 1950s, and inefficiency in the use of capital is now a more serious problem than the sluggish rise in labour productivity. However, over the past ten years or so, increasing attention has been devoted to indicators of capital productivity such as *fondoemkost'* (capital–output ratio), shift coefficients and machine down-time.[8]

Particular attention has been devoted in recent years to the fact that automation has not so far had a great impact on service and repair personnel, who tie up a far greater proportion of factory workforces than is the case in the USA (38 per cent as opposed to 11 per cent in their respective engineering indusries.).[9] Alongside highly automated production lines there remain large pockets of unskilled, manual workers. There is currently a drive to 'mechanise' these areas (a mechanisation target has been built into each enterprise's annual plan since 1979), from the installation of conveyor belts to remove used dishes in canteens, through to an increase in the output of fork-lift trucks.

Marxist economics separates 'productive' from 'unproductive' sectors, a distinction which is dubious even in the capitalist market but even more tendentious in the Soviet context (where there is not a true 'market' upon which goods are 'realised'—Marx's criterion for productive labour.). Despite the opacity of this concept, it does occasionally shape planners' policy preferences. The most positive manifestation of this have been the periodic drives to cut down on the bloated numbers of administrative personnel (which go back to the mid-1920s.). Less useful, however, has been the tendency to treat service personnel (for example, in retailing) as 'unproductive'. From the technical Marxist point of view this may be correct; they are concerned with the distribution, not the production, of the social product. However, economising on the provision of shopping facilities leads to queues, with 'productive' workers taking time off to stand in them.

PRODUCTIVITY AND THE WORKFORCE

If investment and automation are seen as providing the 'objective' framework for improvements in productivity, Soviet economic policy also recognises a 'subjective' side to the problem: that the workers and managers must be stimulated to realise the potential of the machinery. These stimuli operate on both a 'material' and a 'moral' plane.

Material rewards (i.e. wages) consist of two elements: the tariff wage (about 70 per cent of total earnings) and the various bonuses for overfulfilment, innovation, and so on.[10] The tariff system is designed to reward the 'scientifically measurable' contribution of each worker, in accordance with the principle of 'equal pay for equal work', by means of a system of national job evaluation, supplemented by coefficients for unpleasant conditions, inhospitable regions, training, industrial sector, and so on. The drawing up of tariff scales is such a centralised and bureaucratic process that the incentive impact of the tariff wage is barely discernible on the shop floor.

Bonus schemes must therefore play the decisive role in stimulating the workforce to higher productivity. Three problems dog this sphere. First, there is the question of whether the management itself has the incentive to use bonus schemes to improve efficiency. This will be examined in closer detail in the section on organisation below; suffice it to say here that the dominant motivation of managers in disbursing the bonus fund would seem to be to attract and secure reliable workers in conditions of general labour scarcity—a situation conducive to the awarding of high bonus payments but not one in which great care is exercised to ensure that they are justified by higher productivity. In any event, 'the workers who receive bonuses often do not know precisely for what they are receiving them'.[11]

Second, the continuing scarcity of consumer goods undermines the value of monetary rewards. Even the most industrious and innovative worker is unlikely to garner 100 rubles of bonus in a month (average total monthly pay is around 190 rubles). This is roughly the price of a good watch, or one third of the price of a black and white television. Beyond these basic necessities of modern life, the availability of goods plummets and prices rocket. Non-monetary material rewards may be a better instrument for stimulating workers—priority in flat allocation, holiday places, and so forth.

The third problem with the bonus system is its complex and confusing nature. Soviet economists are united in their recognition of this problem but tend to draw somewhat contradictory conclusions. Some argue that managers are so tied down by central regulations that they cannot, for example, offer significant incentives to engineering personnel. Others point to the ease with which managers 'find' bonuses for workers in short supply (as described above). Shkurko even talks of a system of 'resultism' (*vyvodilovka*), whereby managers manipulate the bonus regulations to award bonuses to those workers whom they consider to be 'deserving'.[12]

Either way, the Soviet problem with incentives is not, as is frequently assumed in the West, a result of a distaste for differentials *per se*. The difficulties stem from an inability to so organise the incentive schemes as to reward efficient work.

As for moral incentives, these should be seen as part of the Soviet ideological tradition of seeing economic problems as amenable to political and ideological solutions: an intensification of *effort* and a heightening of politial consciousness will break down the barriers and realise the innate potential for greater efficiency.

'Effort' and 'consciousness' are abstract, politico-psychological categories; how is one to try to relate them to economic performance? The Soviets view consciousness as something which *can* be positively measured, via indices of participation. Thus, for example, the following involvement was claimed for the year 1981:[13]

Social bureaus (economic analysis, design teams, etc.)	4.7m
Inventors' clubs (VOIR)	20.0m
Production conferences:	
directly	5.5m
attending meetings	40.0m
Socialist competition	106.0m

This emphasis on participation extends across the spheres of both politics and economics in the USSR. On the political front, Western commentators have concentrated their critical attention on the formal and ritualistic nature of much of these activities. On the economic side, Soviet writers argue that participation is not only intrinsically valuable (as is also the case for politics) but also that it produces positive economic results. This sort of participation may be divided into two types: involvement in factory decision-making (as in the production conferences, VOIR and economic bureaus in the table above), and participation in mass campaigns—typically, those under the banner of 'socialist competition'. The most serious attempt to promote involvement in decision-making in recent years has been the brigade system, which is the subject of a separate section below.

As for the moral-political campaigns, these involve a wide range of titles, honours and awards for noteworthy performance on the shop floor. In practice, most of the moral incentives are also accompanied by monetary rewards. 'Socialist competition' itself is a process whereby different groups of workers, ranging from individuals up to factories or even entire cities, set themselves specific targets, usually in 'competition' with another group. Considerable attention is devoted to these campaigns, with the winners being lauded in the press, and the results of the periodic national campaigns being discussed at Politburo level. Since 1978 there has been a policy of trying to integrate the targets set in socialist competition with the formal system of plan targets, with the 'socialist obligations' and 'counter plans' which are drawn up by or on behalf of the workers being written into the plan itself.

Running socialist competition is undoubtedly an important part of the party's work at regional and local level, but it is debatable whether it has a significant impact on productivity levels on the shopfloor. The campaigns are run in a formal, ritualistic manner, with the workers barely aware even that they are competing. Even if one does come across a campaign closely tied in to actual performance, one is likely to find that the criteria for success in the socialist competition contradict the principal bonus-determining

plan indicators. Generally speaking, enthusiasm is a blunt instrument when it comes to promoting industrial efficiency. It is
difficult to 'fine tune' it to changing production requirements. In as
much as it works via the building-up of a sense of solidarity
amongst the workforce, it will tend towards egalitarianism,
undermining individual material incentives. Above all, there are
limits to the extent to which people can constantly 'enthuse'. It
may suffice to see the plant through the rush of work to meet plan
targets at the end of the year ('storming', *shturmovshchina*; or 'all
hands on deck!' *avral*!); but in the long run even this spasmodic
display of enthusiasm must start to pall. Thus moral incentives
schemes *may* play a role in promoting a good 'psychological
climate' in the enterprise and in bolstering the CPSU's sense of
purpose, but they are unlikely to be the key to increased
efficiency.

Perhaps the most widely publicised moral 'crusade' of recent
years was the Andropov discipline campaign of 1982–83.[14]
(Although it has come to be associated with his name, it is safe to
assume that it had been planned before he took over as CPSU
General Secretary.) One should recall, however, that these sorts
of campaigns have been a feature of Soviet industrial life for over
half a century. They may have played a role in inculcating some
kind of rudimentary work ethic in the peasants who flocked to the
factories during the early five-year plans. But in a modern
industrial environment, discipline problems stem from a whole
range of complex social problems (alcoholism, poor housing,
blocked career paths, children, etc.) which are not amenable to
direct political assault. It is even doubtful whether the Soviet
political apparatus is itself capable of mounting such a programme.
Consider the following results from a survey of 12,500 discipline
offenders in factories in the Gorky region in 1977:[15]

Q: *Who talked to you about matters of work discipline?*

Foreman	82%
Personnel department	51%
Comrades at work	46%
Shop head	42%
Trade-union worker	26%
Regional cadres commission	8%
Party worker	7%
Komsomol worker	5%

Thus the influence exercised by the political agencies (the Party, Komsomol and trade unions) would seem to be much weaker than Soviet political rhetoric suggests.

PRODUCTIVITY AND ORGANISATION[16]

Finally, we must examine the organisational characteristics of Soviet productivity drives. Efficiency is not seen as the product of invisible economic laws, as under capitalism; it is something which must be realised through specific measures of planning and administration. To do justice to this massive subject would require a multi-volume work; here we will merely attempt to sketch out a few initial hypotheses. We will begin, however, with brief summaries of two case studies of recent innovatory campaigns.

The Shchekino Method: 'Same Output, Fewer Workers'[17]

It is widely recognised that Soviet managers tend to bid for as many inputs as they can cajole out of the central planners, and that incentives to shed excess stocks or labour are weak to non-existent. In 1967 the Ministry of Chemical Production introduced an experiment in the Shchekino combine whereby workers and managers would be allowed to share directly in any savings which may result from running the plant with less than the initially targeted labour force. By 1970 the combine was deemed to have 'saved' some 15 per cent of the workforce, principally by means of better work organisation, with workers taking on more machines or doing jobs previously reserved for other trades.

The scheme was approved by the Council of Ministers and spread steadily across Soviet industry. By 1982 some 21 million workers in over 11,000 enterprises were operating under the method to some degree. However, in the course of the 1970s the scheme came in for some severe criticism. It was argued that the method merely bought out existing inefficiencies and had nothing to offer 'good' plants. Ministry officials seem to have shared this view, for they tended to claw back any savings which firms achieved by raising plan targets in subsequent years. The scheme was most popular in continuous process industries; in engineering it was found to conflict with their already 'tight' production norms. Step by step, these sorts of grouses led to the incorporation of the scheme into standard ministerial procedures.

In 1979 a new method of calculating plans in terms of 'normative net output' (NNO) was introduced, and it included a requirement to calculate 'wage normatives' of labour costs per ruble of output. This is a logical consequence of the way of thinking behind the Shchekino method but is so bewilderingly complicated to operate in practice that there are murmurings (1984) that the NNO technique will be scrapped as discreetly as possible.

Thus, what began as a simple device for cutting through the mass of conventional practices which maintained the inefficient status quo eventually became yet another thread in the dense web of bureaucratic regulations confronting the Soviet manager.

The Brigade System in Soviet Industry[18]

Brigades have been around in Soviet industry for a long time, but previously they had only a formal, political role. Around 1970, however, certain plants and building sites began using the brigade system as a device to raise labour productivity. Work would be allocated not on an individual basis but to the brigade as a whole. This made the foreman's job easier and was expected to lead to greater cooperation and self-discipline amongst the workers. The new system was rapidly taken up by the political leadership; not only did its proponents claim that it raised productivity by between 10 and 15 per cent but also it accorded with their ideological commitment to collectivism and to self-management in the prevailing state of 'developed socialism'.[19] By the end of 1983 some 65 per cent of workers in industry were working in collective contract brigades.[20]

The new brigades have undoubtedly scored some major successes; for example, the Kaluga turbine factory, with its democratic hierarchy of brigade councils, or in the construction of the export gas pipeline—a triumph which catapulted the deputy minister responsible (Yu.P. Batalin) to the headship of the State Committee on Labour and Social Problems.

However, a detailed reading of the Soviet press reveals that the actual performance of brigades has been very mixed. Work study engineers recognise that individual piece-work cannot be beaten as the most efficient incentive structure of certain technological conditions. Also there have been reports of social conflicts within brigades, with individual workers (particularly the highly skilled) resenting the loss of their high individual bonuses. The division of labour between foreman and brigadier is unclear; the latter commands the loyalty of the workers (although he is appointed, not elected), but the foreman still carries formal responsibility for the running of the shop.

Above all, the brigade method has been undermined by pressures from the surrounding economic environment.[21] The much-vaunted Zlobin construction brigades ran aground when supplies failed to materialise, making a nonsense of the idea of fixed completion dates.[22] Management are under such pressure to fulfil output targets that they are not prepared to devote the attention and resources necessary to brigades if they are to succeed. Finally, with labour turnover running at some 20 per cent per annum it is rather difficult to cultivate the stable work collectives which the method presupposes.

The rapid spread of the scheme across Soviet industry can primarily be attributed to its political significance for the Soviet leadership. Even the Central Committee itself felt moved to complain that 'in a number of sectors the formation of brigades has a formal, campaigning character'.[23]

Productivity campaigns in the USSR operate at both enterprise and shopfloor level. Activity at the latter level revolves around the commitment to the 'scientific organisation of work' (NOT). This can be traced back to Lenin's endorsement of Taylorism, and while it fell out of favour during the Stalin era, it has been an important feature of Soviet industrial life since the early 1960s.[24] A vast apparatus of work-study centres is spread across the industrial ministries, drawing up 'normative materials' on the use of all types of machinery and materials. Massive tariff-qualification handbooks attempt to categorise and evaluate each type of job and specify appropriate rates of pay. At enterprise level these normatives are translated into work norms by means of the full panoply of time-and-motion techniques. Calls to promote NOT intensified during the tenth five-year plan (1975–80), and it was credited with one-quarter to one-third of the overall rise in labour productivity during those years.[25]

In practice, problems abound. There is a high degree of purely formal adherence to the central norms; necessarily so, in many cases, since the norms frequently contradict each other (*normy sporyat*). For Western specialists, the idea of scientific work organisation is itself highly controversial; when it is locked into a centralised system of calculation and control, one's doubts about its viability begin to multiply.

The drive to improve work organisation has little momentum of its own; work study engineers, for example, lack the authority to deflect line management from their concentration upon meeting the primary plan targets of output and quality control. The central authorities have to resort to a succession of campaigns to try to maintain some momentum behind the NOT movement: work organisation cards, the certification of workplaces, model workplace designs, personal plans (*lichnye plany*) and so on.

THE IMPACT OF ADMINISTRATIVE INITIATIVES

Above the shop floor, a whole battery of administrative mechanisms come into play to influence managerial behaviour. It is the manager who is ultimately responsible for the efficient combination of the productive resources allocated to the plant. They are subject to pressure along two dimensions. First, there are the basic plan targets laid down by Gosplan. With the passage of time these have tended to increase in number and complexity (despite periodic attempts to check this trend), as attention has broadened beyond crude output to include such indicators as labour productivity, quality control and adherence to sales contracts. Second, there are all sorts of control agencies paralleling Gosplan which also lay down instructions and incentives for plant directors: Gosbank, the State Committee on Science and Technology, and so on.

Thus the Soviet economic system exhibits the well-known bureaucratic characteristic of creating a new institution or organisational channel for each new problem which comes to its attention.[26] One should not imagine that the command economy consists of a set of rigid bureaucratic hierarchies; Zaleski has shown how the Soviet economy from its very inception has been characterised by a constant and disorientating organisational flux, while Schroeder argues that by the 1960s and 1970s they have become locked into a 'treadmill' of spurious reforms.[27] These administrative campaigns are found across the whole spectrum of economic activity—quality control, innovation, labour training, discipline, and so on. One Soviet commentator even managed to turn this plethora of administrative initiatives into a virtue: 'The forms and methods of economic management must be changed as frequently as a child grows out of its clothes'.[28] We shall argue below that the actual situation is far less rosy.

The campaigns follow a broadly similar pattern. They may be initiated at either central or local level, the brainchild of an individual ministerial department or of a particular factory director. At local level they are most likely to come from one of the large, prestigious plants, such as the Lvov electrical factory or the 'Svetlana' association in Leningrad. One should recall that efficiency levels vary considerably between different plants. While some productivity problems are to be found across the board, others may have been tackled much more successfully in some plants than others. Thus the efficiency problem boils down in many cases to raising the general level of industry to that attained in the best enterprises; this is why campaigns frequently take the form of 'the exchange of experience by leading factories'.

The new technique will run for a few years, produce positive results and will be written up in local newspapers. It will be mentioned in reports on the region's performance and may be recommended by the regional party committee or ministry, after which it will start to be adopted by other plants in the area. Some experiments end here, others may go on to feature in the national press, to have books written about them and to be favourably mentioned in the speeches of top Party leaders. The peak of success is to be endorsed by the Central Committee and to be adopted as model practice by a joint resolution of the Council of Ministers, Central Committee and relevant state committee(s).

The political coalition of forces behind these campaigns will vary. Sometimes the local Party apparatus will proudly seize upon the experiment as proof of their efficiency and innovatory skills; in other cases they will see it as a distraction from their efforts to meet the plan and will do nothing to support it. The newspapers are probably the most consistent advocates of these campaigns; after all, it is costless for them to propose these changes. They are also prepared to come forward with critical analysis when the scheme starts to run into problems (as they invariably do). The ministries and state committees are most frequent candidates for the position of opponents of innovation. Initiatives will necessarily be disruptive of their established procedures; even if the industry does make room for the scheme, it will be found to conflict with the set practices governing the relationship between plants and the ministry, and between plants and other ministries and agencies.

Alexander Zinoviev has pointed to the peculiar legal status of all
these directives. They are not expected to be legally binding in the
same sense as is legislation in the West; and if/when they fail, it
will be because their executors have not been sufficiently energetic
in carrying them out.[29]

One should not be too dismissive of the impact of these
campaigns, however. It is true that the 'propaganda of success' to
be found in laudatory newspaper articles cannot be trusted. Data
on rises in productivity, for example, rarely makes clear whether it
may be due to a change in product mix or to the introduction of
new machinery, rather than to the specific initiative being
promoted. But it would be an absurd slander on Soviet managers
and technicians to suggest that these campaigns are completely
devoid of significance. If the centre puts its mind to it, it can devise
new programmes which have a decisive impact on the economic
situation; for example, the development of special 'territorial-
production administrations' to exploit natural resources in inac-
cessible areas, or the massive 1982 Food Programme.

Two general points of evaluation can be assayed. First, there is
what one might call the 'supermarket egg' principle. Some 80 per
cent of damaged eggs are broken by customers checking to see if
they are intact, the point being that in certain circumstances
attempts to check and control may actually be counter-productive.
Arguably the Soviet economy has passed beyond the point at
which the centre can hope to gain from direct attemps to
manipulate managerial behaviour. Yet the dominant actors in the
Soviet political system seem unable to swallow the paradox that if
their aims are to be furthered, they must desist from their current
attempts to realise them.

The second and related observation directs our attention to the
tangled web of economic relationships within the USSR. Campaigns seem to be undermined by problems lying just outside their
sphere of influence—as with the Zlobin construction brigades and
supply shortages, described above. One can detect over the past
twenty years a succession of reforms designed to seek out the key
link in the economic chain. First, in 1957 Khrushchev successfully
assaulted the power of the central ministries, replacing them with a
system of regional councils. The scheme was revoked by 1965
because the councils lacked any satisfactory economic criteria by
which to manage their affairs, and waste and duplication had
resulted.

There followed the Kosygin reforms of 1965, intended to

overhaul the incentive structure facing enterprise directors. However, this ran into the sand because it failed to prevent the ministries' continued reliance upon constant meddling and crude output targets. (A virtual reversal of the situation after 1957.) In the wake of the 1965 reforms, the next reorganisation was pitched at an intermediate level, and involved the introduction of economic 'associations' (1973), bridging the gap between ministry and enterprise. This reform has stuck, but did not succeed in arresting the deteriorating economic situation. Reforming zeal has now turned full circle, back to the role of the central ministries. There is talk of the creation of a dozen or so 'super ministries' to coordinate the unmanageably large body of ministry level institutions (now totalling roughly ninety).

The history of the past twenty years must lead one to question whether it is meaningful to talk of economic reform in the Soviet context. There may be something about the entrenched pattern of institutional relationships which make the economy impervious to reform. As Chawluk has observed, we should be talking solely about economic *policy*, not reform.[30] This is a problem which goes deeper than the oft-recognised issue of political opposition from vested interests within the bureaucracy. The CPSU has shown in the past that it does possess the political muscle to override these vested interests when they deem it necessary. It is also true that they are extraordinarily reluctant to raise politically controversial issues—witness Oleg Bitov's revelation that a series of articles on the brigade system and the Shchekino method had been abruptly terminated on orders from above.[31]

Generally speaking, the CPSU prefers to continue with a stream of piecemeal measures rather than unleash a wide-ranging and systemic reform. It is noticeable, however, that the latest, June 1983 experiment (reducing the degree of regulation of firms in five selected industries—to some extent an application of the 'supermarket egg' principle) has required special procedures to try to insulate the experimenters from the problems dogging the rest of the Soviet economy—primarily in the form of having first claim on deficit materials in the supplies system. However, one cannot prioritize the inputs of every enterprise in the land, so one wonders how the experiment will fare when it is broadened to a further twenty or so ministries, which is being planned for 1986.

CONCLUSION

What are the implications of the above for the future prospects of the Soviet economy? The picture may be bleak as regards the prospects for wholesale reform, but the economy described above is by no means a static or decaying one. The very bureaucratic momentum of the planning system, with the setting of targets 'from the base' (*po baze*), or 'from the achieved level',[32] to some extent provides an in-built guarantee of growth, provided that the planners can avoid the sort of disproportions which led to stagnation in the years 1978–80. Labour productivity in industry has itself shown a recovery in the past two years. The annual percentage rise in labour productivity in industry is shown below:[33]

1971–75	6.8
1976–80	3.4
1981	2.4
1982	2.1
1983	3.5
1984 (first nine months)	3.7

In a long-run perspective it is worth bearing in mind that structural factors rather than administrative mechanisms are likely to play a decisive role in promoting the overall development of the Soviet economy. The active promotion of new products and new sectors is of far more significance than shaving a few kopeks off the labour cost of existing production lines.[34] The problems holding back innovation in the USSR have been thoroughly analysed elsewhere,[35] but it is also worth pointing out that the planners seem to find it more difficult to wind up old production lines than they do to lay down investment in new areas. But these considerations take us beyond the sphere of productivity campaigns, into the broader arena of the formulation of plan priorities and the relationship between the planned economy and developments in world markets.

NOTES

1. For a book-length study of one plant, *see* A.I. Levikov, *Kaluzhski variant* (Moscow, 1980). The most detailed studies of individual plants are to be found in doctoral dissertations. Around forty were written on productivity-related issues in the USSR from 1965 to 1982.
2. *Narodnoe khozyaistvo SSSR 1922–82* (Moscow, 1982), pp.88–121.

3. Figures from Yu.V. Yakovets (ed.), *Povyshenie urovyna planovoi raboty* (Moscow, 1982), Table 2.4, p.44.
4. For a review of the field, *see* I.I. Kuz'minov, *Ekonomicheskii zakon neuklonnogo rosta proizvoditel'nosti truda* (Moscow, 1974).
5. P. Gregory, *Socialist and Non-socialist Industrialization Patterns* (New York, 1970), pp.144–5. In the socialist countries accumulation was 28 per cent of national income, in the OECD 20 per cent.
6. *Ekonomicheskaya gazeta*, no.10, 1984, p.5. Figure refers to the first shift alone.
7. Kuz'minov, *op. cit.*, p.202, attacks other Soviet economists for faltering on this issue.
8. *See* the Supplement in *Ekon. gaz.*, no.13, 1983.
9. G. Kulagin, 'Trudno byt' universalom', in *Pravda*, 8 Dec. 1982, p.2. The figures are for transport, repair and instruments personnel in the engineering industry. One should also recall that about half of the work of transporting materials is done by line personnel themselves (Kuz'minov, *op. cit.*, p.123).
10. On pay structure, *see* L.E. Kunel'skii, *Povyshenie stimuliruyushchei roli zarabotnoi platy i optimizatsiya ee struktury* (Moscow, 1975); *also* S.I. Shkurko, *Stimulirovanie kachestva i effektivnosti proizvodstva* (Moscow, 1977).
11. I. Danilov, 'Material'noe stimulirovanie i napyazhennosti plana', in *Planovoe khozyaistvo*, no.10, Oct. 1982, pp.63–71.
12. Shkurko, *op. cit.*, p.207.
13. E.I. Kapustin (ed.), *Organizatsiya sorevnovaniya i sovershenstvovanie khozyaistvennogo mekhanizma* (Moscow, 1982), p.165. This volume also offers a sound, critical analysis of these campaigns, unlike the bulk of the other hundreds of books on socialist competition.
14. Detailed in L.V. Nikitinski, *Gvozd' khozyaistvennogo stroitel'stva* (Moscow, 1984).
15. G.M. Podorov, *Ditsiplina truda* (Gor'kii, 1979), p.15.
16. For details on efficiency campaigns, *see* Yakovets, *op. cit.*, and I.A. Dzhaparov, *Proizvoditel'nost' truda—reshayushchii faktor effektivnosti proizvodstva* (Frunze, 1980).
17. The details in this section are taken from P. Rutland, 'The Shchekino Method and the Struggle to Raise Labour Productivity in Soviet Industry', in *Soviet Studies*, vol.36, no.3, July 1984, pp.345–65.
18. For further details, *see* P. Rutland, 'The Brigade System in Soviet Industry: An Assessment', paper presented to the annual conference of the National Association for Soviet and East European Studies, Cambridge U.K., 24–6 March, 1984. Useful Soviet sources, apart from *Ekon. gaz.* and *Sotsialisticheskii trud*, include: Levikov, *op. cit.*; V.A. Mironov, *Effektivnost' brigadnogo podryada* (Simferopol, 1981); and A.V. Akhumov and S.A. Kharchenko, *Shagi brigadnogo podryada* (Leningrad, 1984).
19. *See*, for example, the new law on the work collective, in *Pravda*, 19 June 1983, p.1.
20. Yu.P. Batalin, 'Effektivnost' kollektivnogo truda', *Ekon. gaz.*, no.32, 1984, p.2.
21. Yu. Pakhonov, 'Mekhanism khozyaistvovaniya', *Planovoe khozyaist-*

vo, no.10;, Oct. 1982, pp.93–7.

22. Zlobin himself highlights this problem in an interview in *Pravda*, 29 April 1984, p.2.
23. *Ekon. gaz.*, no.50, 1983, p.5.
24. *See*, for example, G.V. Poplov (ed.), *Organizatsiya sovershenstvovaniya upravleniya proizvodstvom* (Moscow, 1977), Chs. 8, 9 on the history of NOT.
25. Goskomtrud, 'Osnovnye napravleniya nauchnykh issledovanii NII truda v oblasti organizatsii, normirovaniya i uslovii truda v XI pyatiletke', mimeo, Moscow, 3 May 1979.
26. *See* M. Albrow, *Bureaucracy*, (London, 1970), p.21.
27. G.E. Schroeder, 'The Soviet Economy on a Treadmill of "Reforms"', US Congress Joint Economic Committee, *Soviet Economy in a Time of Change*, vol.1 (Washington, D.C. 1979), pp.312–41.
28. Kapustin, *op. cit.*, p.24.
29. A. Zinoviev, *The Reality of Communism* (London, 1984), pp.204–6.
30. A. Chawluk, 'Economic policy and economic reforms', *Soviet Studies*, vol.26, no.1, Jan. 1974, pp.98–129.
31. *Sunday Telegraph*, 5 Feb. 1984, pp.8–9. For some of the articles that *did* appear, see *Literaturnaya gazeta*: 10 and 17 May 1978, 12 Dec. 1979, 28 Nov. 1979, 12 Feb. 1980, 27 Feb. 1980, 12 Nov. 1980.
32. I. Birman, '"From the Achieved Level"', *Soviet Studies*, vol.30, no.2, April 1978, pp.153–72.
33. Sources: *Nar. khoz.*, *op. cit.*, pp.59–65, *Ekon. gaz.*, 1983, no.5; 1984, no.6; 1984, no.45.
34. Yakovets, *op. cit.*, pp.91–2, 212, talks of the need to keep up with Western developments and informs us that in 1981 the Council of Ministers gave the go-ahead to the production for mass consumption of remote-control televisions, programmable washing machines and video recorders.
35. J.S. Berliner, *The Innovation Decision in Soviet Industry* (Cambridge, Mass., 1976); V.A. Trapeznikov, *Upravlenie i nauchno-tekhnicheskii progress* (Moscow, 1983).

12 Transition from School to Work: Satisfying Pupils' Aspirations and the Needs of the Economy

SHEILA MARNIE*

The discrepancy in the Soviet Union between the 'pyramid of job preferences' of school-children and the 'nation's pyramid of requirements' has been the subject of much discussion since the mid-1960s, when a series of empirical studies into the educational aspirations and career plans of school-leavers were carried out by the Philosophy Department and the Sociological Laboratory of the Urals State University in Sverdlovsk.[1] Much of the blame for this discrepancy has been placed on the system of general secondary education, which has tended to prepare school-children for higher education and not for production jobs. Those children who fail to get places in higher education either do a one-year course at a technical school (TU) to learn a skill or go straight into a production job. These jobs are on the whole unprestigious and have not matched the aspirations of the young would-be white-collar employees. For those who fail to get into the senior classes of the general secondary school, the opportunities to enter higher education institutions (*vuzy*) through alternative channels (evening classes, vocational schools, correspondence courses) have been possible in theory but limited in practice, and the frustration of young workers is expressed in low levels of motivation and high rates of turnover. In the mid-1970s, studies similar to those carried out in the 1960s seemed to suggest that young people were becoming less *vuzy*-orientated. This paper will attempt to evaluate the results of these and later surveys and will look at recent steps taken by the Soviet government to bring school education and the aspirations of school-children more in line with the economy's labour requirements. From the point of view of the efficient

* European University Institute, Florence. This research was financed by a grant from the British ESRC, under the direction of Prof. David Lane.

utilisation of labour resources, it is crucially important, in the absence of unemployment, to match the demands of school-leavers with the supply of jobs.

The development of this 'mismatch' between the aspirations of young people and the job opportunities available to them can be studied in the context of the history of secondary education in the Soviet Union. In the post-war period the shortage of specialists with higher education means that there was a justified orientation in the secondary schools towards the preparation of school-leavers for higher education. However, even in the early 1950s there were too many applicants for the places available in higher education, and in 1958 a reform was introduced which was aimed at orientating schools towards the training of young people for work in material production.[2] Young people were to obtain both a general secondary education and training in a skill or occupation (*professiya*). All young people over the age of fourteen were to be incorporated in 'feasible socially-useful labour'. One year was added on to the ten-year general education, and the schools were renamed 'general education labour polytechnical schools with industrial training'. Since the growing competition for places at higher educational institutions (*vuzy*) favoured the children of the intelligentsia, preference was given to applicants with at least two years work experience.

The aims of the reform were, however, never quite realised. The general education schools were not equipped to provide vocational education on the scale required by the reform, nor could the necessary links between production and education be established at short notice. The network of vocational schools (PTUs) was not sufficiently developed to provide training for the fifteen-year-old school-leavers, who left school after the eighth class, and they usually started work immediately in production with no *professiya*. This means that they were of little use to many branches of production, or that they were hired and given short makeshift training on the job. Those who stayed on for the ninth and tenth classes also received minimum training in production skills due to the lack of facilities available to schools, and very few (3 to 6 per cent) worked in the *professiya* they had learnt. At the same time, their general education was suffering due to the time allocated for vocational training. A 1966 decree more or less annulled the aims of the 1958 reform;[3] schools were now to give pupils a general education with only preparation for obtaining a production skill. However, it became clear throughout the 1970s that schools were not preparing pupils for production jobs, and that the 'labour-upbringing' aspect of their education was being neglected.

The provision of general ten-year secondary education for every child has been the declared intention of the Soviet government since 1966, and the transition to full secondary education is now almost complete.[4] After the eighth class, pupils divide into those who continue in the ninth and tenth classes and those who switch to a secondary PTU (SPTU), or a secondary, specialised educational institution (SSUZ, or technicum) where general education is combined with a more advanced technical training.[5] The SSUZs provide training for the para-professional occupations (nurses, kindergarten teachers) and various kinds of technicians (e.g. in electronics). The SPTUs combine general education with training in a production skill, whereas ordinary PTUs only provide training: secondary education can be completed at evening schools. TUs provide short one-year training courses for tenth-class leavers. Particularly in the past, attitudes to all kinds of PTUs provide evidence of the low prestige of blue-collar production jobs in comparison with those requiring higher education. It is difficult to get recruits to fill the PTUs, and teachers tend to use them as a threat to make pupils work harder.[6] There has been a tendency for schools to keep on their best pupils for the ninth grade and to 'ship-off' average pupils and the more unruly elements of the class to the PTUs. The fact that it has been difficult for PTU and SSUZ graduates to apply for places in higher education[7] has meant that the eighth class divide is crucial for the future of school pupils. The difference in 'desirability' between jobs requiring specialised or higher education and those using production skills has in some cases been so great that PTUs have almost come to be regarded as schools for the 'failed'.

Tables 12a and 12b show that in 1980, eight-class school-leavers divided into two groups: approximately 40 per cent left for PTUs or SSUZs and 60 per cent stayed on for the ninth and tenth classes. The tenth-class school-leavers can likewise be divided into two groups: approximately 60 per cent went to SSUZs, TUs, or *vuzy* and 40 per cent went straight to work. Since the ninth and tenth classes of the general secondary schools are only concerned with giving pupils a general education, it can be assumed that on average approximately 40 per cent of school-leavers receive no vocational training before starting work. Since, furthermore, this 40 per cent will include those who have failed to get into higher education, a fairly high proportion of these first-time entrants to the labour force not only lack vocational training but also any interest in the job opportunities (mainly blue-collar) open to them.

Table 12.1a: *Destinations of School-children after the eighth grade (per cent)*

Years	Total completing eight grades	Went to work	Conven-tional-type PTU	'Secondary' PTU	Ninth grade	Technicums
1965	100	42.5	12.3	–	40.0	5.2
1975	100	2.3	21.4	10.2	60.9	5.2
1980	100	0.5	13.8	19.3	60.2	6.2

Table 12.1b: *Destinations of the tenth grade (per cent)*

			Admitted to study in day divisions of	
Years	Total completing school (ten or eleven grades)	Went to work	Technical school	Technicums	Higher school
1965	100	16.2	–	42.4	41.4
1975	100	55.3	12.9	16.0	15.8
1980	100	41.2	26.9	15.6	16.3

Source: M. Rutkevich, 'Put Labor into the Secondary School Certificate', *Sovetskaya Rossia*, 21 Sept. 1983; *CDSP*, Vol.XXXV (1983), no.40.

The ten-year general secondary school would seem, then, to provide a form of education which is in many ways inappropriate to the task of ensuring a supply of labour to meet the present requirements of the economy. Despite the statutory labour lessons,[8] children at these schools are prepared for higher education and not for production jobs. Yet only a small proportion of them (14.6 per cent in 1981)[9] will be accepted for full-time study at *vuzy* and many more will have to learn a production skill, either 'on the job' or at a TU. The situation is further complicated by the importance attached to work in Soviet ideology. There is a contradiction between the ideology which claims that work should be a source of satisfaction, a way of fulfilling basic human needs, and the reality of production life, where most jobs are routine and dull. The organisation of production and the content of production jobs cannot live up to the expectations of a better-educated and more demanding young generation of workers. This aspect of the problem was discussed in a recent article in *EKO*.[10] The article is based on an interview with three Leningrad sociologists who have been involved in a survey of young Leningrad workers carried out in 1976, the results of which have not yet been published. In it the contradiction between young people's upbringing and their first experience of work is stated clearly:

From childhood onwards a person is told that his/her future place in society and success in life will be connected with work, that in work, above all else, he will attain dignity, independence and find the meaning of existence. Thus long before he begins work, his attitude to work has to some extent already been formed. . . But when these somewhat idealistic views are brought into contact with reality, reality does not always live up to these youthful dreams and problems arise (p.111).

The result of this contradiction is young people's indifferent attitude to work:

There have been fairy-tales circulating which imply that every boy and girl will one day grow up, study, and find a creative, extraordinarily interesting and pleasant job. But when young people reach production, they find that their work is rather routine and that it is difficult to find any satisfaction in the content of the work. Moreover, for understandable reasons, they are, as a rule, initially given the worst jobs and not much of a salary. So it happens that confrontation with reality, the destruction of their idealised views on life, means that young people turn to the other extreme—a careless, indifferent attitude to work (pp.121–2).

The article suggests that young workers' reaction to this situation is to 'instrumentalise' work. On the basis of this Leningrad survey it is claimed that the young generation express more concern about their conditions of work and rate of pay than about the content of their work. Since the work they are offered has a low status, cannot satisfy their fairly developed demands and usually offers them only limited possibilities for expressing and developing their personalities, fulfilment of many of their basic needs is sought outside the sphere of work. Thus work is not seen as a need, a source of satisfaction, but is 'instrumentalised' into a means of achieving other aims outside the work process. The views expressed by these sociologists tie in with the criticism expressed in the Soviet press of young people's consumerist mentality.[11]

'Labour discipline' becomes a problem, for the worker cannot be sanctioned, as under capitalism, with the loss of job.

There is, however, some evidence that in recent years young people have become more realistic about their future careers and that they are becoming more reconciled to manual type labour. An all-Union sociological study entitled 'Higher Education as a Factor of Change in the Social Structure of Developed Socialist Society', which was carried out from 1973–75,[12] produced results which have been used to suggest that a larger proportion of both eighth- and tenth-class leavers are choosing forms of vocational training.

Let us look first at the eighth-class school-leavers. The eighth-class divide is considered important in the career plans of young people since until now the choice of continuing in the ninth class has meant opting for a career requiring higher education, and if more pupils are diverted into other forms of secondary education and vocational training at this stage, there will be fewer disappointed and untrained tenth-class leavers. Since the late 1960s the system of vocational education has been expanded and there have been more opportunities for eighth-class leavers to obtain 'complete' secondary education as well as vocational training.[13] The development of SPTUs has brought about the most significant changes in this respect. The 1973–75 research was carried out in various parts of the country, including the Sverdlovsk oblast', and it is the figures for this oblast' that are used to make comparisons with the mid-1960s. Tables 12.2a and 12.2b attempt to make sense of figures taken from four main sources.

These figures seem to suggest that there has not been any change in the proportion of eighth-class leavers either intending to, or actually going on to, study in the ninth class. Those who do not enter the ninth class, however, now have more opportunities to combine vocational training with general education. The SPTUs seem to have attracted pupils who would otherwise have gone to SSUZ or PTUs but not necessarily those intending to enter the ninth class. The difference between the regional figures for SPTUs and the all-union figures may be explained by the fact that there are enormous regional differences in the availability of SPTUs. Thus in Leningrad, where SPTUs have been widely introduced, 43 per cent of eighth-class leavers went to SPTUs in 1978, yet the figure for Tadzhikistan is only 9.3 per cent.[14] Filippov's claim (based on 1967 and 1973 figures for Sverdlovsk) that almost as many eighth-class pupils now opt for a combination of secondary and vocational education as opt for the ninth class, would not yet

Table 12.2a: *Intentions of eighth-class leavers (per cent)*

	1965— Nizhnyi Tagil (i)	1973— Nizhnyi Tagil (ii)		1975— USSR (iii)
Ninth class	40.7	42.8		40.8
SSUZ	36.9	29.3	(21.3)	20.5
SPTU	–		(30.0)	11.0
PTU	13.6	17.4	}	4.6
Work and study	7.4	–	}	3.8

Sources:
(i) M.N. Rutkevich (ed.), *The Career Plans of Youth*, (New York: White Plains, 1969), p.38.
(ii) F.R. Filippou, *Vseobshchee srednee obrazovanie v SSSR*, (Moscow, 1976), p.143 (these figures based on a survey of only 656 pupils). Figures in brackets: *Vysshava shkola kak faktor izmeneniya sotsial'noi struktury razyitogo sotsialisticheskogo obshchestva* (Moscow, 1978), p.92.
(iii) F.R. Filippov, 'Rol' vysshei shkoly v izmenenii sotsial'noi struktury sovetskogo obshchestva', in *Sotsiologicheskie issledoyaniya*, no.2, 1977, p.45.

Table 12.2b: *Destinations of eighth-class leavers (per cent)*

	1965— Nizhnyi Tagil (+1969) (i)		1973— Nizhuyi Tagil (ii)	1975— USSR (iii)
Ninth class	62.6	(48.5)	48.0	60.9
SSUZ	12.9	(16.2)	15.1	5.2
SPTU			17.3	10.2
PTU	17.2	(27.5)	16.0	21.4

Sources:
(i) *The Career Plans of Youth*, p.44. Figures in brackets: *Vseobshchee srednee obrazoyanie v SSSR*, p.144.
(ii) *Vseobshchee srednee obrazovanie v SSSR*, p.144.
(iii) M. Rutkevich, 'Trud v attestat zrelasti', *Sovetskaya Rossia* 21 Dept. 1983.

(let alone in 1976) seem to be valid on an all-union level.[15] The SPTUs have greatly increased their intake. In 1975 they took in 10.2 per cent[16] of all eighth-class leavers; in 1980, 19.3 per cent,[17] and by 1985 they are expected to take in 37.5 per cent.[18] Their further development, as well as the conversion of ordinary PTUs into SPTUs was intended to enhance their desirability in comparison to the secondary general school. The Draft Guidelines for the School Reform propose that the number of fifteen year olds entering the SPTU should double.[19] This would mean that the proportion of eighth-class leavers entering the SPTU could be between 52 and 66 per cent. Providing that sufficient facilities are made available for this intended expansion, more than half of the eighth-class leavers (ninth-class leavers after the reform) will have to opt for this combination of secondary and vocational education.

Figures on the tenth-class leavers are less detailed (see below). Filippov's figure of 46 per cent[20] of tenth-class leavers aspiring to *vuzy* in 1975 (almost half of the 1965 figures for Sverdlovsk and Nizhnyi Tagil) would be worrying if, as with his conclusions about eighth-class leavers he was basing it on the Sverdlovsk oblast' alone.[21] He does, however, appear to deduce this figure from the all-union study of 1973–75 which covered Moscow, Estonia, Novosibirsk, Voronezh, Krasnodar, the Odessa oblast', and the Sverdlovsk oblast'. He gives a sample of regional figures for the proportion of secondary school-leavers aspiring to *vuzy*, which suggest that 46 per cent is a reasonable average, provided his regional sample is accepted as representative. The figures are as follows:

Odessa	55.8%
Tallin	55.7%
Tartu	50.0%
Sverdlovsk & Nizhnyi Tagil	47.8%
Moscow	61.8%

Filippov gives further evidence that the plans of school-leavers are coming more into line with 'the objective requirements of Soviet society' when he points out that the competition for *vuz* places has become less fierce. If in 1969, there were 2.52 applicants for every place, in 1975 there were 2.37.[22]

There do not appear to be any more recent all-union figures. Data collected for either Moscow or Leningrad tend to be relied on by commentators. These have tended to distort Filippov's picture of a more realistic generation of school-leavers since a far larger proportion of school-leavers in these two cities aspire to jobs requiring higher education than elsewhere in the country. This is partly because there are many more opportunities to enter higher education in Moscow and Leningrad (Moscow school-leavers make up the basic contingent of students in the capital), and partly because the white-collar and specialist social strata are well represented in both cities. All the sociological research on this subject since the mid-1960s has pointed to the fact that children from non-manual backgrounds are far more likely to aspire to jobs requiring higher education.[23]

A survey of tenth-class leavers from two Moscow districts was carried out in 1981–82 by members of the Department of Labour Resources at the NII Truda.[24] Of their respondents, 81.3 per cent[25] intended continuing full-time study at a *vuz*, and only 4.1 per cent intended starting work in production immediately after school. Sixty per cent were accepted for full-time study[26] and 17.4 per cent went to work in factories. A survey of two or three hundred tenth-class leavers in Leningrad[27] shows that in 1980, 79 per cent of those questioned wished to enter higher educational institutions (*vuzy*) and 42 per cent got places. Three per cent intended starting work immediately after school and 32 per cent actually did. These figures for *vuz*-aspiring tenth-class leavers cannot however be regarded as representative for the whole country and Filippov's figure of 46 per cent is probably more realistic outside of Moscow and Leningrad.

The aspirations of young people do seem to be slightly more realistic than they were in the mid-1960s and early 1970s (Tables 12.2a and 12.2b). This can be partially explained by the expansion of the system of vocational education. The problem nevertheless remains that there are approximately 2.3 applicants for every *vuz* place, and approximately 40 per cent of all school-leavers are entering the labour force with no vocational training and low motivation for the blue-collar production jobs which are open to them. In a society which ensures full employment and where, as David Lane's paper (Ch. one above) has shown, work is considered to meet a social need, this may lead to inefficiency at the place of work. Since school-leavers now represent the only significant annual increase to the labour force, and since it is the unskilled blue-collar jobs which are being vacated by the older generation of workers, Soviet commentators have been calling for school education to be brought more in line with the economy's requirements. The Draft Guidelines for the School Reform, with their proposals for creating a unified system of general and vocational education, are a step in this direction.

In practical terms the most significant change suggested by the guidelines is that the SPTUs are to double their intake.[28] How this can be carried out remains to be seen. In more general terms the Guidelines seem to represent a conscious shift in emphasis away from the 1966 idea that secondary school education should merely provide a general education as a preparation for work; they seem rather to revive the aim of the 1958 Reform that general and vocational education should be provided for all, that the worlds of school and work should be combined. This is not a completely new

Table 12.3a: *Intentions of tenth-class leavers (per cent)*

	Sverdlosk—1965	Sverdlosk—1973	Nizhnyi Tagil—1964	Nizhnyi Tagil—1973	USSR—1965	USSR—1975
Vuz	82.0 (84.6) (94.7)	49.0	86.7	48.6	80–90	46.0
SSUZ	5.0 (6.5) (1.2)	15.0	–	21.3	–	–
TU/PTU	– – –	3.3	–	10.6	–	–
Work	– (14.2) (2.0)	–	–	–	–	–

Source: F.R. Filippov, *Vseobshchee serdnee obrazoyanic* . . .; 'rol' vysshei shkoly . . .', *Sots. issledoyaniya*, no.2, 1977. The figures in brackets are given for separate raion in Sverdlovsk, in *The Career Plans of Youth, op. cit.*, pp.57, 61.

Table 12.3b: *Destinations of tenth-class leavers (per cent)*

	Nizhnyi Tagil—1971	Nizhnyi Tagil—1974	USSR—1965	USSR—1975
Vuz	22.8	19.3	41.4	15.8
SSUZ	12.2	14.2	42.4	16.6
TU/PTU	12.0	21.0	–	12.9
Work	49.2	43.0	16.2	55.3

Source: F.R. Filippov, *Vseobshchee sredne obrazoyanie* . . . (Nizhnyi Tagil); 'Put Labor into the Secondary School Certificate', *op. cit.*

direction, since labour training in general secondary schools was given increasing emphasis throughout the 1970s and early 1980s.[29] Yet there is much evidence that young people do not use the skills they are trained in[30] and the Guidelines' emphasis on labour training may be a sign of an awareness that education will only cater for the economy's labour requirements if there is more interaction between production and education.[31] A practical step in this direction is the statement that every school should have a base enterprise (as PTUs do at present).[32] In the long term the convergence of general and vocational education and the granting of SPTU graduates with equal opportunities to apply for *vuz* places should make the eighth- (now ninth) class divide less crucial. (In the short term there may be fierce competition for places in the senior classes of the general secondary school; such competition would surely favour the children of the intelligentsia and specialists and would make these classes an ever more obvious stepping-stone to higher education, which is potentially socially-divisive.)

Vocational guidance is given passing mention in the guidelines.[33] In the past this has been the task of various bodies (enterprise vocational guidance, cabinets, commissions for the job-placement of young people, Komsomol). It is now to be coordinated by Goskomtrud and experimental vocational guidance centres are to be set up.

From the labour point of view it would be an oversimplification to see the Guidelines as merely representing a method of supplying the economy with additional labour resources,[34] even though articles have been published calling for school-children to pay for their education through productive work, and for the labour code to be changed to allow more forms of child labour provided it is connected with labour education.[35] It has often been suggested in the past that in order to influence school-children's plans, labour training should begin before the ninth class of the general secondary school, when pupils are already orientated towards higher education.[36] The Guidelines suggest that labour training and upbringing be part of every stage of school education. The change in emphasis towards combining work and study could represent a first step towards making education more appropriate to the jobs which are available.

NOTES

1. M.N. Rutkevich (ed.), *Zhiznennye plany molodezhi*, (Sverdlovsk, 1966); English trans.: *The Career Plans of Youth*, (New York, 1969).
2. 'Zakon ob ukreplenii svyazi shkoly s zhizn'yu i o dal'neishem razvitii sistemy narodnogo obrazovaniya v SSSR'. 24 Dec. 1958, in *Narodnoe obrazovanie v SSSR*: Sbornik dokumentov 1917–73 gg. M. 1974, p.55.
3. 'O merakh dal'neishego uluchsheniya rabot u srednei obshche-obrazovatel'noi shkoly', 10 Nov. 1966; *ibid.*, p.219.
4. Of those completing the eighth class in 1982, 98.5 per cent continued in some way to obtain full secondary education, *Byulleten' Normatiynykh Aktov Ministerstva Prosvescheniya SSSR*, no.3, 1983, p.3.
5. I include 'technicums' under the SSUZ heading.
6. This was confirmed once again in V.N. Turchenko, 'Vazhneishaya sostav-lyayushchaya proizvoditel'nykh sil', *EKO*, no.12, 1983, p.88; and in M. Rutkevich, 'Trud v attestat zrelosti', *Sovetskaya Rossia*, 21 Sept. 1983, p.3. (abstracted in *CDSP*, vol.XXXV, no.40).
7. Since June 1972, the most successful trainees at PTUs have had the right to apply for a place at a full-time Vuz. According to F. Kuebart (*Vocational Training in the 1980s*, International Symposium on Soviet Education in the 1980s, London 1982), it has until now been possible for up to 10 per cent of the most successful SPTU graduates to enter high education.
8. Labour training has always been part of the general secondary school curriculum. The December 1977 decree on general education increased the number of hours to be spent on labour training from two to four hours per week.
9. I.E. Zaslavskii, V.A. Kuz'min, R.T. Ostrovskaya, 'Sotsial'nye i professional-'nye ustanovki Moskovskikh Shkol'nikov', *Sotsiologicheskie issledovaniya* no.3, 1983, pp.132–4.
10. 'Molodezh' i trud', interview conducted by M. Levin with Leningrad sociologists V.A. Yadov, A.N. Alekseev and N.Yu. Shcherbakov, *EKO*, no.8, 1983, pp.110–28.
11. *See*, for example, A. Vladislavev in *Kommunist*, no.2, 1984, p.56. Chernenko also criticised 'young people's desire to set themselves apart, not by their knowledge and industry, but by expensive things bought with their parents money', in this report to the June 1983 Party plenum.
12. The results of this research (headed by M.N. Rutkevich) are published in *Vysshaya shkola kak faktor izmeneniya sotsial'noi struktury razvitogo sotsialis-ticheskogo obshchestva* (Moscow, 1979).
13. 'O merakh po dal'neishemu uluchsheniyu podgotovki kvalifitsirovannykh rabochikh v uchebnykh zavedeniyakh sistemy professional'no-tekhnicheskogo obrazovaniya' 2 April 1969, Narodnoe *obrazovanie v SSSR: sbornik dokumentov 1917–73 gg.* (1974), p.129.
14. Kuebart, *op. cit.*, p.5. Taken from *Sotsial'no—ekonomicheskie problemy prodgotovki molodezhi k trudy* (Moscow, 1982). p.93.
15. F.R. Filippov. *Vseobshchee sredne obrazoyanie v SSSR*, (Moscow, 1976), pp.137, 142. He backs up this claim with figures for Sverdlovsk in 1973, where it seems that 43 per cent wanted to go on to the ninth class, 19 per cent to a PTU (12 per cent of which to a SPTU) and 21.6 per cent to a SSUZ (43 per cent for the ninth class v. 40.6 per cent for a combination of secondary and vocational education). The figures both for those aspiring to the ninth class and those aspiring to SSUZ had decreased since 1967, and the number wanting to go to a PTU had risen by 1.6 times.
16. *Sovetskaya Rossia*, 21 Sept. 1982, p.3.
17. *Ibid.*

18. Kuebart, *op. cit.*, p.5.
19. 'Osnovnye napravleniya reformy obshcheobrazovatel'noi i professional'noi shkoly', *Pravda*, 4 Jan. 1984 (sec. 5).
20. F.R. Filippov, 'Rol' vysshei shkoly v izmenenii sotsial'noi struktury sovetskogo obshchestva' *Sotsiologicheskie issledovaniya* no.2, 1977, p.48.
21. Filippov, *op. cit.*, p.49.
22. *Ibid.*, p.48.
23. See: Rutkevich, 1979, *op. cit.*; *Vysshaya Shkola, op. cit.*, pp.88–97. The latter reports on the basis of the 1973–75 all-union study that of those eighth-class pupils choosing careers which require higher education, 51.2 per cent came from the white-collar and specialist group, and 34.4 per cent from worker backgrounds. Of the tenth-class leavers aspiring to higher education, 74.4 per cent came from the white-collar and specialist group and 38.3 per cent from worker backgrounds. It is also pointed out that pupils from better-educated families are less likely to opt for SPTUs.
24. *Sotsiologicheskie issledovaniya*, no.3, 1983, pp.132–4. Of the tenth-class school-leavers, 72.8 per cent in the Leninskii *raion* of Moscow, and 85.4 per cent in the Kalininskii *raion* were questioned in 1981, and in 1982 the same young people were asked to fill in forms aimed at establishing the extent to which their plans for the future had been realised; 46 per cent of all the forms were returned.
25. This figure is difficult to reconcile with Filippov's figure of 61.8 per cent for the whole of Moscow in 1975 (*Sotsiologicheskie issledovaniya*, no.2, 1977, p.49). The Leninskii *raion* is central and presumably houses a large proportion of intellectual and white-collar workers. The Kalininskii *raion*, on the other hand, appears to be industrial, so the sample of school-leavers may be representative for Moscow. The 81.3 per cent figure is more credible if compared with that quoted for 1974 by L.P. Korolev in *Trudovye resursy i ikh ispol'zovanie* (Moscow, 1981), pp.63–64. He claims that a similar study of school-leavers from one Moscow *raion* in 1974 showed that 83.8 per cent of the tenth-year leavers intended continuing full-time study at a *Vuz*, but only 44.4 per cent could carry out this intention. It is, however, difficult to judge how representative one *raion* is for Moscow, let alone the rest of the country.
26. This suggests that these Moscow figures are not representative, since in the country as a whole in 1981, only 14.6 per cent of secondary school-leavers were accepted for full-time study at *vuzy*.
27. *Shkola—PTU—zavod*; (Moscow, 1982), p.52. These figures are used by N. Turchenko, *EKO* no.12, 1983, p.88, to reject claims made by Filippov (among others) that less school-leavers are aspiring to jobs requiring higher education. In support of this plea for productive labour to become an integral part of all secondary school education, he claims that the actual number of tenth-class leavers wishing to enter *vuzy* has not dropped at all, but is, in fact, rising. He points out that in 1965, 913,000 pupils graduated from the secondary general schools. In 1975 the overall number of secondary school graduates had doubled and was 2,716,000. The numbeer of *vuz*-oriented pupils in this age group had not diminished, but increased, and by the mid-1970s not 46 per cent but between 65 and 88 per cent of tenth-class leavers wanted to enter a *vuz*. It seems, however, difficult to believe that the increase in numbers would justify such a high figure, and the Leningrad figure (Turchenko fails to mention that he is quoting figures specifically based on a Leningrad survey) cannot be regarded as representative for the country as a whole.
28. Sec. 1, para. 5 of the Draft Guidelines.
29. Inter-school production training combines were set up by a decree in 1974 ('on the organisation of inter-school study-production combines for labour training and vocational guidance') to provide training for ninth-class pupils, who can then go onto work in factories in the tenth class. They are equipped and staffed

by local enterprises. There are now apparently 2,482 such combines in the country (*Uchitelskaya gazeta*, 6 Oct. 1983, p.1; *CDSP*, vol.XXXV (1983) no.40, p.8). The decree of 29 Dec. 1977 ('On Further Improving the Teaching and Upbringing of Pupils in General Education Schools and their Training for Work') doubled the amount of time to be spent on labour training to four hours per week, demanded more links with local enterprises and better career guidance. (*Pravda*, 29 Dec. 1977).

30. *See*, for example, F. Filippov, 'Shkola i professiya: vzglyad v budushchee', *Sovetskaya Rossiya* 22 Jan 1984 'Sociological studies at enterprises in the Belorussian Republic Gorky Province, and other parts of the country have shown that only half of the workers who have the appropriate training for highly skilled labour are in fact performing it'.

A low proportion of secondary school graduates are said to use the skill they learn at the study-production combine. The average is less than 40 per cent (*Pravda*, 14 Jan. 1983, p.3). The training given at the combines is also not always recognised by enterprises employing school-leavers (*Sotsiologicheskie issledovaniya*, no.3, 1983, p.133).

31. A recent article in *Kommunist* ('Sistema nepreryvnogo obrazovaniya— sostoyanie i perspektivy' by A. Vladislavlev, *Kommunist* no.2, 1984, pp.54– 64), advocates a system of 'uninterrupted education'. Education should not be a pre-work activity, and adult education should not just compensate for the inadequacies of pre-work general and vocational education. There should not be such fixed boundaries: production labour should penetrate the sphere of education, and education should penetrate the sphere of social production. The amount of knowledge required for modern production cannot always be covered with SSUZ or *vuz* courses and young specialists often cover unnecessary or outdated subject matter. It would be better to train specialists at these institutes as they are required. The emphasis on pre-work education means that poor use is made of specialists and that there is a danger of a polarisation occurring in society between those who have had some form of further education (and who are most likely to want to continue their educational development) and those who have had a further education and can see no point in pursuing any educational pursuits once they have begun their working life. Education must become more flexible. The school reform provides an opportunity to start work on 'uninterrupted education'.

32. Sect. IV, para. 22 of the Guidelines. This is in fact a re-emphasis of a similar demand made in the December 1977 decree.

33. *Ibid.*, para. 21.

34. *See* Sergei Voronitsyn, 'Discussion of the Draft School Reform Begins', *Radio Liberty*, 16/84, (Munich, 1984).

35. *See*, for example, *EKO*, no.12, 1983, p.77.

36. See *Pravda*, 14 Jan. 1983, p.3.

13 Underemployment and Potential Unemployment of the Technical Intelligentsia: Distortions Between Education and Occupation

EDUARD GLOECKNER*

Underemployment may be defined as a discrepancy between the pattern of professional qualifications or level of educational attainment and the empirically based demand for technically skilled and trained specialists in industry. At present it is often the case that the working conditions of specialists require less than half of their present level of knowledge.

There are several reasons for this. The scale of knowledge appears too narrow in profile because the application of Taylorism in the Soviet Union of the 1920s and 1930s has meant that Soviet engineering trades are—according to the educational pattern at universities and higher technical colleges—scheduled in a rather strict and limited mode.[1] But there are many other reasons for those discrepancies and distortions between educational and occupational profiles, between the skills of specialists and the needs of the work place. One important cause can obviously be located in the numerous organisational deficits of the Soviet economy and in particular of industrial plants. One major result of those striking disproportions and distortions seems to be that industrial plants suffer from an excessive supply of specialists and from the inefficient use of their labour.

EFFICIENCY OF TECHNICAL SPECIALISTS AND ANALYSES OF WORK-TIME BUDGETS

In Soviet sociological literature, the engineering and technical intelligentsia in the industrial sphere is mostly designated as engineering and technical personnel (i.e. Inzhenerno-

* Freie Universität Berlin, Institut für Internationale Politik.

tekhnicheskie rabotniki, or ITR). Many technicians with secondary specialist education are included in that professional-social
category in Soviet statistics. In Soviet labour economics, the
engineers' low degree of efficiency and the overmanning and
wrong personnel placement in their jobs have been ascertained
with the aid of work-time budget analyses. If one takes productive
activity to be dependent on the extent to which the work-time of
engineers is used economically, that is, to what extent the
work-time budget of engineers is characterised by the use of their
qualifications, then a concept of productivity results which is more
input-orientated than conditional on output. The Soviet engineer's
manual states, 'Working hours have a great social value which we
must try to use more rationally and in conformity with the
engineer's qualification wherever possible'.[2]

Various analyses of work-time budgets of Soviet engineers and
technicians in the 1960s and 1970s confirm previous observations
that deficits in the organisation of work, specific to the Soviet
system, were partly responsible for the significantly unproductive
use of working hours. The results of Kugel and Nikandrov's study,
which ascertained and analysed the work-time budgets of young
engineers in Leningrad's industry, have been substantially confirmed by the results of an investigation of engineer's work-time
structures in Novosibirsk and Leningrad. (See Mangutov's study,
annex of tables). Mangutov's samples demonstrate that very
differing values are placed on the individual departments and
functional groups of ITR. The coefficients of productive use of
engineers' working hours calculated by him vary between 0.66 and
0.83, whereby the average coefficient is 0.75.[3] A quarter of
engineers' working time was and is—according to this study—
used unproductively. This general conclusion has also been
reached in more recent calculations by the time-budget research of
Patrushev. According to him between 25 and 30 per cent of
unproductive work-time is registered amongst urban employees,
which has led in practice to a thirty-hour week instead of a
forty-one-hour week.[4] The diagram segments show in detail the
empirical results of ITR time-budget distribution (Figure 3).[5]

In the mid-1970s a sociological research study which covered
a sample of over one thousand engineers and technicians in
scientific research institutions and projecting-planning bureaus in
Leningrad, produced similar results. These showed that between
40 and 50 per cent of engineers are systematically used for work
which is unrelated to their educational-professional profile. Their

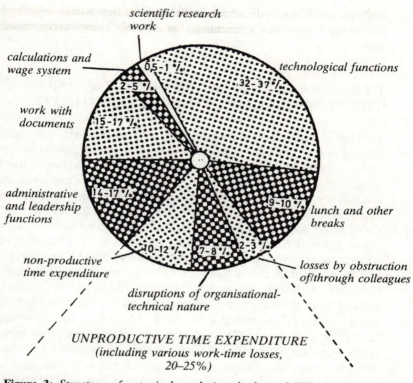

scientific research work

calculations and wage system

technological functions

work with documents

0.5–1 %

32–37 %

2–5 %

15–17 %

administrative and leadership functions

14–17 %

9–10 %

lunch and other breaks

non-productive time expenditure

10–12 %

7–8 %

2–3 %

losses by obstruction of/through colleagues

disruptions of organisational-technical nature

UNPRODUCTIVE TIME EXPENDITURE
(including various work-time losses, 20–25%)

Figure 3: *Structure of a typical work-time budget of ITR cadres in an industrial plant*

Source: I.S. Mangutov, *Inzhener. Sotsiologo-ekonomicheskii ocherk*, (Moscow, 1973), p.81.

superiors estimated that 37 per cent of their work-time was spent on unproductive work, unrelated to their qualifications.[6]

ITR personnel are often subdivided into two basic categories: leadership cadres (management) and specialists (professionals). A study shows that the organisational-administrative and socio-educational aspects of the management cadres' work dominate; for the ITR specialists (departmental engineers) the technological and operative aspects predominate.[7] But in both cases, with a typical bias on the management side, the operational aspects (i.e. the unproductive elements of work-time budgets) have a remarkably high ranking. There has been no obvious change in these work-time structures. But one should also take into account that the more ITR cadres and specialists who receive training in those abilities and skills, the shorter the work-time that will be required for those activities ('learning by doing' obviously takes more time).

DISCREPANCY BETWEEN TRAINING AND THE PROFESSIONAL PROFILES OF THE ITR

To what extent is the Soviet engineer equipped with the necessary knowledge for his job? Various sociological investigations in the 1970s clearly demonstrated the fragmentary and overspecialised educational background of the engineers and technicians in comparison with the requirements of their everyday work. The engineers' specialisation (*spetsial'nost*) compared favourably, but they had to acquire their administrative abilities on the job; 17.6 per cent felt their training at the polytechnics for the function of plant manager to be 'good', 23.4 per cent considered it 'mediocre', and 59 per cent said they had received poor training in this area.[8] Research engineers, whose scientific knowledge was in demand, showed in all analyses the strongest correlation between training profile and professional practice (e.g. 66.3 per cent of young Leningrad engineers).[9] The majority of upper engineering management cadres maintained that there was no discrepancy between college-learned knowledge and professional practice. Podmarkov drew attention to the requirement-profiles of nine ITR official positions, which were described with the aid of four education and qualification grades. He came to the conclusion that—with the exception of the plant's managerial level—almost all functional groups did not require higher educational standards but rather only secondary special education or a lower qualification.[10]

Despite all the differences between branches of industry, size of enterprises, plants or works, and functional levels, one fact came to the fore time and time again: the ITR specialists and management cadres can display good engineering and specialist knowledge, but they suffer from a lack of ability in the organisational area. Only 32.5 per cent of former students of the Kostroma Institute of Technology assessed their ability to lead people (which should have been transmitted by the college), to steer group dynamic processes in the factories, as 'good to very good'.[11] Soviet empirical results show the great problem confronting the technical inelligentsia in Soviet industry: a lack of specialists for managerial positions and inappropriate kinds of

Table 13.1: *Correlation between requirement and training profiles of engineers (Leningrad sample, per cent of all ITR categories questioned)*

Office positions	Activity corresponds completely to training
Higher management branch/level	60.0
Polytechnic teaching staff	92.3
Works and department managers/deputies	77.1
Higher engineers (seniors)	65.7
Engineers (rank and file)	48.1
Office managers, group leaders	50.0
Master craftsmen	37.5
Average all groups	62.2

Source: Otsenka kachestva podgotovki spetsialistov, (Leningrad, 1977), p.76.

training. There is, in addition, a fear of responsibility and of social conflicts.[12] The result is that ITR managerial cadres share the responsibility with other ITRs, which leads to a proliferation of positions. Many ITR positions are upgraded. Technicians often become 'engineers', engineers become 'higher' or 'senior engineers' (*starshii inzhener*) and craftsmen become 'master craftsmen', which also leads to higher salaries.

An attempt by labour economists to set up a 'rational time budget' for engineers (i.e. in the chief technologist's department) led to the following result: of the thirty-seven managers and engineers, only thirteen were actually necessary. On the other hand, twelve technicians were necessary (but none were present) and three (instead of two) technical anxiliaries. According to this study there was a surplus of twenty-four engineers and a deficit of twelve technicians.[13] The actual number of ITR specialists and ITR management cadres in fifteen mechanical engineering plants and twenty tool-making plants was contrasted with the computed norms and the corresponding deviations from the norm. The distribution chart shows larger ITR surpluses than deficits as the final result (Table 13.2).[14]

UNDERQUALIFICATION AND OVERQUALIFICATION OF THE TECHNICAL INTELLIGENTSIA

In this section we ask the question 'Is a policy of increasing

Table 13.2: *Distribution of deviations from the calculated norms in the actual number of ITR (management cadres in the corresponding areas of employment (based on a sample of fifteen mechanical engineering plants and twenty tool-making plants)*

Management function	Less Than −30	−30	−20	−10	−5	+5	+10	+20	+30	More than +30
1. Overall management of basic production (line)	–	–	1	1	2	2	3	2	2	2
2. Improvement of production organisation and management	2	1	2	2	1	1	–	–	1	5
3. Economic leadership (administrational staff)	1	–	3	2	–	1	–	2	2	4
4. ITR and clerks in plant	–	–	–	2	3	3	2	3	2	–
Mechanical engineerng	3	1	6	7	6	7	5	7	7	11
Tool-making	7	8	6	7	7	9	7	5	7	17
1. Overall management of basic production (line)	–	–	3	4	1	3	2	3	1	3
2. Improvement of production organisation and management	6	3	–	–	2	–	–	1	1	7
3. Economic leadership (administrational staff)	1	5	1	2	2	1	1	–	2	5
4. ITR and clerks in plant	–	–	2	1	2	5	4	1	3	2
Sum of both industries	10	9	12	14	13	16	12	12	14	28

Source: A.Yu. Dmitriev and V.M. Pukshanski, 'Opredelenie chislennosti ITR po funktsiyam upravleniya promyshlennym predpriyatiyem', in *Chelovek i obshchestvo*, Vyp. XI (Leningrad, 1973), p.138.

potential unemployment of people with higher (academic) education appropriate?'

In Soviet sociological literature a specialist is defined as someone who has higher or secondary special education and can apply his knowledge through work activity in his everyday professional life.[15] This definitive description only applies to part of the technical intelligentsia in Soviet industry.

Two groups form the exception: the ITR 'practitioners' and the 'worker-intellectuals'. The sub-group of practitioners is composed of those ITR who do not have higher or secondary special education but only general secondary or primary school education. (The official statistics in Moscow attempt to limit the *praktiki* to those ITR persons who have only incomplete secondary school education.)[16] Consequently, their share of the ITR and management cadres employed in the national economy has changed since 1970 (Table 13.3).

Table 13.3: *Educational level of the management cadres and the ITR specialists in Soviet economy (only higher and secondary special education, in per cent of each group, according to census)*

ITR groups	1970	1979
Upper management and organisational substructures	69.7	81.6
Engineering and technical personnel (strict criteria)	68.3	79.7
Lower economic management personnel (local industry etc.)	12.4	24.3

Source: Vestnik statistiki, May 1981, p.66; and Dec 1983, p.60.

In upper management the proportion of practitioners drops from about 30 to 20 per cent, the actual ITR specialists from somewhat more than 30 to 20 per cent and the lower management category from almost 90 per cent to about 75 per cent. Therefore altogether only one-fifth of practitioners are employed amongst the ITR managers and ITR specialists of the national economy. Among the lower management the proportion of practitioners is significantly higher: in a study carried out in 1980 in mechanical engineering plants in Novosibirsk, between 25 and 37.6 per cent of these ITR cadres (the majority are master craftsmen) were practitioners.[17] This phenomenon of underqualification emphasises that in the everyday routine of ITR the quality of the work must be adjusted to these unskilled 'specialists'. Moreover, the practitioners deflect potential applicants for such positions by pointing to their seniority, their organisational ability (party or union career) and their everyday experience of industry, which younger persons do not have. Those younger graduates of a technical school or a polytechnic (*vuz*) then have to switch to other professional positions. This can occur in two different ways. First, those ITR who have received a technician's training can be placed in engineers' positions. In 1981 one-fifth of engineers' jobs were occupied by technicians. In research institutes and construction offices this distortion can be seen even more clearly; there—admittedly ten years previously—30 to 40 per cent of all engineers' posts were in the hands of technicians.[18] On the other hand, many technicians and even engineers choose to work in the sphere of production; they become industrial workers despite their specialist profile. In Soviet sociological literature these would-be engineers and technicians are called 'worker-intellectuals' (*rabochie-intelligenty*). According to official statements, this group 'within the working class' numbered 1.7 million in 1975, in 1981 it was already 7 million and in 1983 about 8 million.[19] Its proportion in the individual branches of industry grew in the 1970s (Table 13.4).[20]

Table 13.4: *Specialists in industrial workers' positions by branches of industry (per cent)*

Branch of industry	Specialists in blue-collar job positions in relation to all specialists in industry/branch			Workers with specialists' profiles in relat. to all workers	
	1968	1970	1973	1973	1979
Overall industry:	15	19	.	5.6	12.6
Electroenergetics	15	.	23	9.5	.
Chemical industry	23	28	33	9.1	15.3
Non-ferrous metall.	22	.	34	7.9 both	12.8
Ferrous metallurgy	28	33	39	8.7	.
Oil refineries	35	.	44	12.7	.
Oil production	27	32	.	.	.
Mechanical engineering/ mach.bldg	12	.	18	5.9	12.6
Coalmining	13	.	23	4.9	11.8

Source: See reference 20 below.

On the basis of the 1970 census data, the Soviet sociologist Klopov combined about a dozen workers' trades into a group of occupations which he characterised as 'occupations with a high ratio of "workers-specialists". Between 165 per thousand and 90 per thousand workers had admitted having higher or secondary special education (i.e. that they were specialists but working in blue-collar occupations).[21]

The official reason for this phenomenon of overqualification, which could also be called 'hidden academic unemployment' or specialists' unemployment, is as follows: the technical situation often requires knowledge to such an extent that certain jobs can only be accomplished by a worker with the special knowledge of a technical school or *tekhnikum*; sometimes they require an engineer's knowledge. The example of a steel-worker at an electric blast furnace shows that 83 per cent of the work is mental effort. For an installater (fitter, equipper) of automatic lines whose work requires between 93 and 96 per cent mental effort, a specialist who is 'predominantly concerned with mental activity' is required.[22] When worker-specialists were questioned, it was found that only a small proportion of them met these requirements.[23]

At the beginning of the 1970s an investigation in the Moscow area showed that only 5 per cent of engineers and only 10 per cent of technicians thought that their work conformed to the profile and the qualification of a specialist. At the start of the 1980s a similar analysis in Novosibirsk (15 August 1981) showed that 10 per cent and 14 per cent, respectively, thought that their work conformed completely to the educational level and/or profile; a further 29 per cent and 50 per cent, respectively, spoke of a partial conformity. For engineers who were employed as workers, the training profile and level conformed wholly or partially in 20 per cent and 46 per cent of the cases, respectively.[24] An investigation carried out in seven Soviet towns at the end of the 1970s showed that 56 per cent of the engineer-mechanics, 43 per cent of the engineer-technologists and 34 per cent of the electro-engineers had not found work commensurate with their higher educational specialisation.[25]

There are great losses to the national economy arising from this occupational distortion; educational investments of from about five to six thousand rubles per engineer and about three to four thousand rubles per technician are lost. Training for a skilled worker would have cost about a tenth of that.[26] A further drawback of this distortion and overqualification is lower job satisfaction and a propensity to labour turnover among worker specialists; they are also more dissatisfied than other workers with their material conditions and their situation in life. But there are also some advantages: the worker-intellectuals, according to another study, demonstrate a stronger social orientation than the normal ITR or workers. They strive for better pay but have almost the same consumer orientation as the other ITRs.

How has the official sociology and ideology in the USSR reacted to the increasing phenomenon of underemployment of specialists, on the one hand, and of overqualification in blue-collar jobs on the other? Is overqualification equivalent to potential 'academic unemployment'? By the 1960s labour economists reacted to the phenomenon of overqualification (i.e. of 'worker-intellectuals') by saying that non-technical or non-economical profiles of education prevailed there. By 1977 this false interpretation had to be rectified. About one-fifth of a sample of worker-intellectuals with secondary specialist education confirmed that their educational or training profile did not correspond to their present occupation. The overwhelming majority of worker-intellectuals could even have been employed as technicians or engineers if there were appropriate jobs. In the same sample, in 1977, over one third of all technicians coming from a secondary technical school (*tekhnikum*) were already occupied in workers' trades. The assumption that they followed material incentives according to the prevailing income-motive to work (because many skilled workers can earn more money in the Soviet industry than lower echelons of technicians and engineers) did not prove to be be correct or decisive, because only 20 per cent of the sample admitted that motive. The majority in the occupational category could not find suitable working places as specialists—for the reason already mentioned.[28]

In the meantime, an increasing number of workers' trades now require higher or technical special education. In September 1977 the State Committee for Labour and Social Questions (Goskomtrud) stipulated a secondary special education as a prerequisite for 388 worker trades (instead of 37 as previously); it referred to positions using automatic calculators, control-panels and other units with complicated technology.[29] The problem of excesses of specialists in Soviet industry has been diminished but not solved through this change. A further attempt at a solution is to be seen in the resolution of the CC of CPSU and the Council of Ministers on the 'further improvement of general secondary education', which has as its aim the stricter limitation of demand for university or *vuz* places, in order to reduce the excessive supply of specialists.[30]

In 1982, 156,500 young engineers and 324,700 young technicians left colleges and technical schools. In the academic year 1982/83, 31.5 per cent of all college students (i.e. 1,676,000) and 32.2 per cent of the students at establishments with secondary special education studied engineering sciences with the aim of achieving a technical diploma.[31] Of the 31 million specialists employed in the Soviet economy as a whole in 1982, only 5,370,000 worked as ITR cadres and specialists in industry. The problem will thus remain topical because a quarter of the specialists employed in the national economy are not using their training profiles or degrees, and this is not just a question of statistical classification.[32]

Since the end of the 1970s ideologists have also been turning their attention to the worker intelligentsia. The discussion about this 'new marginal' or 'transitional' class between the working class and the intelligentsia culminated in two conferences on the role and structure of the Soviet intelligentsia in Moscow (1978) and in Novosibirsk (1979). Two schools of thought were formed and confronted each other on the matter of a further social differentiation. The conservative group (under the leadership of Stepanyan of the Moscow Academy's Institute of Philosophy) was of the opinion that a new 'marginal class' (the worker-intelligentsia) could not emerge in a society with an alleged tendency to increasing social homogeneity; there could only be a professional differentiation, not a social one. The advocates of the marginal class concept (at the Academy Institute for Sociological Research in Moscow), on the other hand, rejected Stepanyan's objections.[33] The theoretical journal of the CPSU, *Kommunist*, supported the sociologists with their thesis of a further differentiation and demanded more realistic sociological investigations of the economy and society in their 'microstructure'.[34]

SOME OBJECTIONS AND CONCLUSIONS

When considering the disproportions between individuals' qualifications and work performed in the USSR, one has to remember that in other industrial societies similar phenomena also occur. The purpose of the above arguments and data is to show that the Soviet Union has entered the growing community of industrialised societies, with all the accompanying positive and negative effects—perhaps some more negative and some more positive, depending on one's outlook. The Soviet case is a special one. From the economic perspective it cannot be argued that overqualification may be reduced to the consumer level of education (i.e. 'cultural wealth'). But it is possible that work dissatisfaction could also lead to a higher evaluation of week-end leisure-time in Soviet society.

The too-narrow profiles of specialists could be bridged by better work organisation or by training on a broader scale, as has been shown by the Leningrad training system. The phenomenon of overqualification does not automatically mean that there is a strong tendency towards potential unemployment. Conformity of the educational profile with the occupational one should at least be called the 'labour market optimum'. With regard to the increasing number of students, we have to realise that the Soviet (as well as any other) labour market cannot meet all the demands for preferred occupations for several reasons. The system of employment does not seem as flexible as it should be. The majority of young specialists apparently wish to find work in big cities which offer a large selection of cultural activities, leisure-time opportunities and mobility. The large modern enterprises in big cities are particularly overmanned with qualified specialists (as are research institutes), whereas the provincial plants are obviously short of those personnel, so that there is a chance for the 'practitioners' category' to survive. The result seems to be that many specialists earn money as blue-collar workers as long as there are not suitable jobs available in those localities. Even if the blue-collar misuse of ITRs is worrying, it should be realised that there is an overproduction of ITR (and other) specialists in many Eastern (as well as Western) societies. This may be considered an economic failure in the light of education costs, and a social failure because of the increasing potential for dissatisfied highly skilled people not to be used appropriately, while demanding participation in administrative affairs because of their competence. This problem of over-supply of specialists would not decrease if underemployment in ITR spheres of work were reduced (as the Shchekino experiment demonstrated), but it will prevail. It remains to be seen whether the recently announced reform of the education system (and the limitations on access to it) will result in effective remedial measures being taken.

NOTES

1. *See* 'Directives and Resolutions of the Central Committee of the CPSU' of June 1983, Jan. 1984 and April 1984, *Pravda*, 13 and 14 April, 1984. This reform apparently aims to bridge the growing

discrepancy between the output of specialist cadres from the higher educational establishments and industry's demand for specialists and qualified, skilled workers. Blue-collar occupations are once more to be recommended to pupils rather than white-collar professions with their higher educational levels. The reform does not, however, go as far as that of Khrushchev, who in 1958/9 partially transferred the training of specialists to production. In the technical colleges attached to factories, the practice of production was to be imparted to prospective engineers or technicians from the start. After 1964—after the fall of the promoter of this reform—this was again revised. Aiming at the system-optimal effects of the 'scientific-technical revolution', the emphasis was placed on theoretical knowledge and the performance principle. Since then 90 per cent of prospective school-leavers from the secondary school (tenth or eleventh class) have wanted to continue their studies at an establishment for higher education (*vuz*). In the middle of the 1970s the rush for the title of engineer or for a specialist's degree abated amongst half those completing secondary school (54 per cent). See: N.M. Blinov, in 'Sotsiologiya molodezhi: dostizheniya, problemy', in *Sotsiologicheskiye issledovaniya*, 2/1982, p.14.

2. *Inzhenernyi trud v sotsialisticheskom obshchestve*. Izd. 3-e. Uchebnoe posobye dlya inzhenerno-tekhnicheskikh rabotnikov (Moscow, 1978), p.71.

3. I.S. Mangutov, *Inshener. Sotsiologo-ekonomicheskii ocherk* (Moscow, 1973), pp.192–3.

4. V.D. Patrushev, 'Osnovnye itogi i zadachi issledovaniya byudzhetov vremeni v SSSR', in *Sotsiol. issled.*, 3/1981, p.17.

5. See Mangutov, *op. cit.*, p.81.

6. See V.A. Yadov (ed.), *Sotsial'no-psikhologicheskii portret inzhenera* (Moscow, 1977), p.28.

7. My own calculations based on S.P. Tikhonova, 'Sotsial'no-professional'nye razlichiya mezhdu rabotnikami umstvennogo truda na promyshlennom predpriyatii', in *Sotsializm i ravenstvo* (Sverdlovsk, 1970), pp.99f.

8. L.Ya. Rubina, 'Formirovanie professional'noi morali v period obucheniya studencheskoi molodezhi v VUZe, in *Sotsial'nye problemy truda v sotsialisticheskom obshchestve* (Sverdlovsk, 1976), p.87.

9. S.A. Kugel', and O.M. Nikandrov, *Molodye inzhenery* (Moscow, 1971), p.139.

10. V.G. Podmarkov, *Vvedenie v promyshlennuyu sotsiologiyu* (Moscow, 1973), p.172.

11. See M.I. Skarzhinskii, *Kvalifikatsiya i trud inzhenera* (Yaroslavl', 1975), p.69.

12. See Davidovitch, Ya.A and S.G. Klimonova, 'Orientatsiya ITR na dolzhnostnoe prodvizhenie', in *Sotsiol. issled.*, 2/1984, pp.111–13.

13. V.I. Golikov (ed.), *Effektivnost' upravlencheskogo truda* (Kiev, 1974), pp.78–9.

14. Yu.A. Dmitriev and V.M. Pukshanski, 'Opredelenie chislennosti ITR po funktsiyam upravleniya promyshlennym predpriyatiyem', in *Chelovek i obshchestvo*, Vyp. XI (Leningrad, 1973), p.138.

15. M.N. Rutkevitch, *Dialektika i sotsiologiya* (Moscow, 1980), p.259.
16. See *Vestnik statistiki*, 12/1983, p.60/footnote 2.
17. E.M. Bezrodnyi, 'Ob ispol'zovaniy kadrov s vysshim i srednim spetsial'nym obrazovaniyem na rabochikh mestakh', in *Sotsiol. issled.*, 1/1982, p.102; See E. Gloeckner, *Der sowjetishche Ingenieur in der Industriellen Arbeitswelt* (The Soviet Engineer in the Industrial Sphere of Work), Bd. 18 (Berlin, 1981), pp.67–71, 238–48.
18. See P.N. Zavlin, A.I. Shcherbakov and M.A. Yudelevitch, *Trud v sfere nauki* (Moscow, 1973), p.233; Yadov, *op.cit.*, p.28; M.N. Rutkevitch, 'Prestizh inzhenera', in *Sotsialisticheskaya industriya*, 8 Jan. 1982.
19. M.N. Rutkevitch, 'Sovetskaya intelligentsia: struktura i tendentsiy razvitiya na sovremennom etape', in *Sotsiol. issled.*, 2/1980, p.71; Rutkevitch, 1982, *op. cit.*
20. *Vestnik statistiki*, 7/1974, pp.93–5; *Vestnik statistiki*, 5/1981, p.65; A.M. Gelyuta and S.P. Gogolykhin, 'Formirovaniye i rost' sloya rabochikh-intelligentov', in *Problemy razvitiya sotsial'noy struktury obshchestva v Sovetskom Soyuze i Pol'she* (Moscow, 1976), p.120.
21. E. Klopov, 'Rabochiy klass SSSR na etape razvitogo sotsializma', in *Razvitie rabochego klassa stran sotsialisticheskogo sodruzhestva*, Sbornik nauchnykh trudov (Budapest, 1978), pp.350–2.
22. See Rutkevitch, 2/1980, *op. cit.*, p.70.
23. E.R. Sarukhanov, *Sotsial'no-ekonomicheskie problemy upravleniya trudovykh sil v sotsializme* (Leningrad, 1981), pp.42f.
24. Bezrodny, *op. cit.*, p.102; L.S. Blyakhman and O.I. Shkaratan: *NTR, rabochii klass, intelligentsia* (Moscow, 1973), p.266; L.V. Kozlovskaya, *Sotsial'nye aspekty razmeshcheniya promyshlennosti* (Minsk, 1977), p.112.
25. N.A. Aitov and R.T. Nasibullin, 'Professional'naya mobil'nost' intelligentsii', in *Sotsiol. issled.*, 2/1980, p.107.
26. See *Vestnik statistiki*, 3/1977, p.95.
27. A.A. Kostin, 'Sotsial'no-kul'turnye kharakteristiki rabochikh-intelligentov', in *Sotsiol. issled*, 2/1980, pp.113f.
28. M.N. Rutkevitch, 'Sblizhenie rabochego klassa i inzhenerno-tekhnicheskoi intelligentsii', in *Sotsiol. issled.*, 4/1980, p.33.
29. See Sarukhanov, *op. cit.*, p.46–6.
30. *Pravda*, 29 April 1984, pp.1, 3.
31. *Vestnik statistiki*, 8/1983, pp.63f.
32. *Narodnoye khozyaystvo SSSR* (Moscow, 1983), p.372, p.124.
33. See Ts.A. Stepanyan, 'Besspornoe i spornoe v diskussii o sotsial'noi strukture sovetskogo obshchestva', in *Sotsiol. issled.*, 4/1980, pp.85–7; 'Otredaktsii', in *Sotsiol. issled.*, no.4, 1980, p.94.
34. V. Petchenev, in *Kommunist*, 11/1982, pp.32–40.

PART IV

Labour and the Law

14 The USSR Law on Work Collectives: Workers' Control or Workers Controlled?

ELIZABETH TEAGUE*

As might be expected of a workers' state that is heir to a revolution ostensibly carried out on behalf of the working class, the USSR claims as part of its ideology that the working class plays a key role in Soviet society. One of the distinguishing characteristics of 'developed socialism', the term used to describe the USSR's current phase of evolution, is said to be the expansion of 'socialist democracy'; that is, 'the ever broader participation of citizens in managing the affairs of society and the state'.[1] In this framework, 'the primary cell not only of the economic but also of [the] entire social organisation' is said to be the work collective:[2]

The work collective . . . is the place where Soviet people implement most of the social, economic and political rights granted them by the USSR constitution. This is also the place where they perform their main constitutional duties.[3]

As our society moves towards communism . . . the social activity of the workers steadily increases. . . . The participation of the workers in the management of production is realised primarily through the work collective.[4]

The work collective received formal recognition when a new article describing its role in Soviet society was included in the constitution of 1977. Article 8 reads:

Work collectives take part in discussing and deciding state and public affairs; in planning production and social development; in training and

---

* Radio Liberty and Centre for Russian and East European Studies, University of Birmingham. The author wishes to thank Dr Julian Cooper and Dr Philip Hanson for their comments on this paper. Responsibility for the overall interpretation rests, however, with the author alone.

placing personnel; and in discussing and deciding matters pertaining to the management of enterprises and institutions, the improvement of living and working conditions, and the use of funds allocated both for developing production and for social and cultural purposes and financial incentives.

Work collectives promote socialist competition, the spread of progressive methods of work, and the strengthening of production discipline; educate their members in the spirit of communist morality; and strive to enhance their political consciousness and raise their cultural level, skills, and qualifications.

It was the introduction of this new article into the constitution of 1977 that necessitated the subsequent adoption of legislation detailing the rights and duties of the work collectives. A new law, On Work Collectives and Increasing Their Role in the Management of Enterprises, Institutions, and Organisations, accordingly came into effect on 1 August 1983.[5]

This is not, as has been suggested by some Western observers, 'the Soviet Union's answer to Solidarity'. It is part of a larger body of new legislation brought about by the provisions of the new constitution. The fact that new legislation on this topic was 'under preparation by the USSR Council of Ministers with the participation of the All-Union Central Council of Trade Unions and the Central Committee of the CPSU' was announced as early as 1978,[6] and the legislation was then scheduled for adoption in February 1980. The publication of much of the new legislation described as under preparation at that time has, however, since been delayed. It is not impossible therefore that, as a number of Western journalists have already suggested, the adoption of the new law on work collectives was speeded up by the leadership of Yurii Andropov at least partly in response to the events in neighbouring Poland.

The new law was published in draft form in April 1983.[7] In line with recent practice, the authorities invited a general public discussion of the document. This was widely reported in the pages of the Soviet press over the course of the next two months.

Introducing the law in its final form to a session of the USSR Supreme Soviet on 17 June 1983, First Deputy Premier Geidar Aliev announced that no fewer than 110 million people (almost the entire working population) had taken part in the discussion, that 130,000 proposals for additions to or amendments in the draft law had been made, and that the final version of the law incorporated some seventy alterations, with only two of the law's twenty-three clauses remaining unchanged.[8] This statement may well be true. A comparison of the draft law and the final version of it, however, reveals few changes of substance and suggests that a large number of those made were of a merely propagandistic nature.

The law has been hailed in the Soviet media as evidence of the increasing democratisation of Soviet society and of its progress towards self-management. The preamble states:

In the conditions of mature[9] socialism, the role of the work collectives in production and social and state life is enhanced; opportunities for active participation by workers, kolkhoz members, and the intelligentsia in the management of enterprises, institutions, and organisations are widened; *and genuine socialist self-management* [samoupravlenie], *which develops in the course of building communism, is realised.* [Emphasis added to indicate words not included in the draft but inserted in the final version.]

Although the law itself is new, it in fact codifies already standard practices at a number of leading Soviet plants and factories, sovkhozes, and kolkhozes. In its editorial of 21 April 1983, for example, *Pravda* singled out the Kaluga turbine plant, the Likhachev motor vehicle plant in Moscow, the 'Gigant' sovkhoz in Rostov, and the Minsk tractor plant. These practices, previously regulated by a multitude of legal ordinances, are now covered by a single, comprehensive law and given nation-wide recognition and endorsement.

POWERS OF THE WORK COLLECTIVE: SCOPE AND LIMITS

A basic provision of the new law is that the powers of the work collective (defined as the aggregate, or union, of all enterprise personnel, including managerial, technical, and administrative staffs) are to be exercised at periodic mass meetings. These meetings must be held not less than once every six months (article 20).[10]

General meetings will have force only if attended by at least half the workers at the enterprise (article 20). The workers will be consulted on a wide range of matters, and their recommendations—adopted by a simple majority on a show of hands—will be binding on the collective and also on the management (articles 19 and 21).

The range of topics on which the workers are to be consulted

seems at first sight to be impressive and truly to grant them
enhanced participation in the management of their enterprises.
They are to be consulted on a large number of matters relating to
the planning and running of production, such as the distribution of
rewards and penalties (up to and including dismissal), the
appointment of shopfloor managers and the allocation of enterprise housing and other funds. In future, the enterprise's production plan will be adopted only after it has been approved by the
work collective at a general meeting. Workers are also given the
right to complain about their managers if they perform badly (thus
adding a new level of control to the existing system). They may
propose candidates for election to the soviets at all levels, and they
have the right to check subsequently on the performance of these
officials.

On closer examination, though, the extensive powers granted to
the work collective under the new law turn out to be of a
consultative and advisory nature only. The legislation is carefully
worded to ensure that the collectives are granted no more than a
participatory voice in the decision-making process. The key words
used are 'propose', 'ratify', 'advise', 'suggest', 'monitor'. The work
collectives will 'participate in the . . . discussion of . . . economic
and social plans'. They will 'hear reports from the management',
'make proposals . . . aimed at . . . utilising internal reserves',
'discuss the state of labour discipline', 'ratify the proposals of
management and the trade unions on the internal organisation of
work', 'discuss the state of communal and medical services',
'endorse measures for raising labour productivity', 'approve the
eligibility of workers . . . [to receive] material assistance', 'consent
to the management's appointment of brigade leaders', 'propose
the names of workers as candidates for bonuses', 'propose
punishment for those guilty of infringing labour discipline' and
'recommend the lifting of such punishments' if the guilty workers
mend their ways. They may 'propose measures for the adoption of
progressive forms of work', 'check the implementation of safety
regulations', 'participate in drawing up plans for economic and
social development', and so on and so forth.

The sole right to 'adopt decisions' given the collectives under the
new law involves the determination of certain allocations—
namely, those relating to 'the construction of housing, children's
preschool institutions, and other cultural and consumer
facilities'—from the enterprise social-culture fund (article 16).

The management, for its part, will be obliged to 'consider' and 'respond to' the workers' suggestions, and the opinion of the work collective will be 'taken into account'. Clearly, the enterprise management and the Communist Party organisation will retain the final, controlling say in the decision-making process. This is ensured by article 1 of the new law, which states that the work collectives must operate 'under the leadership of the organisations of the CPSU' and that their 'duty and obligation' includes 'the implementation of Party decisions'. In addition, the new legislation reaffirms the principle of one-man management (*edinonachalie*) in Soviet enterprises (article 4), whereby responsibility for the affairs of the entire enterprise is borne by its director. This further limits the scope of influence of the work collective, but not that of the Communist Party; the director of an enterprise of any size will invariably be a Party member, and he himself will therefore be under effective Party supervision.

The statement in article 21 that 'the decisions of meetings of the work collective . . . are binding on members of the collective and on the management of the enterprise' must therefore be viewed in terms of the pre-eminence that is accorded Party decisions by article 1.[11] In general, the wording of the new legislation ensures that the work collectives will be permitted only to *participate*—that is, to be consulted by management—in the making of decisions.

This is made even clearer by the fact that those rights that the new law grants to the workers are without any means of enforcement. Article 21 stipulates that the management must 'consider' decisions taken by the work collectives and respond to them within one month. But nowhere in the law is there mention of any action open to the workers if the management ignores their recommendations. A right that is not enforceable is not a right at all.

In addition, the new law states (articles 1 and 21) that the decisions, recommendations and proposals of the work collectives will have force only when they are in accordance with existing legislation. While this would seem to be a reasonable enough condition, it should be borne in mind that an enterprise's production plan itself has the force of law in the Soviet Union. Literally interpreted, therefore, this provision could be taken to mean that the workers will be allowed to make no proposals that the management might claim would create difficulties in meeting plan targets.

The importance of this qualification is suggested by a far from untypical letter published in the trade-union newspaper *Trud* on 23 March 1983. In the letter a worker complains that it has become the rule at his factory to work on Saturdays and Sundays, not because the workers want to work overtime but because the management insists that this is the only way in which the plan can be met. Those who have refused to cooperate are said to have been threatened with punishment or even dismissal. The writer himself had been taken off the list for housing and deprived of his thirteenth-month salary. Management's legal obligation to meet monthly plan targets, complicated by the generally chaotic situation with erratic deliveries and supplies of raw materials and spare parts, is probably the reason most frequently cited in the Soviet press for failure to observe existing regulations on working conditions—especiallay safety regulations—in enterprises. For example, a brigade leader in Tajikistan was recently reported to have refused to clear child-workers from cotton fields that were about to be sprayed by aircraft with chemical defoliants because he had to fulfil the plan.[12]

Another way in which the powers of the work collectives are circumscribed by the new legislation is that their decisions are to be taken at general meetings to be held 'when the need arises' but not less than twice a year (article 20). The collectives may therefore be expected to meet at roughly six-monthly intervals, and their meetings will not be permanent institutions but more or less *ad hoc* gatherings. Moreover, article 20 of the new law further stipulates that it is the trade union and the enterprise management that have the right to convene a meeting of the workers: *the workers themselves do not.* (However, individual members of the collectives, as well as the management, Party, trade-union, and other social organisations do have the right 'to submit questions for examination by meetings of work collectives' (article 20).) Voting at general meetings is to be by open ballot, and decisions are to be adopted by absolute majority.

No provision is made in the new law for the setting up of any permanent representative body that would, in the period between the meetings of the work collective, be empowered to check up and follow through on the management's execution of the workers' recommendations. Quite the reverse, in fact: article 19 stipulates that in the intervals (which may well be as long as six months) between general meetings, the powers of the collective will be exercised not by the workers' elected representatives but by the management, acting in conjunction with the Party, trade-union, and Komsomol organisations.

In only one area is this not the case; that is, the powers of the work collective as detailed in article 5, which include the right of the collective to consider draft decisions of the local soviets, nominate candidates for election to the soviets, elect members of comrades' courts, and so on.[13] On matters that concern the day-to-day running of the enterprise, however, the management and Party may exercise the rights of the work collective between general meetings. It is perhaps superfluous to point out that decisions in this area are likely to have the most effect on the workers' working and living conditions.

Although the final version of the law was amended to require the management and the trade-union committee 'systematically to inform members of the work collective of their activity in exercising the work collective's powers in the period between general meetings' (article 19), no formal mechanism has been created to facilitate this exchange of information or to enable the collective to protest should it feel that its instructions are being ignored.

Indeed, it was not immediately clear just how the new law would operate. One commentator noted that further legislation was needed to spell out the details of what actual legal force the work collective's decisions would have.[14] The new law has accordingly been criticised by Western observers on the grounds of its vagueness. Even a commentator who describes it as progressive seems to have some doubts about how it will be implemented. Thus, the Moscow correspondent of the French Communist Party daily *L'Humanité* commented wryly, 'There's no shortage of progressive legislation in the Soviet Union . . . but whether it's observed or not is another matter'.[15]

Certainly the new law will entail an extension of the activity of the 'social organisations' (that is, the Party *buro*, the trade-union committee and the Komsomol committee of each enterprise), since it is they who are to exercise the functions of the work collective during much of the year. The new tasks of the trade-union organisations were detailed by a plenum of the All-Union Central Council of Trade Unions.[16] It is to be the trade-union committees that will be responsible for informing the workers of the date and agenda of general meetings and, after each meeting has taken place, for checking on the management's execution of the workers' decisions. During the periods between meetings, too, it is the union committee's responsibility to ensure that the *workers* fulfil not only the tasks decided upon at the last meeting but also 'Party and government decisions'. The trade-union committee is also instructed to keep a check on whether or not the management fulfils its contractual obligations under the provisions of the collective agreement between management and workers and, in cases where the management fails in its responsibilities in this regard, to raise the matter with the trade union's central committee and with the appropriate government ministry. The trade-union committee must, moreover, 'keep the workers regularly informed of progress in the execution of their decisions'.

An enormous amount of attention was given to the new law by the Soviet media, particularly during the months from April to June 1983, when the draft was under nation-wide discussion. This discussion focused largely on two subjects, the first being the issue of labour discipline. The new law has been seen by some cynical Western observers as aimed primarily at increasing control over the workforce, its purpose being to get the work collectives to police the workers themselves and formally mobilise public opinion in the work-place in support of official attempts to tighten up slack labour discipline.

That labour discipline in the USSR is lax seems clear: workers are frequently apathetic, alienated and simply unwilling to work. It is not possible to be sure whether or not the situation deteriorated during the immobilism of Leonid Brezhnev's last years, though it certainly seems likely that this was the case. However, the question of poor labour discipline has undoubtedly become a political issue in the USSR and is clearly viewed with concern by the authorities. In the words of Seweryn Bialer, this is 'because it impinges heavily on the ability of the political directors of the system to achieve their economic goals, and because, in a police state, these forms of deviant social behavior are seen as a mass expression of political disaffection'.[17]

THE WORK COLLECTIVE AND THE PROBLEM OF LABOUR DISCIPLINE

Immediately after Yurii Andropov's election as Party leader in November 1982, a campaign was launched to raise sagging labour productivity by tightening up labour discipline. Following the publication of the draft law on work collectives in April, much of the discussion of it was devoted not to its specific provisions but to the problem of how labour discipline was to be improved. It was reported that 'the largest number of suggestions submitted in the course of the discussion of the draft law . . . pertained, in one way or another, to the problem of strengthening discipline'.[18] A lawyer writing in *Izvestia* on 27 May 1983 was highly critical of the number of suggestions relating to labour discipline, saying that such proposals were all very well in a discussion of other legislation, such as the labour code, but that they had no place in the discussion at hand.

The debate on labour discipline was conducted on two levels: the simplistic and the sophisticated. On the one hand, the workers were represented in the media as being in the forefront of those calling for tougher measures and less leniency for shirkers, idlers, slackers and drunkards. Outraged workers wrote to the press demanding that the worker guilty of producing shoddy goods should be fined, that persistent slackers or those who changed jobs frequently should no longer be allowed to change jobs at will, that workers in one enterprise should have the right to veto the hiring of people who had earlier been sacked for reasons of discipline elsewhere or to insist on their being hired at reduced rates of pay, that feckless workers be deprived of vacation rights, bonus payments and their places on the waiting list for housing, that young workers should be required to sign contracts for periods of not less than two to three years, and that details of a person's work record should be entered in his or her internal passport (which cannot be so conveniently 'lost' as a work book because of the greater problems involved in its replacement). Many of the suggestions put forward—ostensibly by the workers themselves—were a great deal harsher than the measures ultimately adopted in August of 1983.[19]

The prominence given by the media throughout the spring of 1983 to calls for tougher measures against errant workers suggested that tightening of social controls occupied a high priority for Party and state authorities. At the same time, the fact that the measures eventually adopted were less severe than many that had been proposed indicated that a compromise had been reached between those calling for harsh measures and those who, though in an apparent minority, had been pointing out quietly but clearly that fecklessness on the part of the workers was only one factor contributing to the sluggish performance of the Soviet economy and that the main cause should be sought elsewhere. Writing in *Literaturnaya gazeta*, for example, a law professor pointed out that

'Infringements of labour discipline may also occur because of poor organisation of production, lack of prospects for professional advancement, administrative inattention to improving working conditions and a poor psychological climate'.[20] A worker from a Moscow automobile plant wrote to *Pravda* to point out that mere discipline was not enough; what was also needed, he said, was order. It was not just a matter of coming to work on time and staying until the time to go home: the workers must have adequate tools and supplies to enable them to work efficiently while they were on the job.[21] A workers' meeting in a Chelyabinsk factory complained that it was not always the workers' fault if they stood around idle; it was the management's responsibility to keep the workforce supplied with equipment, tools and materials, and this responsibility needed to be more strictly enforced.[22]

THE QUESTION OF WORKERS' PARTICIPATION IN MANAGEMENT

In some important respects the debate on the draft law on work collectives did appear to reflect a genuine desire to increase workers' participation in management. Numerous suggestions were made during the course of the discussion that the new law should give workers the right to elect their immediate superiors: not the top-level managers but the brigadiers or leaders of the teams (brigades) into which the Soviet workforce is commonly divided. At present, brigade leaders are generally appointed by the management.

The new law, as adopted, states that brigades shall have the right 'to consent to the management's appointment of a brigade leader and to demand that the management relieve a brigade leader of his duties if he fails to justify the collective's trust' (article 18). During the public discussion of the law, however, many individuals had proposed that this provision should be altered. For example, a Komsomol activist wrote that it should surely be the brigade that made the choice and the management that gave its consent rather than the other way around. This was already the established procedure in some workshops, he reported.[23] A worker on the BAM construction project wrote that the same practice was common there and that it worked well. He suggested that workers should be given more say in the selection not only of brigade leaders but also of middle management.[24] *Pravda* wrote of an interesting experiment in a Riga plant where work collectives could nominate their own candidates for lower managerial posts (master, shop foreman) and then vote at a general meeting for the candidate of their choice from a list containing several names.[25]

In the event, the law as finally adopted was not changed, and the workers were not given the right to elect their own leaders. This was in a way surprising since the proposal had received widespread support. *Sovetskaya kul'tura* had noted that 'In practice, the custom of electing brigadiers has already taken root. Where brigadiers are elected, the social and economic benefits are greater than where they are nominated [from above]'.[26] 'It has been shown', commented *Sovetskaya Rossiya*, 'that the best brigades turn out to be those where decisions are decided in the most democratic way—for example, when the brigade elects its own brigadier, instead of accepting someone on recommendation from above'.[27]

Some time after the law had been adopted, *Trud* judged it necessary to clarify the matter: 'If the brigade members refuse their consent to a worker's appointment, then that worker should not be appointed brigadier. The brigade collective also has the right to demand that the management release a brigadier from his position as leader of the brigade should he fail to reward their trust. Justified demands should be met'.[28]

Another indication that some people wanted to see more participation for workers was contained in a letter addressed to *Izvestia* by a lawyer named V. Kikot', who suggested that work collectives should be represented during the intervals between their general meetings not by the management but by the PDPS (standing production conference, which is elected annually by the work collective at its general meeting). Kikot' pleaded, moreover, that the collectives should be given the right to propose their own initiatives and 'not merely discuss and approve proposals made by the management'.[29]

Many similar suggestions were made. To cite just a few: workers at the Kaluga turbine plant suggested that the powers of the work collectives should devolve during the periods between meetings not only on the management, the Party, trade unions and the Komsomol but also on the councils of brigadies (a specific innovation of the Kaluga brigade system that is fast gaining ground in other enterprises).[30] A worker from Kazakhstan suggested instead that between general meetings the work collective's powers should be exercised by a specially elected body composed of representatives of the management, the Party and social organisations and of leading workers.[31] More radically, a law lecturer from the Kazakh State University Law School proposed, 'the creation of a special coordinating organ, made up of elected representatives of the workers, who would represent the interests of the work collective and act as a link between the collective, the management and the social organisations. This council of the work collective would assume plenary powers in the period between workers' meetings'.[32] Sporadic calls were heard during the discussion for work collectives to be granted greater rights and for the immediate transfer of some administrative and managerial functions to them. A Moscow lawyer named G. Ermoshin complained, for example, about the use in the draft law of words such as 'participates', 'elaborates', 'takes measures', 'raises questions', and so on, since, he said, these words are so vague as to have no force of law. Similarly, he complained, the law does not make it sufficiently clear just which body—the workers' general meeting, the management, the trade-union organisation—is responsible for the actual adoption of decisions. 'The law on work collectives is supposed to enhance the role of the collectives in management', he wrote, 'but this is quite impossible without clarification of the legal competence of every organ representing the collective and without clarification of the exact legal forms that the actions of each of these organs should assume'.[33]

The most far-reaching and significant intervention in this debate was made by E. Torkanovsky, a legal specialist on the staff of the Institute of Economics, writing in the authoritative journal of the Central Committee of the CPSU, *Kommunist*.[34] Torkanovsky criticises the new law for not going far enough in giving workers authentic powers of decision. He writes that self-management on an advisory level already exists in the USSR but that, though workers are allowed to participate in the preparatory stages of decision-making, they have no real control over the final decision, and their advice and opinions can easily be ignored by the management. He pleads that workers should not be relegated to the role of mere 'advisors'. 'What kind of self-management is it', he asks, 'when workers do not work out their own decisions but merely receive them ready-made from management?' Torkanovsky calls instead for 'a qualitative change' whereby workers would be given authentic powers of decision not only over distribution but also over production. Only then, he says, will the workers feel that the decisions taken by the collective are really 'their own'.

Torkanovsky's article suggests that, for all its vagueness and limitations, the new law on work collectives should not be dismissed as simply another attempt by the authorities to pull the wool over the workers' eyes. In the first place, it should be borne in mind that some Western observers view the new legislation with guarded approval, pointing out that for some categories of Soviet workers the new law may signify an important advance. For industrial workers—particularly those in large, well-managed plants—the law promises no extension of the consultative rights they already enjoy. Other groups of workers—such as those in small offices or retail outlets—may now, however, find themselves being consulted by their managers for the first time in their working lives.

Moreover, there have been under the leadership of both Yurii Andropov and Konstantin Chernenko persistent hints that a limited restructuring of the economic mechanism is being planned. This seems to have been foreshadowed by the economic experiment introduced on 1 January 1984, which granted greater autonomy to enterprises in certain industries. Soviet leaders have stated that, if successful, the experiment will be generalised in the five-year plan period due to begin in 1986. An extension of autonomy at the enterprise level would call for an increase of initiative not only of managers but also of workers. In his speech introducing the law on work collectives at the session of the USSR Supreme Soviet in June 1983, Aliev stressed the point that the new law would dovetail with the economic experiment, which, at that time, was still in the planning stage.[35] It may therefore prove that the new law will provide the legal framework for an eventual expansion of worker participation. It is perhaps for this very reason that the workers' new rights have been so cautiously and closely circumscribed.

Another important aspect of the new law is that it gives official recognition for the first time to the 'brigade', or team, as an organisational unit within the Soviet enterprise. A feature of Soviet industry for decades, the brigade form of labour organisation has received significant encouragement in the last few years. As a result of many complaints made during the course of the public discussion that the definition of the work collective contained in the draft law was too vague, article 1 was amended as follows: 'In accordance with the structure of the enterprise, institution or organisation, the collectives of shops, departments, sectors, brigades and other subunits operate within a single work collective.' In addition to the recognition granted to the brigade as a form of work collective by article 1, article 18 goes on to describe the 'production brigade' as 'the primary component in the work collective of an enterprise or organisation'. The law clearly envisages a further enhancement of the role of the brigade in the Soviet enterprise.

Finally, the materials examined here provide clear evidence of the existence within the Soviet establishment of a vocal lobby of reform-minded lawyers advocating the liberalisation of the law's tenets. The process that led to the adoption of the new law appears to have embraced a genuine debate between different opinion groupings: those in authority who, like those in authority everywhere, are extremely reluctant to see their power diluted in any way, and those who advocate the granting of a greater role to workers. The form of the law as eventually adopted suggests, however, that the reform-orientated lobby is able to exercise relatively little influence when pitted against powerful vested interests.

THE INITIAL EFFECT OF THE NEW LAW

It is clear from press reports published since the adoption of the new law that in some enterprises the workers are taking their new responsibilities very seriously, particularly as regards the enforcement of labour discipline. *Trud* reported on 5 November 1983 that 'the USSR law on work collectives has significantly raised the workers' activity in the management of production and in the resolution of social problems, but the role of the collective has particularly grown in the strengthening of labour discipline'. As an example, a case was described in a machine-building factory in Chelyabinsk oblast' where the workshop collective had met to consider the behaviour of a worker who had missed a day's work. He admitted that he had got drunk the previous evening and been unable to come to work the next day. As a punishment, and 'in the spirit of the law [on work collectives]', his workmates deprived him of his thirteenth-month salary (worth about two hundred rubles) and told him he would be allowed to take his annual holiday only in the winter. He was also required to make up the lost day by working in his free time. This case supports the predictions of many Western observers that the new law would be used largely as an instrument of social control; that is, as a means of getting the workers to police themselves.

Izvestia of 18 November 1983 bore the same message: the director of the Taganrog metallurgical factory reported that 'the struggle against infringements of labour discipline . . . has been especially stepped up since the plenum of the Central Committee of the CPSU in June and the adoption of the law on work collectives. And, most importantly, the majority of cases concerning labour discipline are now coming before the collective for punishment. On 15 November 1983 *Trud* voiced the first words of criticism concerning the implementation of the new law. *Trud*'s correspondents all over the country were asked to send in reports on how, three months after its adoption, the new law was being put into practice. Naturally enough there were words of praise and enthusiasm from some quarters. It was said, for instance, 'In a number of sections [at an automobile plant in Minsk oblast'], workers' meetings are now being held every month, whereas they were previously held only sporadically. . . A monthly report is now being presented by the management to the trade-union committee'. But while there were five good reports, three were bad, which by the standards of the Soviet media seems a high proportion and suggests fairly widespread failure to put the new law into effect in the way the authorities intended.

'Some trade-union committees have done no more than propagandise', *Trud* complained, 'and they have shown no initiative in the concrete application of [the law's] provisions'. In a factory in Tyumen', *Trud* found evidence only of 'formalistic merasures, which might look very good in reports but which in reality change nothing'. Workers at a machine-building factory in Ivanovo, *Trud* reported, had made many suggestions of how chronic discipline problems related to drunkenness could be tackled. 'All these suggestions the representatives of the management and the trade-union committee assiduously noted down and just as assiduously forgot.' Too many enterprises, *Trud* concluded, seemed merely to be 'waiting for orders from above'.

POSTSCRIPT

It has been suggested here that the law on work collectives was perceived as an integral part of a package of cautious innovations introduced under the leadership of Yurii Andropov and intended to improve the functioning of the Soviet economy. The idea, it has been argued, is that if and when greater powers of decision are devolved to enterprise managers, a new level of control— exercised by the workforce at general meetings of the collective— will already be in operation. It is therefore of obvious importance that the first (and so far only) public criticism of the way in which the law on work collectives is being put into effect came from Mikhail Gorbachev. Speaking at a Party ideology conference in Moscow in December 1984, Gorbachev said:

The available evidence shows that many collectives are not fully exercising their rights and are making only sporadic use of the sanctions, benefits, and material and moral incentives provided for by the law.[36]

More importantly, Gorbachev went on to complain, enterprise managers are not allowing workers the participatory role in running their enterprises that the law demands:

Managers do not always listen to the workers' proposals, and trade-union committees are not showing the necessary persistence. One sometimes hears it said that some question or other could either be discussed at a meeting of the workers, or it could be decided within a narrow circle; that perhaps the enterprise director should be required to give an account of his work before the work collective or that perhaps this necessity could be dispensed with.

Significantly, Gorbachev's critical remarks were repeated in a front-page editorial published in *Pravda* on 17 March 1985, that is, within days of his election to the post of Party general secretary. This fact alone confirms the importance being attached to the new legislation by the present leaders of the USSR.

NOTES

1. Article 9 of the USSR constitution of 1977.
2. This phrase was used by Geidar Aliev, First Deputy Premier of the USSR, in an article in *Problemy mira i sotsializma*, no.3, 1984, pp.5–11.
3. *Moscow News*, 24 April 1983.
4. A. Vasil'ev, 'Razvitie form uchastiya trudyashchikhsya v upravlenii proizvodstvom', *Politicheskoe samoobrazovanie*, no.11, 1981, pp.28–36.
5. The text of the law was published in *Pravda* on 19 June 1983.
6. *Konstitutsiya obshchenarodnogo gosudarstva* (Moscow, 1978), p.192.

7. For the text of the draft law, see *Pravda*, 12 April 1983.
8. *Pravda*, 18 June 1983.
9. The word used in the draft was *razvitoi* (developed); this was changed to *zrelyi* (mature) in the final version. The reason for the change is unclear since, in this context, the two words are generally considered synonymous (*see* F.N. Gel'bukh, 'O razvitom, zrelom i real'nom sotsializme', *Politicheskoe samoobrazovanie*, no.6, 1982, pp.111–14).
10. In exceptional circumstances—for instance, where sections of an enterprise are located far apart from each other—provision is made for workers to elect delegates to represent them at a special conference (article 20).
11. There appears to have been some toning down of the Party's pre-eminence. The draft law spoke of the work collectives' duty 'to execute unswervingly the Party's decisions', while the final version calls merely for 'the implementation of Party decisions'. The significance of this change is not clear. In any case, *Izvestia* made it clear in its issue of 12 August 1983 that 'the Party organisation is the leading and guiding force and political nucleus of the work collective'.
12. *Pamir*, no.2, 1984, pp.93–120, cited in *Radio Liberty Research*, 175/84, 'Tajik Schoolchildren Exposed to Chemical Defoliants', 2 May 1984. (Munich, 1984).
13. V.A. Maslennikov, 'Zakon o trudovykh kollektivakh', *Sovetskoe gosudarstvo i pravo*, no.10, 1983, pp.3–9.
14. *Ibid.*
15. As quoted in *Le Monde*, 13 October 1983.
16. *Trud*, 19 July 1983.
17. Seweryn Bialer, *The USSR After Brezhnev*, New York, Foreign Policy Association Headline Series, no.265, 1983, p.23.
18. *Kommunist*, no.14, 1983, pp.3–12.
19. *Pravda*, 7 August 1983.
20. *Literaturnaya gazeta*, no.15, 1983, p.13.
21. *Pravda*, 18 April 1983.
22. *Sovetskaya Rossiya*, 26 April 1983.
23. *Komsomol'skaya pravda*, 8 May 1983.
24. *Izvestia*, 28 April 1983.
25. *Pravda*, 5 April 1983.
26. *Sovetskaya kul'tura*, 28 April 1983.
27. *Sovetskaya Rossiya*, 29 April 1983.
28. *Trud*, 4 November 1983.
29. *Izvestia*, 27 May 1983.
30. *Literaturnaya gazeta*, 4 May 1983.
31. *Pravda*, 8 May 1983.
32. *Kazakhstanskaya pravda*, 29 April 1983.
33. *Literaturnaya gazeta*, 27 April 1983.
34. E. Torkanovsky, 'Razvitie demokraticheskikh nachal v upravlenii proizvodstvom', *Kommunist*, no.8, 1983, pp.36–46.
35. *Pravda*, 18 June 1983.
36. M.S. Gorbachev, *Zhivoe tvorchestvo naroda* (Moscow, 1984), pp.29–30.

15 Job Security and the Law in the USSR[1]

NICK LAMPERT*

It has sometimes been said that an important source of full employment in the USSR derives from constitutional and legal guarantees. Together with certain features of the Soviet planning mechanism which encourage inflated demands for labour, these legal guarantees ensure that people will not only get a job but will be protected once they are in it. It has indeed been argued that the Soviet legal provisions cause considerable problems because in the USSR managers have the greatest difficulty getting rid of unproductive employees. The purpose of this article is to ask to what extent that image is appropriate. My intention is not to question the stark contrast between Soviet-type and capitalist societies in relation to job protection in the broad sense—a contrast which is of great political importance—but to consider how far the *law* creates the conditions for such protection in the Soviet Union.[2]

The gist of the argument is this. I shall accept as a background assumption that there is in the USSR a strong political commitment to full employment, which is embodied in the constitutional right, and indeed the legal duty, to work.[3] In that sense the law can be said to underpin the security of labour. But it is another matter to say that the law protects the particular jobs of particular people once they are employed. The Soviet Union has a highly codified framework of labour law which is designed, in part, to protect employees from arbitrary action by management that might threaten their jobs. But it would be misleading to say that this body of law, and the agencies established to implement it, act as a serious constraint on managers in their dealings with employees. At least, this is a question that deserves a close investigation, and

* Centre for Russian and East European Studies, University of Birmingham.

is of more than academic interest since it may tell one something about the conditions under which a 'right to work' might be made more effective.

The discussion proceeds as follows. In section 1, I outline the formal provisions of Soviet labour law that lay down managerial disciplinary and dismissal powers and the provisions that regulate disputes in this connection. Section 2 looks at the effects of management attitudes towards the workforce on job security. In section 3, I briefly examine the role of the trade unions in disputes over dismissal, and in section 4, at greater length, the role of the courts in dealing with claims for reinstatement.

PENALTIES, DISMISSALS AND WORK DISPUTES IN SOVIET LAW

Soviet labour law is noteworthy for being backed up by a constitutional right to work. It is also notable for its highly 'positive' and comprehensive character: it specifies in detail the rights and duties of the employing organisation and employees and the role of trade unions and courts—the two main agencies that have been given the task of resolving work disputes.[4] The range of formal management powers in relation to the workforce, like other aspects of labour law, is closely defined in the 1970 Principles of Labour Law and in the 1971 Labour Code.[5] These specify all permissible disciplinary sanctions and provide a complete list of grounds for dismissal.[6] The main disciplinary measures are (a) reproofs or reprimands, (b) withdrawal of bonuses for unsatisfactory work, (c) transfer to lower paid work or demotion to a lower position for a period of three months and (d) dismissal.

Dismissal for broadly disciplinary reasons is provided for on the following main grounds: first, in the case of 'systematic non-fulfilment of work duties' (if this is to be applied, there must have been at least one other violation of discipline in the course of the past year); second, in the case of 'absence without good cause' (this means absence for more than three hours, or appearing at work drunk); third, there are additional disciplinary grounds for dismissal for people with special responsibility for money or goods (they can be dismissed because of 'loss of trust'), and also for people with educational functions, who can be fired for an 'amoral misdemeanour'.

In addition to these, there are certain non-disciplinary grounds for termination of contract. These include provision for loss of jobs because of 'staff reductions', which enterprises are on occasion instructed to carry out in the interests of economy and a more rational use of labour. It is, in the words of one authoritative source, 'one of the measures to improve the work of the enterprise, and also to staff it with more qualified cadres'.[7] In the event of such a dismissal, the management must offer the employee suitable alternative work in the same organisation, or be able to show that no other such work is available or that the employee has refused a suitable offer. Also, managers must take into account qualifications and length of service in making the decision. Employees can also be declared 'unsuitable for the post' and dismissed if they cannot fulfil their duties for health reasons or if they are judged to be no longer qualified for the job. In the case of non-manual personnel, this judgement may be reached on the basis of a periodical (every three to five years) certification test (*attestatsiya*). The latter measure was introduced after a USSR Council of Ministers recommendation in 1973, 'with the aim of increasing the effectiveness and responsibility of the work of executives, engineering-technical workers and other specialists'.[8] Decisions about implementation are made by individual ministries. Certification commissions, appointed by the administration, are staffed by managers and specialists, together with Komsomol, Party and trade-union representatives.

These rules are intended both to protect Soviet workers from arbitrary action by management and to ensure that workers carry out their duties: that they come to work on time, stay sober, do a fair day's work and, where necessary, keep their qualifications up to scratch. If employees believe they have been unfairly treated, they can make appeal through the procedures on work disputes which are also laid down in detail in legislation. In Soviet law, work disputes occur when either an employee or the management of an organisation wish to challenge the actions of the other side, on grounds set out in the Labour Code. Disputes can occur over disciplinary sanctions; termination of contracts; payment of wages, salaries and bonuses; holiday entitlements; compensation for damages; acceptance of technical innovations by employees. Disputes do not take the form of collective industrial action. They involve an individual (or an organisation acting as an individual) appealing to rights and duties and norms specified in law which are alleged to have been violated.[9]

The main agencies responsible in law for the resolution of work disputes are the trade unions and the courts—though in dismissal cases, as we shall see, certain categories of employee cannot appeal to these agencies but only to administrative superiors. Most disputes are subject to initial discussion by a commission on work disputes, which is made up of half management and half trade-union representatives. If the commission fails to give satisfaction to the plaintiff, the matter passes to the trade-union committee. If the union committee decides against the plaintiff, she can appeal to a People's Court, comprising one presiding judge and two lay assessors. Both plaintiffs and defendants can have legal representation in work disputes, and in hearings on reinstatement it is obligatory for a representative of the procuracy to be present to give an opinion on the legal aspects of the case. The decisions of the court are binding but can be contested, either by means of an individual appealing to a higher court or by means of judicial review of lower court decisions by higher courts. In addition, both managerial and court decisions in work disputes can be 'protested' (though not reversed) by the procuracy, acting in its capacity as 'supreme supervisor' over legality as a whole.[10]

For the purpose of my discussion the most important disputes are those arising from dismissals on disciplinary and non-disciplinary grounds and from other disciplinary sanctions. The commissions on work disputes do not appear to play a significant role in this context and are not entitled to discuss appeals against dismissals.[11] I shall therefore leave them out of this account and focus on the trade-union committees and the courts. In most cases the agreement of the trade union is necessary before issuing a dismissal notice. Thereafter, with important exceptions to be noted later, one can appeal to a court for reinstatement. But before discussing the role of these agencies of labour-law enforcement, it is important to look first at the effect of management attitudes towards the workforce on the security of labour.

MANAGEMENT ATTITUDES AND THE SECURITY OF WORK

We have seen that the codification of management powers provides a tight guaranteee on paper against arbitrary action in relation to employees, as well as legal backing for labour discipline. How far does managerial practice in the USSR conform to these rules, and what are the implications of that practice for job security?

It is commonly said by both Soviet and Western observers that the managers of Soviet organisations are inclined to tolerate behaviour by their workforces which according to law they should not tolerate. Soviet workers get away with an inordinate amount of drunkenness, shoddy work, absenteeism and bad time-keeping. It is also widely agreed that special problems of work motivation arise from labour shortages in Soviet-type economies, however such shortages are defined or explained.[12] The result, it seems, is that the work regime is not authoritarian but based on a type of informal bargain in which employees will put in the effort necessary to meet plan targets (for example, turn up at the end of the month and do a lot of overtime) but in return can enjoy a definite tolerance towards formal transgressions of the disciplinary code.

If this is right, then it can be seen that the behaviour of Soviet managers tends in one sense to create a greater security of labour than is intended in law. Managers are typically reluctant to dismiss workers because they cannot easily be replaced. But it does not of course follow from this that managers are deterred in all circumstances from getting rid of their employees. In 1981, according to a Soviet trade union official, 'about 800,000 persons were dismissed for disciplinary reasons from organisations of industry, building, transport and communications' (i.e. 1.3 per cent of the workforce of those branches).[13] This figure excludes dismissals on non-disciplinary grounds (e.g. staff cuts) and also a certain proportion of voluntary quits, where management has put pressure on employees to leave 'voluntarily'. Thus the numbers involved are not negligible and are difficult to square with the image of the Soviet manager bound hand and foot by the law.

It seems to me probable that in the great majority of cases those who are dismissed are seen by management as 'troublemakers' in a broad sense—either because they have flagrantly neglected their work duties and thereby failed to meet their side of the bargain or else because they have fallen out with their superiors and have thus become an embarrassment. It is in this second type of case that the most serious disputes are likely to arise, because management action will be seen as more akin to retribution than to an attempt to impose discipline. But in either case it is not so much the violation of law that causes the problem but the breakdown of informal relationships and expectations.

Without systematic information about managerial motives it would be difficult to demonstrate this point conclusively. But one can point to a number of things in support. First, there is plenty of anecdotal evidence from the Soviet press that where personal conflicts develop between management and employees, the former will have few compunctions about trying to oust an uncooperative subordinate. The conflict is likely to be especially sharp where an employee tries publicly to expose management breaches of law, whether in the pursuit of a personal grievance or for more disinterested reasons. This is not an uncommon phenomenon in Soviet organisations, and one which attracts a lot of press coverage.[14] Typically, such 'whistleblowers' will incur some kind of reprisal; for example, transfer to a less desirable job or loss of bonus, a reprimand or dismissal—measures that were designed as weapons against unproductive workers, not against people who had become an embarrassment to the organisation. The law says that it is strictly impermissible to act against an employee for reasons of personal hostility; indeed, it is defined as a criminal offence.[15] But this carries little weight in practice, as hinted at recently by a member of the USSR Supreme Court, who commented that 'materials on court practice show that there are still cases of gross violation of the labour rights of citizens, in particular illegal transfers and dismissals, sometimes by way of retaliation for critical statements, signals about abuses by people in official positions.'[16] As an alternative to the use of disciplinary clauses, a director could resort to other measures to secure a dismissal, especially in the case of administrative or technical personnel who have been defined as undesirable. 'Staff cuts' seems to be the most popular tactic in this context.[17] But 'unsuitability for the post' is also used. An employee in a construction organisation, who was discharged after failing a certification test (*attestatsiya*), took the view that certification was being used as a 'new form of dismissal of employees'.[18] Specialists are vulnerable in this situation since it is difficult, in the face of another opinion, to prove that one is still sufficiently qualified for the job. One informant, who had worked as an engineer in a radio plant, put it this way:

If he (the director) had wanted to dismiss me, he could have done it very simply. He would have written a note . . . that I wasn't coping with the work. . . It is impossible to prove (that you are working well) . . . with a lathe operator, you can see what he has done . . . but with a designer you can always say that he's not coping, that he's not suitable etc. . . . You can say that his level used to be high, but has become lower than two years ago.[19]

It is possible, then, to use the formal provisions of the labour law in order to dispose of unwanted employees. As implied earlier, a final dismissal notice may indeed be unnecessary, since one may choose to leave 'voluntarily' or, to use an ironic Soviet expression for it, 'by the voluntary decision of the bosses' (*po sobstvennomu zhelaniyu nachal'stva*). This is no doubt the preferred option for management because it avoids possible legal complications, and it seems that this is what a liberal sprinkling of reprimands is often designed to achieve.

A second indication of a somewhat casual attitude by management towards legal guarantees of job security can be found in comments from the higher levels of the Soviet judiciary about appeals for reinstatement that have come before the courts. The most recent systematic comment of this kind relates to 1975. The USSR Supreme Court studied a sample survey of more than 4,000 claims for reinstatement that had come before the courts in that year. The conclusion was that there was still not enough respect for some basic formalities when dismissing people. According to the survey, legal norms were most often violated when people were dismissed in connection with violations of discipline (that is, 'systematic non-fulfilment of work duties' or 'absenteeism'), or in connection with staff cuts. Together these made up 63 per cent of the stated reasons for dismissals, as the following figures based on the survey indicate (1975):[20]

	%
Staff cuts	16.9
Unsuitable for the post	5.6
Systematic non-fulfilment of work duties	13.5
Absenteeism (including drunkenness)	32.3
Loss of trust	9.5
Amoral misdemeanour	1.2
Transfer to other work	7.2
Other reasons	13.8

Managements were still frequently ignoring the requirement to get trade-union agreement for dismissals, a requirement which has been described as one of the 'legal guarantees of the right to work'.[21] In the USSR as a whole, one out of three dismissals in the survey had been carried out without trade-union agreement, and in Azerbaidzhan, Turkestan and Uzbekistan, about one in two.[22] Furthermore, employees were sometimes being fired for reasons and in ways not provided for in law:

Contrary to law, employees were fired for systematic non-fulfilment of work duties for a single misdemeanour, or more than one month after the discovery of the misdemeanour, or sometimes even six months later. There were frequent dismissals for absenteeism when the reasons for the absence had not been checked, or dismissals for failure to carry out an illegal directive on transfer to different work.[23]

Finally, in carrying out staff cuts, measures were not always taken to transfer the dismissed employees to other work.[24]

The following picture emerges from this discussion. On the one hand, managers are reluctant to impose sanctions on employees who break the official rules that define labour discipline. On the other hand, they are quite willing to penalise subordinates who are not prepared to play by the informal rules and who get in the way of the task at hand as understood by their superiors. These are two sides of the same coin, which reflect the dominant role of informal relationships and understandings in Soviet organisations. In his book on Soviet managers, Andrle aptly describes the Soviet manager as a 'benevolent boss', who can dispense favours to selected employees, strengthen loyalties and thus hold on to needed members of the workforce.[25] But the same benevolent boss can turn 'malevolent' when people fail to play the game. It should not be concluded from this that there is anything especially vindictive about Soviet managers. It is just that the pattern of labour relations has been established to a large extent without reference to law. Those who undermine the informal rules and practices cannot expect indulgence.

THE ROLE OF THE TRADE UNIONS

One of the main functions of trade-union officials within an organisation is to defend workers from arbitrary action by management. Except in those cases where employees must rely on appeal to superiors—I shall discuss these in the next section— dismissals are legally valid only if sanctioned by the union committee, which is supposed to withdraw its agreement if a proposed dismissal is contrary to law. Soviet sources do not provide much detailed information on the behaviour of trade unions in disputes that impinge most directly on the security of work. But it would, I think, be safe to generalise that where there is a definite element of personal conflict, then the trade union is extremely unlikely to speak up for employees threatened with disciplinary sanctions or dismissal. In a sample of seventy press stories dealing with disputes that had arisen from personal conflicts,[26] there were two in which the union was said to have failed to support the management in their efforts to dispose of an employee. In one of the cases a rift had developed in the organisation between supporters and opponents of the director, collective letters of complaint had been written to the city Party committee, and the Party secretary had also come out against the director. The other case was about a building organisation in which a worker had publicly criticised the boss for his 'immodest style of life': he already had a posh establishment but was now, among other things, building a 'huge separate house with a garage and a bath', when there was a long queue of workers for housing. The worker was offered a transfer to the job of night guard, which it was clear he would refuse because his wife was ill, and was then given his notice. But the trade-union chairman refused to sanction this.[27]

Both of these cases are interesting as exceptions. Where a dismissal is less contentious, less 'political' in the broad sense, it may be that trade-union organisers and committees will not be so ready to jump to the defence of management.[28] Also, the strength of the union committee seems to be much greater in some sectors and organisations than in others. In the view of one informant, who had long trade-union experience in machine-tool plants, the amount of influence was likely to depend greatly on the 'professional level of the workers' and 'the strength of the collective'.[29] But where management is intent on disciplining or dismissing an employee, the trade union is very unlikely to resist.

The reluctance of the unions to defend employees in the more serious disputes over disciplinary matters and over dismissals is not surprising, but it deserves some comment. First, one should remember that trade-union officials bear joint responsibility with management and the enterprise Party committee for the results of the organisation's activities. One of their tasks is to assist the enterprise in meeting targets. Union organisers will therefore, broadly speaking, share the management definition of the situation. If the administration has defined an employee as troublesome to the organisation, union officials are scarcely likely to quarrel with that judgement.

Second, although members of a trade-union committee are formally elected, in practice it seems that nominees for the committee are usually selected by the administration in alliance with the Party secretary, and that such nominees are rarely turned down at annual trade-union meetings when elections are held. The nominees are therefore beholden both to the administration and to the Party secretary. If the director has the support of the Party secretary, which is usually the case, the trade-union official will have very little room for manoeuvre.

Finally, union organisers have something to gain materially from their positions. Being a union official brings a number of material privileges and career advantages which incumbents may not want to forgo by making themselves unpopular. If they fall out of step, they may fail to gain re-election the next time round.

In sum, trade-union officials at enterprise level simply do not have the independence from management that they would need in order to offer any serious challenge when conflicts develop and an employee needs support from within the organisation.

THE ROLE OF THE COURTS

Since the trade unions tend to rubber-stamp management decisions, considerable weight is put on the Soviet courts to defend people against unfair dismissal and other illegal managerial decisions affecting the security of work. A very small proportion of dismissed employees in fact take the trouble to appeal to a court—about 2 per cent according to a reliable estimate.[30] But the court response in these cases is an important indicator of the strength of legal protection of jobs. It is impossible to give a full account of that response in the absence of sufficient published data on court decisions. But by gathering together some of the available pieces of information one can draw a rough picture and make some inferences.

The possibility of defending yourself in court against arbitrary action by managers or officials is now a constitutional right of Soviet citizens. Article 58 of the 1977 constitution says that 'The actions of officials committed in violation of law, in excess of their powers and impinging on the rights of citizens, may be appealed to a court in accordance with the procedure established by law'. In

similar vein, article 57 states that 'Citizens of the USSR shall have
the right to judicial protection against infringements on their
honour and dignity, life and health, personal freedom and
property'.[31]

In the light of these provisions it is important to note that people
in certain categories of jobs are *not* entitled to appeal to a court for
reinstatement or for redress of other disciplinary penalties. The
most important of these categories are defined in a 'List No.1' and
'List No.2', which were appended to the Regulations on Work
Disputes drawn up in May 1974.[32] They cover those with
administrative responsibility down to the level of foreman,
together with staff of elected bodies and social (e.g. Party and
trade union) organisations and some employees in scientific
research, educational institutions and the media. People in these
positions must rely on a complaint to a superior within their own
administrative hierarchy, a process which by all accounts is highly
unlikely to succeed.[33] It has been clearly said by some Soviet legal
specialists that it is now unconstitutional not to give the categories
in these lists the right of judicial defence, and that the law should
be brought into line with the constitution.[34] But so far there have
been no moves in this direction.

The effect of these provisions is that people in administrative
and technical positions are relatively more vulnerable to arbitrary
management action. If one considers too that administrative and
technical staff are much more likely to be affected by 'staff cuts'
than manual workers and that 'unsuitability for the post' is a
provision usually applied to specialists, the upshot must be that the
jobs of the intelligentsia, broadly defined, are less protected than
the jobs of the working class.

If we now set aside this problem and consider those who are
entitled to appeal to a court for reinstatement, what are the
chances of getting a decision in one's favour, and what will that
decision depend on? In the period between 1960 and 1980 the rate
of reinstatement remained fairly stable at between 50 and 60 per
cent for the USSR as a whole.[35] The figures have been higher,
however, in some republics. For example, a large sample review
by the USSR Supreme Court in 1975 showed that 55 per cent of
plaintiffs were successful in the USSR as a whole, but more than
70 per cent in Uzbekistan and more than 60 per cent in Armenia,
Kirgizia, Georgia and Azerbaidzhan.[36]

Soviet commentators do not regard a high rate of reinstatement
as a good thing in itself. If large numbers of management decisions

are being reversed in the courts, it means that managers are showing too little respect for labour law. This is logical enough, and it may well be that the management attitude to these matters is more casual in Central Asia and Transcaucasia than in the RSFSR and European republics. With these criteria in mind, one local Party secretary pointed with pride to the fact that in Ivanovo province in 1974, 102 out of 207 claims for reinstatement were successful, whereas in the first half of 1981, only 1 out of 35 such claims had succeeded.[37]

Following this line of thought, one would have to say that the lower the rate of reinstatement, the better. But the issue takes on a different significance in the light of a good deal of criticism of the Soviet courts for their failure to give an adequate response to claims against illegal dismissal and thus to ensure that the legal right of job security is fully observed. Given this criticism, which I shall discuss presently, one wants to know more about what lies behind the general figures on reinstatement. The important thing is not just the general chances of success but what the chances depend on. For example, what kind of organisations were involved? (How big a fish was the director?) What were the reasons for dismissal? What kind of jobs did the plaintiffs occupy? What reasons were given for accepting or rejecting the claim? Did the court consider the possibility that the management was 'taking reprisals for criticism'? In the absence of detailed published information, these questions cannot be answered in the way that one would ideally like. But a few suggestions will be offered that may at least begin to tackle the issue.

In the event of blatant disregard of correct procedure by management, the chances of reinstatement are probably very high, because when considering dismissal cases the Soviet courts seem to put a heavy emphasis on procedural correctness. However, the amount of care and objectivity that the courts bring to work disputes seems to vary greatly. One can point to contrasting pieces of evidence on this score. Over recent years USSR Supreme Court resolutions and reviews of court practice have recurrently noted an improvement in the 'role of the judicial organs in strengthening socialist legality in the sphere of labour relations'.[38] In support of such statements, Soviet commentators can point to a general decline over the past twenty years in the number of work disputes coming before the courts and, in particular, to a decline in the number of dismissal cases.[39] It has been argued that this change is due to an increasing level of legal awareness on the part of managers, which in turn, according to one resolution, is 'to a certain extent a result of the activity of the courts in the struggle against violations of labour law'.[40] There are additional factors which could help to explain this decline. For example, it may be that dismissal for disciplinary reasons (which is recorded in one's work book) has become less of an impediment in finding a new job, given an increasingly tight labour market, so that there is less incentive to seek reinstatement. The decline could also have been affected by an expansion in the 1970s in the range of people excluded from the courts as a source of appeal.[41] However, there is no reason to doubt that the level of observance of law by management has indeed increased, or that the role of the courts in reinstating people may have contributed to this development.

I would add to this that some personal experience listening to cases dealing with dismissals in Moscow and Leningrad courts suggested that the court procedure, at least in principle, allows room for a thorough, informal and fair investigation of the claim, with plenty of scope for the plaintiff and the plaintiff's lawyers to defend their case.[42] But against this there is a lot of criticism by the USSR Supreme Court of the handling of work disputes, and dismissals in particular. Recurrent references have been made to 'serious shortcomings' and violations of procedure by the lower courts.[43]

The most frequent criticism is superficiality in court examination of dismissals and other work disputes, and it is clear from USSR Supreme Court judgements that this superficiality generally works against the interests of the plaintiffs. In almost all the dismissal cases reviewed on appeal by the USSR Supreme Court, the plaintiffs are defended against superficial or prejudicial decisions by lower-level courts and are sent down again for a new hearing.[44] As one resolution put it, 'the most widespread reason for incorrect decisions on claims for reinstatement . . . is the lack of a thorough investigation by the court of the actual circumstances of the dispute'.[45] In a review of court practice in 1973 the meaning of such observations was spelt out. The courts were criticised for sometimes failing to examine properly the arguments for reinstatement in cases of dismissal on grounds of staff cuts, unsuitability for the post, systematic non-fulfilment of work duties and absenteeism. The courts did not always check properly that there were no alternative jobs for 'reduced' staff nor that those dismissed under a certification procedure were indeed 'unsuitable'; they sometimes failed to check that violations of discipline had been 'systematic' or to investigate the real reasons behind somebody's failure to appear at work. On occasion, too, the courts ignored the lack of prior agreement to a dismissal from the trade union.[46]

A second criticism has been that the courts have generally failed to take action against managements that have dismissed an employee in clear violation of the law. In such cases the courts are instructed to recover from individual managers some of the damages incurred by the enterprise in paying for the involuntary absence of the plaintiff. But 'the courts rarely [do this] even when the dismissal occurs without the agreement of the trade-union committee'.[47] In 1974, in only a quarter of cases where this agreement was lacking, were any damages recovered at all, and in only 14 per cent of such cases were managers personally penalised.[48] The courts are also instructed to issue special rulings where clear violations of labour law have taken place. The purpose of the rulings is to comment on the conditions giving rise to illegal management decisions and to help managers to mend their ways. These too, it is said, are issued all too rarely.[49] In 1975, special rulings were issued in 16 per cent of cases where it would have been appropriate, and it was lower than this in many republics.[50]

In addition to these problems, all raised by the higher judicial authorities, it is worth asking to what extent the courts consider the possibility that the formal grounds on which a person has been dismissed are simply pretexts, and that the real reason has to do with personal animosities, perhaps as a result of 'criticism from below'.

In law the courts are supposed to consider the possibility that the plaintiff has been disciplined or dismissed for personal reasons since, as we have seen, it is regarded as a serious offence. If this is revealed during the court hearing, the court is instructed to issue a special ruling and, if necessary, to raise the question of bringing a criminal charge.[51] But my impression, both from a reading of legal sources and from some experience listening to dismissal cases in Soviet courts, is that judges are not generally prepared to enter into a discussion of motives and tend to stick strictly to procedural matters. Special rulings are rare in this connection, and I have come across no case in which a manager was dismissed (under the provisions of article 138 of the RSFSR Criminal Code) as a result of a violation of this kind. In 1981 the USSR Supreme Court reviewed a sample of 327 cases on reinstatement. It noted that in 153 of these the plaintiffs had indicated that the reason for dismissal had to do with criticism. But in only 12 cases did the court issue a special ruling, and in no case raised the question of a criminal charge, although there were grounds for doing so.[53]

All this is understandable. It is difficult to sort out rights and wrongs when there is a breakdown in personal relationships. It is difficult to sort out the origins of personal animosities. But it is also clear that the court cannot do its job of understanding the real reasons for the dispute unless it is prepared to examine this aspect of the matter. The high degree of codification of Soviet law is here ambiguous in its effects. In one sense it favours employees, because managers cannot simply get rid of an employee without finding some formal pretext. But it also makes it easier for the administration superficially to abide by the rules while obscuring the real basis of its behaviour.

This review of court practice suggests that the chances of reinstatement are quite good, if one considers simply the general proportion of successful claims. But it also emerges that Soviet judges, though they put great emphasis on procedural matters, often fail to observe the requirements laid down by the highest judicial authorities and are not over-concerned to get to the root of a dispute. There are no doubt quite wide variations in this respect between different republics and regions of the USSR. But this is not the only issue. The attitude of the court will depend upon the size and importance of the organisation and the prestige and influence of the director. If the enterprise is relatively small and unprominent, the court is less likely to worry about offending the director or his supporters within officialdom by reinstating an employee. The basic problem here is a general problem in the relationship between the Soviet courts and local political power. Heads of enterprises of any size or prominence will be on the party *nomenklatura*, the list of responsible positions that are filled on the authority of the relevant Party committee (the more responsible the position, the higher the Party organisation in whose *nomenklatura* it comes). Such a manager will typically have the support of local party officials. Although the Party does not apparently interfere in a detailed way in the affairs of the courts, they are undoubtedly subject to local political influences and cannot lightly ignore them. Without day-to-day interference, the courts have a good idea of the kind of legal intervention that will incur the wrath of Party officials and tend to limit their intervention accordingly. This observation is difficult to demonstrate directly, but some evidence can be brought to bear on it.

First, it seems that the great majority of successful claims for

reinstatement come from relatively small and unprestigous organisations, very often, one suspects, where the director was either
very low on the Party *nomenklatura* or not 'nomenklatured' at
all.[53] This is no doubt partly because few illegal dismissals occur in
large organisations where legal services are more developed and
managements more conscious of legal problems. But the explanation is also that the court will want to avoid decisions in favour of
reinstatement if this is going to reflect badly on a 'big fish'. Such a
big fish will typically have the support of the local Party secretary,
whom the judge cannot lightly ignore. One informant, a former
legal consultant, had a comment about this:

Undoubtedly this [i.e. the prominence of the enterprise] had a significance. This was not blatant, it was not emphasised, but it was significant
. . . for example, the director of Z (an agricultural procurements
organisation) where I worked to begin with, was a small figure in the
district. . . [On the other hand] the director of the ship-building factory
. . . was a member of the *raikom* buro. The judge who examines cases
involving this factory . . . will not usually be a member of the buro. He
might be a member of the *raikom*, but even that not always. But he is
unfailingly a Party member. From this point of view, from the point of
view of one's position within the Party, the director stands five heads
higher than the judge. . . And, of course, the judge feels this all the time
when he is examining cases concerning this factory.[54]

A very similar observation was made by another informant, a
former journalist, who was familiar with cases in which, even when
an employee had been reinstated by a district People's Court, the
management refused to reinstate or procrastinated. In this event
the court could in theory start criminal proceedings against the
manager, but there were difficulties:

There is of course another possibility, to bring a criminal charge against
[such a director]. But this is another and complex matter . . . connected
with the Soviet *nomenklatura*. A district judge is, let's say, in position
no.8 on the *nomenklatura*, whereas the director of a big factory is say,
no.6. This means that the chairman of the court cannot simply start
criminal proceedings. He must ring up the district Party secretary, usually
the third, and tell him that this swine is not carrying out my decision. But
the district Party secretary will say: no, no, that's not how to settle such
things . . . such cases are so normal that anecdotes cannot convey their
typicality.[55]

The importance of the director's position and influence is
strongly suggested also by the fact that in some cases an enterprise

administration reinstates an employee on a court order only to find the next suitable pretext to issue another dismissal notice. If a management can regard legal intervention as only a temporary setback and continues with its efforts to get rid of an undesirable employee, this must mean that the director has the necessary support or indulgence of his own superiors or of local Party officials.[56]

A NOTE ON OTHER CHANNELS OF APPEAL

We have seen that the enterprise trade-union bodies are in a weak position to support employees faced with dismissal and that there are definite limits to the power of the courts in this context. These limitations help to explain the frequent pursuit of claims for reinstatement through other channels—through the higher trade union agencies, the procuracy, the Party organisations and the press. The higher trade-union bodies (the central or local trade-union councils) receive a large number of submissions on a wide variety of matters relating to labour law, including disputes, and they are obliged to respond.[57] The procuracy is also an important source of appeal for employees with claims under labour law, and procuratorial 'protests' in cases of illegal transfer and dismissal are not uncommon.[58] Again, the Party and the press receive numerous complaints concerning the handling of disputes about dismissals and are in a position, if they so decide, to put pressure on other agencies to get something done. All these channels deserve a separate discussion, for which there is not space in this contribution. But enough has been said, perhaps, to indicate some of the limits to job security that arise from management attitudes and from the activities of the agencies chiefly responsible for the enforcement of this aspect of labour law.

CONCLUSIONS

The main points that have emerged from this discussion can be summarised as follows. The Soviet law on disputes seems admirably fair and well worked out, and legal guarantees of job security are strong on paper. But in practice these guarantees impinge much less on work relations than appears on the surface.

This is not to say that Soviet law in this field is simply a vast figleaf covering a reality of complete arbitrariness; that would clearly be a distortion. The rules embodied in Soviet labour law evidently establish limits to the role of managerial whim, as well as providing one instrument in the pursuit of labour discipline. But Soviet labour relations remain heavily influenced by informal under-standings and reciprocal favours. The formalities required by the Labour Code in relation to dismissal must be taken into account, but it is not so difficult to get round them.

The importance of informal understandings means that, on the one hand, employees are more protected than the legislation intended; the management acts indulgently towards formal viola-tions of labour discipline. On the other hand, people are less protected than the law intends. They are highly dependent on the good-will or ill-will of the boss. One can break the written rules and get away with it. But in the event of a breakdown in personal relationships, an employee who has fallen out of favour cannot expect indulgence.

The trade unions are supposed to defend employees in the event of arbitrary actions by management but simply lack the independ-ence they would need to develop a view of the situation different from the administration and to impose that view. This gives the courts, which are the second main institutional source of support for employees, a correspondingly important role to play. They do indeed act in the defence of people who are in dispute with management. But that defence is likely to be selective and partial. This is suggested by numerous criticisms of the courts by the higher judicial authorities themselves. Where the organisation is small and the management relatively uninfluential, one can expect the courts to act objectively. The procedure itself allows full scope for a thorough examination of the case. But in other situations the outcome is much less certain, because of the subordination of law enforcement to local political influences.

The difficulties are especially great for non-manual workers. There are more provisions in law itself for their dismissal, and a significant proportion of such employees cannot appeal to the courts for support. The intelligentsia is less protected in the Soviet Union than the working class and is especially dependent on the personal benevolence of the management.

If these observations are correct, they suggest that one should distinguish carefully between the 'right to work' that has been established *de facto* in the Soviet Union as a result of certain fundamental features of the economic mechanism, and the 'right to work' in the sense of legal protection for particular people in particular jobs. For the majority of Soviet employees, this is perhaps a distinction that would not be seen as having much practical relevance; as long as they abide by the informal rules of the game, they are not likely to suffer any threat to their jobs. Indeed, needed workers may be able to extract a favourable bargain from management, which will overlook their formal transgressions. But if a conflict arises, the weakness of the legal guarantees will make itself felt. Soviet commentators recognise that there are difficulties in this area and generally appeal for efforts to inculcate in managers a stronger consciousness of law. But it seems that the problems are more deep-seated than this and cannot be adequatelay confronted on that level. One condition, at least, for a more effective right to work must lie in a greater political independence for law and for the agencies that have been asked to implement it. This is hardly a surprising conclusion, but it is obscured by the undoubted security of work that arises from full employment.

NOTES

1. This essay draws on some material and argument presented in a recently published study by N. Lampert, *Whistleblowing in the Soviet Union* (London, 1985): I would like to thank the publishers for permission to make use of it. The book explores the causes and consequences of complaints by employees about managerial behaviour. Such initiatives frequently lead to the dismissal of the people involved, and this problem led me on to consider the wider question of legal protection for jobs. Together with Soviet published sources, I have used a few interviews held with former Soviet citizens in Israel. These are referred to in the notes as 'interview'. The article has benefitted from comments on an earlier draft by members of the Soviet labour group at the Centre of Russian and East European Studies, Birmingham University, from the response at Mario Nuti's seminar at the European University Institute, Florence, and from the discussion at the conference on which the present book is based. My thanks are also due to Ger P. Van Den Berg who drew my attention to some important material.

2. This issue is touched on in some Western texts; for example, E.C. Brown, *Soviet Trade Unions and Labour Relations* (Cambridge, MA 1966); M. McAuley, *Labour Disputes in Soviet Russia* (Cambridge, 1969); B. Ruble, *Soviet Trade Unions* (Cambridge, 1981). But a special focus on it seems warranted, especially in relation to more

recent developments in Soviet labour relations. Much information relevant to the present discussion has been skilfully brought together in Ger P. Van Den Berg, 'Judicial settlement of individual labour disputes in the Soviet Union', *Review of Socialist Law*, 1983, no.2, pp.125–64.

3. Article 40, Soviet constitution, *Collected Legislation of the USSR and the Constituent Republics* (New York, 1980), Release 2; article 209, RSFSR Criminal Code, *Ugolovnyi Kodeks RSFSR* (Moscow, 1978), p.69.

4. This provides a marked contrast with Britain, which historically has lacked a positive framework of legislation defining the functions of employer, employee and organised labour. Trade unions have established the ability to exist and to engage in industrial action by gaining immunity from criminal prosecution and from civil damages, not by having their rights and functions positively defined in statute. In recent years changes have occurred: corporatist trends have increased the arena of labour legislation; for example in health and safety, in rules on unfair dismissal, on compensation for redundancy and in attempts to delimit in statute the forms of permissible industrial action. In this sense there has been a certain convergence. But Soviet labour law remains unusually comprehensive in scope. *See*, for example, O. Kahn-Freund, *Labour and the Law* (London, 1977).

5. There are separate Labour Codes for each Soviet republic, but these vary only in minor ways. The Labour Code of the RSFSR (Russian republic) is translated in W.B. Simons (ed.), *The Soviet Codes of Law* (Alphen aan den Rijn, 1980).

6. *See* the provisions outlined in *Sovetskoe zakonodatel'stvo o trude* (Moscow, 1980), pp.71–93. Recent legislative changes arising out of the 1983 labour discipline campaign have modified the Labour Code by strengthening sanctions against violation of discipline. *See Vedomosti Verkhovnogo Soveta* SSSR, 1983, no.33, item 507.

7. *Sovetskoe zakonodatel'stvo o trude* (Moscow, 1980), p.71.

8. *Ibid.*, p.77.

9. In theory disputes can arise not only out of individual claims but also in connection with collective agreements about conditions of work between the enterprise administration and the trade-union committee. But in practice the vast majority of disputes are claims by individuals for the implementation of existing rules and agreements; *see* V.I. Smolyarchuk, *Zakonodatel'stvo o trudovykh sporakh*, (Moscow, 1966).

10. For an account of the functions of the procuracy, *see* G.B. Smith, *The Soviet Procuracy and the Supervision of Administration*, (Alphen aan den Rijn, 1980).

11. *Trudovoe Pravo*, Entsiklopedicheskii slovar', (Moscow, 1979), pp.178–79.

12. *See*, for example, the pieces by Hanson, Harrison and Pietsch in this volume.

13. V. Veretennikov in *Sovetskie Profsoyuzy*, 1982, no.9, p.22f, cited in Ger P. Van Den Berg, *op. cit.*, p.136.

14. This is discussed in detail in N. Lampert, *op. cit.*

15. Article 138 of the RSFSR Criminal Code, *Ugolovnyi Kodeks RSFSR* (Moscow, 1978), p.48.
16. *Bulleten' Verkhovnogo Suda SSSR* (Henceforth *BVS SSSR*), 1980, no.6, p.3.
17. For example, *Pravda*, 6 July 1979, p.3; 5 Oct. 1979, p.3; 15 Oct. 1979, p.3; 15 Aug. 1981, p.2; *Sotsialisticheskaya Industriya*, 14 June 1979, p.2.
18. *Sotsialisticheskaya Industriya*, 15 Aug. 1979, p.4.
19. Interview with a former engineer from Novgorod province.
20. *BVS SSSR*, 1977, no.3, pp.29–37.
21. *Sovetskoe Zakonodatel'stvo*, p.66.
22. *BVS SSSR*, 1977, no.3, p.30.
23. *Ibid.*, p.29.
24. *Ibid.*
25. V. Andrle, *Managerial Power in the Soviet Union* (Westmead, 1976).
26. The seventy stories were all taken from the national press, mainly from *Pravda*, in the period 1979–83.
27. *Pravda*, 28 Mar. 1981, p.3 (report about an electronics factory, Prokhladnyi, Kabardino-Balkarskaya ASSR); *Pravda*, 13 April 1982, p.3 (Inter-kolkhoz mobile mechanised column, Saratov province).
28. A survey in 1967 covering 50 large enterprises in Rostov province showed that out of 639 proposed dismissals, the trade union failed to give its agreement in 111 cases (i.e. 17 per cent). V.I. Nikitinskii, *Effektivnost' norm trudovogo prava* (Moscow, 1971), pp.117–18.
29. Interview with a former engineer at a machine tool plant, Ukraine.
30. Ger P. Van Den Berg, *op. cit.*, p.136.
31. *Collected Legislation of the USSR and the Constitutent Republics* (New York, 1980), Release 2.
32. For a full discussion, *see Sovetskoe Zakonodatel'stvo o trude* (Moscow, 1980), pp.420–28.
33. *See* the remarks on this by S.A. Ivanov and R.Z.Livshits in *Sovetskoe Gosudarstvo i Pravo*, 1978, no.4, pp.14–24.
34. *Ibid.; also* A.D. Zaikin, quoted in 'Delo ob uvol'nenii', *Literaturnaya Gazeta*, 10 Jan. 1979, p.11.
35. Ger P. Van Den Berg, *op. cit.*, p.149.
36. *BVS SSSR*, 1977, no.3, p.29.
37. Discussion with first secretary of the Ivanovo province Party committee, *Pravda*, 7 Sept. 1981, p.2.
38. For example, USSR Supreme Court resolutions of 1971, 1974 anu 1976 in *Sbornik Postanovlenii Plenuma Verkhovnogo Suda SSSR*, part 1 (Moscow, 1980), pp.236–58; review of court decisions in *BVS SSSR*, 1977, no.3, pp.29–37.
39. Ger P. Van Den Berg, *op. cit.*, pp.149–50.
40. USSR Supreme Court Plenum resolution 1971, *Sbornik Postanovlenii* (1980), p.236.
41. Compare the single list established in 1957, defining the categories of employee who could not appeal to the courts in the event of dismissal, with the two lists established in 1974. *Vedomosti Verkhovnogo Soveta SSSR*, 1957, no.4, item 58; 1974, 22, item 325.
42. The cases were heard in Leningrad in 1979 and in Moscow in 1981.

43. USSR Supreme Court Plenum resolutions 1974 and 1976, *Sbornik Postanovlenii*, (1980), pp.240, 256; *BVS SSSR*, 1974, pp.45–6.
44. For a few examples, see *BVS SSSR*, 1971, no.4, pp.7–9; 1971, no.6, pp.26–7; 1973, no.2, pp.26–8; 1974, no.4, pp.21–·22; 1974, no.6, pp.3–5.
45. 1974 USSR Supreme Court Plenum resolution, *Sbornik Postanovlenii*, (1980), p.240.
46. *BVS SSSR*, 1974, no.4, pp.33–9; similar criticisms were made five years later in *BVS SSSR*, 1980, no.6, p.3.
47. USSR Supreme Court resolution 1974, *Sbornik Postanovlenii*, (1980), p.241.
48. *BVS SSSR*, 1977, no.3, p.35.
49. 1974 USSR Supreme Court Plenum resolution, *Sbornik Postanovlenii*, (1980), p.24.
50. *BVS SSSR*, 1977, no.3, p.37.
51. USSR Supreme Court Plenum statement, quoted in *Pravda*, 30 Aug. 1981, p.2.
52. *Ibid*.
53. All the dismissal cases reviewed in the Bulletin of the USSR Supreme Court between 1971 and 1982 related to small organisations in non-priority sectors. *See also* the discussion by Nikitinskii of two surveys of dismissals in Rostov and Moscow provinces in 1967, which show that the great majority of reinstated employees come from small enterprises. V.I. Nikitinskii, *op. cit.*, p.119.
54. Interview with a former legal consultant, Ukraine.
55. Interview with a former journalist with a major republic Party daily.
56. A vivid example of such a 'ping pong' match between management and the judiciary was provided in one of the reviews by the USSR Supreme Court, where the director of a sanatorium in Alma Ata, Kazakhstan, seemed determined to get rid of one of his nurses even after repeated intervention at the highest level by the procuracy and the judiciary: *BVS SSSR*, 1974, no.6, pp.3–5; 1982, no.4, pp.27–30.
57. For some remarks about letters and complaints to the higher trade-union bodies, *see* a speech by the secretary of the Soviet TUC in *Trud*, 30 July, 1981, pp.1-2.
58. In a few of the reports about whistleblowing, the procuracy came to the defence of people who were judged to be illegally transferred or dismissed. For example, *Pravda*, 2 Oct. 1979, p.2; *Sotsialisticheskaya Industriya*, 12 June 1979, p.4; 14 June 1979, p.3.

Index

Absenteeism 61
Accumulation 75;
  see also overaccumulation
Agriculture 179, 184
Alienation 4–5, 8, 10, 76, 80
Aliev 240, 251
Altai krai 130
Andropov 198, 240, 246, 251
Arrow-Debreu 114
Attestatsiya 258, 261
Automation 194

BAM 172
Barber 2
Bell 6
Birthrates 149, 180
Bitov 205
Bialer 246
Blauner 10
Bonus 134, 195
Braverman 5
Brezhnev 9, 70, 246
Brigades 11, 200–2, 242, 248, 251–2
Budget 124, 224–5
Burkharin 31

Campaigns 197, 201–4
Capitalism 20, 113
Central Asia 153, 167, 169, 178, 182–4;
  unemployment in 184–5, 189
Charemza 99
Chawluk 205
Chelyabinsk 159
Chernenko 181, 251
Class structure under capitalism 4
Cobb-Douglas 95, 96, 100
Collective farms 54; supply of workers
  for industry from 52–6
Collectivisation 45, 146
Constitutions of USSR 8–9, 70, 239,
  240, 265
Consumption 3, 13–14, 75, 196
Corporatism 114

Dahrendorf 6

Demography:
  trends 124, 177
Deskilling 5, 60
Depler 106n6
Decentralisation 106
Differentials
  see wage differentials
Discipline 3, 14, 131, 150, 198, 200,
  242, 247, 252, 257, 260, 263; *see also*
  under labour
Dismissals 88, 257–9, 260, 262, 266,
  267
Displacement
  labour law on 132 *see also*
  redundancy
Division of labour 5
Durkheim 3
Dyker 107n8

Education 92, 129, 209; aspirations
  for 217; vocational 210
Efficiency 3, 73, 80, 86, 89–93, 122,
  193, 195, 199, 203
Employment 112, 188; costs of
  full 80; full 84, 116, 118, 145; and
  migration 167–70
Employment system 149
Engels 70
Engineers: training of 226–7
Ermoshin 250
Expansion drive 177, 186
Experiments, economic 251
Exploitation 4

Feshbach 184
Filippov 216, 217, 220n15, 221n27,
  222n30
Five Year Plans 50–1
Food Programme 204
Forced labour 58
Fringe benefits 135

Gastarbeiter 181
Gilbert 107n17
Goskomtrud 131, 150, 219

Gosplan   22, 25, 27–8, 37–8, 45, 52, 56, 115, 202

Habermas   9
Hanson   117
Helgeson   187
Hicks   114

Incentives   13, 76, 168, 194, 196
Ideology   1–2, 11–13, 69, 193, 212, 232
Industrial society   233
Industrialization   1, 50, 70, 74, 146
Inflation   80
Innovation   206
Intelligentsia   223, 229, 273
Investment   74, 102, 105, 112, 113, 127 194; overinvestment   74

Jahoda   6
Japan   85, 89–92
Job Security
   see security

Kalecki   112, 113
Khrushchev   152, 204, 235n1
Kikot   249
Klopov   230
Kolkhozy
   see collective farms
Komsomol   147, 172, 245
Kornai   83, 94, 102, 176, 177, 182, 185–6, 188, 189
Kosygin reforms   204–5
Kotlyar   171
Kraval   25, 31
Krzhizhanovsky   28
Kuibyshev   25

Labour:
   Absenteeism   59, 61–2,77; abundance   104; code   257–8, 275n5; demand for   146; discipline   59–63, 77, 86; direction of   73; forced   58–9, 72; hoarding   75, 83, 88, 92–3, 117
Labour markets:
   heterogeneous   125; primary   132, 135, 136–7; secondary   128, 129, 132, 134–137; *see also* markets
Labour participation   178–9, 182
Labour process   7–8, 10, 14, 191
Labour policy   177
Labour resources   115, 177–81
Labour shortage   31, 51–2, 83–4, 93–106, 116–19, 149, 169, 170, 187–9, 260
Labour surplus   102, 152, 159, 224
Labour turnover   60, 91, 123–5, 128, 130, 146
Labour-exchange   23, 28–9, 36–7, 40, 70
Lane   217
Larin   27

Law   85–6, 132, 252–3, 273; and courts, 265–73; and labour code, 257–8; and job security   256
Legitimacy   13, 14, 69
Lenin   7, 10, 194, 201

McAuley   180, 187
Malle   11, 86, 106n8
Malmygin   108n18
Management   102, 129, 229, 242, 244, 245, 260, 264
Manning levels   93
Manpower supply   51–2
Market   4, 29, 32, 56, 69, 90, 118, 123, 137n2, 189, 195, 234
Marx   3, 5, 193, 194, 195
Marxism-Leninism   1, 2, 12
Migration   23–24, 37, 52, 53, 55, 72–3, 145, 161, 167; *see also* population
Mints   31, 49
Mobility   91
Mode of production   4, 9–11
Modernisation   21

Narkomtrud   28, 30, 31, 51, 55
Needs   4, 12, 212
New Economic Policy (NEP)   21, 23, 25, 45, 51
Newspapers   203
Nomenklatura   270–1
Norms   201, 262
Novosibirsk   87, 130, 224, 229, 231, 233
Nuti   94

Offe   6, 9
Opposition   205
Ordzhonikize   128
Orgnabor   52–5, 147–8, 172
Overaccumulation   114–16
Overmanning
   see labour surplus
Overproduction   20

Parasites   86–7
Parkinson's law   177
Participation   197, 234, 243, 248–52
Party   13–14, 26–7, 88, 115, 192, 198, 203, 242, 243, 244, 247, 264
Passports   107n12, 147–8, 247
Patrushev   224
Payroll-tax   118, 120
Peasants   7
Pensioners   180–1
People's court   259
Pietsch   86, 89, 94, 108n23
Planning   12, 14, 112, 146, 176, 194
Podmarkov   226
Policy, economic   205
Politbureau   197
Population   182;
   1959–1970   151–61; 1970–1979   161–6
Prices   76

Productivity   11-12, 26, 71, 77, 83, 94–
    6, 120, 136, 191–2, 194, 206
Production functions   119–20
Profit   119
Promotion   130–1
Propiska   147, 150
Protestant ethic   7

Razryad (skill-rating)   126, 128, 130,
    133
Redundancy   84–6, 107n8, 186, 258
Reforms, economic   204–5, 206
Regling   106n6
Reserve army   30
Residence   171–2
Rights   8, 69–70, 78, 81, 257, 273–4
Rogachevskaya   35n64

Sabsovich   27
Schwalberg   95, 104
Schroeder   94, 109n23, 117, 202
Security:
    of jobs   84–6, 90, 92, 124, 262
Seeman   10
Shchekino   102, 108n19, 117, 199–200,
    205
Shkurko   196
Shortages see labour shortages
Siberia   149, 183
Socialism   9, 12, 19–20, 32, 76, 113,
    193, 200, 239, 241
Socialist competition   53, 61, 197
Sovnarkom   31, 52, 55–6
Soyuzstroi   54
Stakhanovism   50
Stalin   2, 8, 26, 31, 52, 55, 72–4, 194,
    201
Stalinism   7
Standing production conference   249
State planning commission see Gosplan
State labour reserves   57–8, 63
Stepanyan   233
Strumilin   27
Suvorov   35n64
Sverdlov   8
Sverdlovsk   88, 159
Sycheva   35n64

Taylorism   7, 8, 10, 223
Temporary jobs   37
Thatcherism (in 1929/30)   29
Tobin   32n3
Torkanovsky   250–1

Trade unions   37, 245, 253, 260, 263–5,
    273
Trotsky   27
Turnover see labour turnover

Uglanov   31
Underconsumption   19
Underemployment in USSR   21, 70–1,
    223, 231, 234
Underqualification   229
Unemployment   37, 87, 107n14, 177,
    184, 234; in capitalist societies   6,
    19, 20, 79, 113, 176, 178; data
    sources   36; 'disguised'   77; (in
    1920s & 30s)   22–31;
    registration   37; voluntary 87
United opposition   26–7

Verdoorn   117
Vesenkha   25, 38, 45
Vocational education
    see education; guidance   219
Vogel   108n23

Wages   195
Wage control   182
Wage differentials   133–6, 196
War   57
Weber   3
Weitzman   96, 100, 109n37
Women   10; and employment   24, 70,
    78–9, 179–80; and
    unemployment   38
Work:
    aspirations for   11; collective   239;
    ethic   8; hours worked in   71, 96–
    9; Marxist and Soviet attitude to   1,
    2, 3, 6, 12, 69, 213; motivation
    to   75; under mature socialism   9,
    13
Workers   243; attitudes to work   188,
    233; education and training   128–
    30; movement to industry   52–3;
    participation, see participation;
    reasons for dismissal   88
Workers – intellectuals   230, 231, 233
Working class   233, 239, 273

Yadov   11, 188
Yugoslavia   85

Zaleski   202
Zaslavskaya   105
Zdravomyslov   11